POLITICS FOR A PILGRIM CHURCH

Politics for a Pilgrim Church

A Thomistic Theory of Civic Virtue

Thomas J. Bushlack

WILLIAM B. EERDMANS PUBLISHING COMPANY

GRAND RAPIDS, MICHIGAN / CAMBRIDGE, U.K.

Published 2015 by

Wm. B. Eerdmans Publishing Co.

2140 Oak Industrial Drive N.E., Grand Rapids, Michigan 49505 /

P.O. Box 163, Cambridge CB3 9PU U.K.

Printed in the United States of America

21 20 19 18 17 16 15   7 6 5 4 3 2 1

Library of Congress Cataloging-in-Publication Data

Bushlack, Thomas J.

Politics for a pilgrim church: a Thomistic theory of civic virtue /
Thomas J. Bushlack.

pages   cm

Includes bibliographical references and index.

ISBN 978-0-8028-7090-2 (pbk.: alk. paper)

1. Thomas, Aquinas, Saint, 1225?-1274.   2. Christianity and politics.
3. Christianity and justice.   I. Title.

B765.T54B87   2015

241′.62 — dc23

2015015088

www.eerdmans.com

Contents

Acknowledgments

As I began my professional studies in theology and ethics, I was intrigued by one simple question: What is the nature of the relationship between virtue ethics and social ethics in Christian ethics, especially in Catholic social thought? This book is the result of contemplating that relationship. Whatever insights may have emerged from pondering this question in the pages that follow have only been made possible with the generous support of many helpful guides, mentors, friends, and family along the way.

First, I wish to thank Jean Porter and the rest of my dissertation committee, including Jerry McKenny, David Clairmont, and Joseph Wawrykow, for nurturing the first seeds of an idea into my doctoral dissertation. That work provided enough ideas and left enough questions unanswered to continue the research that is now *Politics for a Pilgrim Church*. Joseph Wawrykow deserves particular credit for suggesting the importance of Henri de Lubac's work on the relationship between nature and grace as a foundational theological issue for considering how Christians engage in politics in the twenty-first century. I would also like to thank those colleagues at the University of St. Thomas who provided ongoing support, advice, and feedback in the writing and revising of the manuscript. In particular, I am grateful to those who read and commented on drafts and chapters of the book: Gary Anderson, Billy Junker, Meg Wilkes-Karraker, Paul Wojda, Massimo Faggioli, and Steve Laumakis (who invited me to submit what is now Chapter 6 to the Common Good Colloquium in the philosophy department in the spring of 2014). Since my knowledge of ecclesiology was quite limited, Massimo Faggioli was particularly helpful in providing a reading list and feedback for incorporating the ecclesiological notion of a pilgrim church into the manuscript.

I have also been fortunate to receive comments and encouragement in this project from several other fine scholars; I solicited advice from some of them via email, and they responded with great intellectual generosity and magnanimity. Russell Hittinger provided some very helpful citations and comments for understanding the history and development of Catholic social thought since the late eighteenth century. Eugene Garver's work and comments on drafts provided valuable insight into the nature of Aristotle's *Rhetoric* and its ongoing significance in contemporary democratic politics and culture. And James Davison Hunter's work was particularly helpful for my understanding of the nature of the relationship between politics and culture and its significance for Christian engagement in the late modern world. Professor Hunter very graciously provided comments on the later chapters amid a very busy research and lecturing schedule. His comments saved me from misrepresenting his work and that of others on key issues related to the sociological study of culture. Any insights from these scholars are entirely owed to their generosity, and any oversights are entirely my own.

Of course, none of this would have been possible without the generous support and endless patience of my wife, Anna Marie, without whose love and encouragement to keep writing I would still be sitting in the Hesburgh Library finishing the manuscript. She has been not only a constant source of support and encouragement but also a sounding board at the dinner table for many of the ideas contained in this book (and a reason why many of those poor ideas have been discarded). I am also grateful to my three children, Sean, Audrey, and Frances, who consistently call me back from research and writing in order to be present with them as they play and grow into their own expressions of joy, love, and virtue (civic, or otherwise). Of any and all testaments to the grace of God, my family remains the greatest witness, and to them I am deeply grateful.

Finally, I wish to thank you, the reader, for picking up this book and journeying with me in seeking to discern the best way for us as Christians and as citizens to witness to Christian civic virtue in the dizzying maze of late modern culture and politics. It is my sincere hope that you find something in the pages that follow that provides you with new insight or inspiration to carry on the work of seeking justice and the common good in this pilgrimage through life. Should you find such inspiration, it would bring me great joy to know that you will pass it on and share it with others.

Introduction

For here we have no lasting city, but we are looking for the city that is to come.

Hebrews 13:14 (NRSV)

But seek the welfare of the city where I have sent you into exile, and pray for the LORD on its behalf, for in its welfare you will find your welfare.

Jeremiah 29:7

The People of God on Pilgrimage

The Christian life understood as a pilgrimage through this world presents a paradox. On the one hand, pilgrims are a people who are fully present to each stage on their journey and depend on one another for their survival in the liminal space of journey away from the safety of their true home. As Pope Francis recently noted, "We must never forget that we are pilgrims journeying alongside one another. This means that we must have sincere trust in our fellow pilgrims, putting aside all suspicion or mistrust, and turn our gaze to what we are seeking: the radiant peace of God's face."[1] Thus a pilgrim people also look forward to a goal of seeing God face to face in friendship, a goal that transcends the present moment. This final goal of the journey holds out the promises of reward and rest, and it provides a sense

---

1. Francis, *Evangelii gaudium* (Vatican City: Libreria Editrice Vaticana, 2013), §244.

of hope and courage amid the inevitable setbacks and moments of doubt on any arduous pilgrimage. At the same time the final goal unites the traveling companions in a common aim and sense of solidarity. As Robin Gill says, "Pilgrims are clearly still part of this world, yet they have their sight set steadily beyond this world."[2] Thus, the Christian pilgrim lives within this paradoxical tension of commitment to seeking the good that can be found on this earthly journey, while also recognizing that she is destined for the final goal of the kingdom of God that both fulfills and transcends the ambiguities and paradoxes of this earthly existence.

Indeed, all of the Christian life can be seen in one form or another as a pilgrimage, as the following examples demonstrate. Christians, along with Jews and Muslims, trace the biblical roots of monotheistic faith to Abram and Sarai's journey from Ur to the land of Canaan promised by God (see Genesis 12–25). Pilgrimages to the Holy Land or the Camino de Compostello in Spain remain popular for many Christians today. As the title of his spiritual autobiography suggests, Ignatius of Loyola referred to himself as "the pilgrim" and began his life after conversion with a pilgrimage to the Holy Land. Thomas Aquinas frequently refers to the human person as a *homo viator* — a wayfarer or pilgrim on a journey home to God.[3] Making pilgrimage is a way of deepening a commitment to one's faith and of growing in deeper appreciation for the significance of faith in this life and its necessity for reaching the final goal. It implies a dual loyalty to seeking the good things that can be found and appreciated in this life while also looking forward to a perfect, future good that transcends the current moment and functions as an architectonic goal for each step along the way.

If the Christian life is viewed as a pilgrimage, then Christians claim a paradoxical dual citizenship in this world, one that was classically articulated by Augustine's two cities in *The City of God*. Christians count themselves among the people of God striving toward the heavenly city and among the common humanity of those who belong to the earthly city. Cathleen Kaveny suggests that when attempting to live faithfully to one's dual citizenship in political life "Christians need to keep two values in creative tension by honoring the insights of two groups of devout Catholics, which I call the prophets and the

---

2. Robin Gill, *Churchgoing and Christian Ethics* (Cambridge: Cambridge University Press, 1999), p. 22.

3. A search of *viator* in the Index Thomisticus indicates that Aquinas frequently uses the term to refer to Christ's human nature, as contrasted with his divine nature in which he is already *comprehensor*. Thus, Christ is the perfect image of the paradox of the human person as wayfarer called to a more perfect completion by grace.

pilgrims."[4] Kaveny explains that prophets witness to an uncompromising commitment to the absolute justice of the kingdom of God and an unwillingness to cooperate with the evils of the times. Pilgrims maintain that the current conditions of sin, injustice, and suffering call for loving engagement in the unjust and imperfect structures of the world to ameliorate human suffering while awaiting the final arrival of God's kingdom. Both are necessary stances for Christian political witness and engagement, but my defense of civic virtue in what follows fits more closely with the image of pilgrimage, as the title of this book suggests.

The Thomistic account of civic virtue that I develop in what follows pays close attention to Aquinas's method, aims, and historical context, to understand how insights gained from his theological work continue to have practical value today. In his thirteenth-century context, Aquinas was interested in demonstrating how the penultimate goals of this earthly life might be harmonized with the transcendent goals of the Christian pilgrim. Aquinas states this plainly when he writes that "a human being is not only a citizen of the earthly city but also a member of the heavenly city of Jerusalem" (*De virtutibus* a. 9).[5] A Thomistic account of civic virtue likewise seeks to integrate these two commitments — the one eschatological, the other immanent — in the life of the people of God within a pilgrim church.

I begin with the image of the pilgrim church from chapter VII of *Lumen gentium* (Dogmatic Constitution on the Church).[6] *Lumen gentium* expresses the Christian paradox in the following manner. On the one hand, the council fathers affirm that "the pilgrim church, in its sacraments and institutions, which belong to this present age, carries the mark of this world which will pass, and it takes its place among the creatures which groan and until now suffer the pains of childbirth and await the revelation of the children of God

---

4. M. Cathleen Kaveny, "Catholics as Citizens: Today's Ethical Challenges Call for New Moral Thinking," *America* 203, no. 121 (2010), *Expanded Academic ASAP*, Web, December 17, 2013.

5. Aquinas repeats this theme in his defense of the mendicants against the seculars at the University of Paris, when he writes that "one and the same person can be a citizen of two cities" (*Contra impugnantes* II.2). I am grateful for these citations provided by Bonnie Kent in "Reinventing Augustine's Ethics: The Afterlife of the *City of God*," in *Augustine's City of God: A Critical Guide*, ed. James Wetzel (New York: Cambridge University Press, 2012), pp. 225-44.

6. English quotations of the Vatican II documents are taken from *The Basic Sixteen Documents of Vatican Council II: Constitutions, Decrees, Declarations*, ed. Austin Flannery, O.P. (Northport, N.Y.: Costello, 1996).

(see Rom 8:19-22)."[7] On the other hand, however, "while on earth it journeys in a foreign land away from the Lord (see 2 Cor 5:6), the church sees itself as an exile. It seeks and is concerned about those things which are above."[8] The text adds further, paraphrasing the thirteenth chapter of the letter to the Hebrews, that the "people of God has here no lasting city but looks to that which is to come."[9] How can a Christian resolve the tension between this dual commitment to "this present age" and "to that which is to come"? This book presents a response to that question as embodied in a Thomistic theory of civic virtue that seeks to integrate this dual commitment within the political practices of a pilgrim church.

My engagement with postconciliar Catholic ecclesiology is born of a belief that one's ecclesiological stance is significant for the manner in which one engages in the common good of the political community. Those who are involved in political theology often operate with implicit assumptions about the church that are not always well defined, but are rather assumed to be shared by all Christians. But even a brief foray into postconciliar ecclesiological debates indicates that one cannot assume one, univocal image of the church operating among those who wish to reflect on the political significance of the pilgrim church. My desire to use the image of the pilgrim church from *Lumen gentium* as a hermeneutical lens for Christian civic virtue in the late modern world based on Aquinas's notion of justice requires some justification from the outset. My purpose in this introduction is to defend the claim that the texts of Vatican II can be read as embodying certain key elements of a Thomistic ecclesiology and moral theology, and that the image of the pilgrim church is consistent with Aquinas's understanding of the role of the church in cultivating the virtues necessary to sustain the human wayfarer on her journey to God. Therefore, the ecclesiology of a pilgrim church provides a fitting hermeneutical paradigm for the practice of civic virtue in early twenty-first-century liberal democracies.

I begin by noting that Aquinas does not develop an explicit ecclesiology. Nor is there a section or question in the *Summa theologiae* on the organization of the church as such. Aquinas wrote no *De ecclesia*. Indeed, tractates dedicated explicitly to the nature of the church do not preoccupy scholastic theologians and canonists until the fourteenth century.[10] Rather, there are impor-

---

7. *Lumen gentium*, §48.

8. *Lumen gentium*, §6.

9. *Lumen gentium*, §44.

10. George Sabra writes, for example, that "the theological outlook of the thirteenth century was replaced or overcome by a juridico-political one" in the fourteenth century,

tant implications of Aquinas's approach to theology for understanding the nature of the church as the space within which the Christian wayfarer learns to receive and to hear the Word of God, to participate in the sacramental life of the church, and to embark on her pilgrimage toward God. In his seminal article on Aquinas's ecclesiology Yves Congar writes, for example, that it is more fitting to speak of a "treatise [on the church] which *could be* written with the guidance of his principles."[11] Indeed, Aquinas's notion of church is so thoroughly integrated into his entire approach to theology that Martin Grabmann has claimed that the church functions as "a kind of 'architectonic law' which governs and underlies the whole of his work," and Congar adds that everything can be understood as ecclesiological in Aquinas's thought.[12] Therefore, although Aquinas does not have an explicit ecclesiology, it is possible to discern the main contours of a theology of the church that undergirds his mature work and bears directly on his understanding of the wayfarer's return to God, a journey that is lived in the practice of the virtues.

My analysis thus far suggests two distinct but interrelated questions that need to be addressed in order to propose Vatican II's image of the pilgrim church as a model for Thomistic civic virtue and Christian political engagement. Although each of these questions could easily fill a separate monograph, I want to state at the outset how I understand my use of this image embedded in the ecclesiology of Vatican II to be congruent with Thomistic notions of virtue. First, the status and fate of Thomas Aquinas's body of work, and of the various strands or schools of Thomistic thought — what Pope Leo XIII referred to as "those purest streams of wisdom flowing inexhaustibly from the precious fountainhead of the Angelic Doctor"[13] — before, during, and after Vatican II is quite complex. Some scholars, for example, see Vatican II as the end of Thomism tout court (accompanied with a collective sigh of relief). Others hail it as a new moment of renewal in Thomistic thought. For these latter scholars, Vatican II expresses certain aspects of Aquinas's methodological approach to theology, one that remains capable of breathing new life into

---

and that this juridical model became even more pronounced after Trent and the Counter-Reformation, up until the twentieth century (*Thomas Aquinas's Vision of the Church: Fundamentals of an Ecumenical Ecclesiology* [Mainz: Matthias-Grünewald-Verlag, 1987], p. 31).

11. Yves Congar, O.P., "The Idea of the Church in St. Thomas Aquinas," in *The Mystery of the Church* trans. A. V. Littledale (Baltimore: Helicon, 1960), pp. 97-117, pp. 115-16, italics added. The original French article is "L'idee de l'Eglise chez saint Thomas d'Aquin," *Revue des sciences philosophiques et theologiques* 29 (1940): 31-58.

12. Quoted in Sabra, *Thomas Aquinas's Vision of the Church*, p. 27.

13. Leo XIII, *Aeterni Patris*, §26.

the church in the modern world in the manner of Pope John XXIII's notion of *aggiornamento* — that is, bringing up to date the means of the church's communication of the gospel. The former group resisted the highly speculative and rigid form of Thomism typically referred to as neo-Thomism, or neo-scholasticism more broadly, while this latter view can be found especially in the followers of what came to be called the *nouvelle théologie*. With a bit of historical and exegetical work, however, certain aspects of Aquinas's ecclesiological vision and its relationship to the practice of the virtues can be seen as expressed within and congruent with the texts of Vatican II.

A second but related question must also be explored at the outset of my project, and that is the question of the interpretation and reception of the texts of Vatican II themselves, with particular emphasis on the ecclesiology present in them. In many respects, the question of the nature of the church has become the central, and most hotly contested, issue of postconciliar theological debate. Even as the notion of *communio* ecclesiology has become a central postconciliar ecclesiological theme, not all scholars agree on what *communio* is or means. However one interprets the ecclesiology of Vatican II, one's ecclesiology bears directly on how one understands the kind of spirituality and morality that is promoted among the people of God.[14] Therefore, the spirituality and morality fostered by ecclesiological assumptions has direct implications for the practice of Christian civic virtue.

The search for a unified ecclesiological vision of Vatican II raises two additional challenges to address in this introduction. The first has to do with the difficulty of applying a consistent, internal principle for interpreting the texts of Vatican II as a whole. This involves the search for what might be called a hermeneutic of Vatican II. The second has to do with the best means of holding together the various images of the church within the texts of Vatican II. These are distinct yet related challenges. In fact, as I argue below, the two questions merge into one focal point for the interpretation of Vatican II. For if it is not possible to discern a coherent internal principle for interpreting the entire corpus of Vatican II texts, then it becomes much easier to dismiss the multitude of images and metaphors for understanding the church as lacking a coherent internal principle of unity as well. The converse is also true. Without a unified vision of the church it becomes difficult to discern a coherent unity of the entire corpus of Vatican II as a whole.

---

14. *Lumen gentium* explicitly ties together ecclesiology, sacraments, and virtues, as in the following: "The sacred character and organic structure of the priestly community are brought into being through the sacraments and the virtues" (§11).

Thomas, Thomism, and Thomisms at Vatican II

Etienne Gilson once bemoaned what he witnessed as "the Thomist problem of the council."[15] The place of Aquinas in the renewal of the church in the modern world was vigorously contested during the sessions of the council. My claim is that elements of Aquinas's (implicit) ecclesiology can be seen in the texts of Vatican II, as some of the council fathers drew on a historically sensitive reading of Aquinas, while others placed renewed attention to many of the same biblical, patristic, and early medieval sources as did Aquinas. This may appear to some to be a strange claim, as certain interpretations of Vatican II see the council as the final overcoming of the rigid styles of Thomistic, neo-scholastic theology that developed in the period between Trent (1545-63) and Vatican II (1962-65) and reached its pinnacle during Vatican I (1869-70) and with the publication of Pope Leo XIII's *Aeterni Patris* (1879). Gerald McCool writes, for example, that the "history of the modern neo-Thomist movement, whose *magna charta* was *Aeterni Patris,* reached its end at the Second Vatican Council."[16] The central question, however, is what kind of Thomism was overcome at Vatican II? If one kind of Thomism was deliberately abandoned at Vatican II, is there a form of Thomism or strands of Thomistic thought that continue to breathe life into the intellectual and spiritual life of the church, one that can still be discovered in the texts and *ethos* of the council? My aim is to demonstrate that there is.

Joseph Komonchak notes that two initial schemas prepared by the Commission on Studies and Seminaries and by the Theological Commission (two bodies responsible for preparing the initial reports and drafts that later became the documents of Vatican II) recommended Aquinas's theological method as the paradigm to be utilized for the ongoing intellectual formation of pastors and for the reform of the church.[17] These initial suggestions, however, were quickly challenged and rejected by the council fathers. They expressed deep reservations about endorsing Aquinas's distinctive method and form of theology in conciliar documents that would place his thought and methodology

15. Cited by M. Fourcade in "Thomisme et antithomisme a l'heure de Vatican II," *Revue Thomiste* 108 (2006): 301-25, p. 304. This and all subsequent translations from the French are mine.

16. Gerald A. McCool, *From Unity to Pluralism: The Internal Evolution of Thomism* (New York: Fordham University Press, 1989), p. 230.

17. Joseph A. Komonchak, "Thomism and the Second Vatican Council," in *Continuity and Plurality in Catholic Theology: Essays in Honor of Gerald A. McCool, S.J.,* ed. Anthony J. Cernera (Fairfield, Conn.: Sacred Heart University Press, 1998), pp. 53-73, p. 54.

above other great thinkers of the tradition. Indeed, in Pope Paul VI's address to the members of the Sixth International Thomistic Congress meeting in Rome during the final session of the council in 1965, he stated that "in declaring [Aquinas] 'Common Doctor' and in making his doctrine the foundation of ecclesiological teaching, the magisterium of the church did not intend to make him an exclusive master, nor to impose each of his theses, nor to exclude the legitimate diversity of schools and systems."[18] The council fathers feared, with good reason, that the endorsement of an ecumenical council could have been interpreted as lending support to the imposition of a particular form and style of philosophy, metaphysics, and theology developed in early medieval Europe onto a more self-consciously global and pluralistic church.

The question of Aquinas's influence on Vatican II is made even more problematic by the fact that there is not one monolithic school of thought that could be designated as Thomism. Rather, there are many different kinds of Thomisms. By Thomisms I mean systems of thought that have been self-consciously developed out of an attempt to remain loyal to the method and fundamental principles of Aquinas himself. Pope Leo XII recognized these as the "streams of wisdom" that trace their roots back to the scholastic master. Ultimately, what was rejected at Vatican II was a rigidly imposed, ahistorical, and ideological neo-Thomism that had arisen in the interim between Vatican I and Vatican II. McCool notes that one of the problems that beset many of the neo-Thomists in the aftermath of *Aeterni Patris* was a lack of attention to the historical and contextual nature of ideas. He writes of "two great weaknesses . . . [of] the early neo-scholastics: lack of historical sense and blindness to the role of historical development in theology."[19] This form of Thomism tended toward abstract idealism and it essentialized Aquinas's use of Aristotelian philosophy into a rigid system of metaphysics that enabled a timeless deduction of truth. This style of theology, referred to by some as the "Roman system,"[20] was thought by the defenders of neo-Thomism to be capable of producing a universal "conclusion-theology" in which timeless truths are discovered independent of context, history, or the historical development of thought.[21] This approach tended to stifle creative

---

18. Cited by Fourcade in "Thomisme et antithomisme," p. 313.

19. McCool, *From Unity to Pluralism*, p. 24.

20. Fourcade, "Thomisme et antithomisme," p. 305. In a personal letter to Jacques Maritain, Father Georges Cotter writes that "the roman theologians have rendered a terrible service to St. Thomas" (p. 305).

21. The term "conclusion-theology" is derived from Johannes Beumer and cited by McCool, *From Unity to Pluralism*, p. 11.

theological reflection in service to ongoing development of doctrine for changing historical circumstances. In moral theology, it tended to produce textbooks and manuals that were safe from ecclesiastical censure, but did little to inspire pastoral or theological flexibility. Unfortunately, "the defeat of the Roman doctors above all opened the way to reject other 'families' of Thomism" at the council.[22]

Other forms of Thomism developed, however, partly in response to neo-Thomism. Many of these scholars of Aquinas were much more attentive to historical context and the historical development of ideas than the Roman school of neo-Thomists had been. James Keenan refers to these as the "revisionist" schools of Thomism that came to fruition especially in the *nouvelle théologie* of the early twentieth century. These schools of thought can be traced back to Odon Lottin (1880-1965),[23] and reached a certain pinnacle of historical consciousness in the work of M.-D. Chenu. Chenu argued that Aquinas's significance can only be appreciated when his work is read not as rigidly imposed dogmatic conclusions, but rather within the context of the thirteenth-century renaissance of scholastic thought and Christian humanism. Aquinas's synthesis is the culmination of an organic assimilation of the wisdom of the biblical, patristic, and spiritual sources of Christian tradition at the time, combined with new insight from a critical reading of Aristotle and his Muslim and Jewish commentators. Furthermore, it was developed to address the social, political, spiritual, and practical needs of his times.[24] Aquinas never considered his work as a means of forestalling future development in new historical contexts.[25] Indeed, as I argue especially in Chapter 4, Aquinas's conception of natural law would never allow for that kind of rigidity. This renewed study of Thomism was flexible and creative, while remaining true to and developing the central doctrines of the faith, in response to the needs of the times. Chenu and others demonstrated that earlier forms of neo-Thomism had fallen short of Aquinas's method and vision in every one of these ways, but that the creative genius of Thomas himself could and indeed must survive the death of neo-Thomism. This more

---

22. Fourcade, "Thomisme et antithomisme," p. 305.

23. James Keenan, S.J., *A History of Catholic Moral Theology in the Twentieth Century: From Confessing Sins to Liberating Consciences* (New York: Continuum, 2010), p. 38. Lottin was succeeded by others in the French *ressourcement* movement such as M.-D. Chenu, O.P., Henri de Lubac, S.J., Yves Congar, O.P., Etienne Gilson, and Jean Danielou, S.J., among others.

24. See Komonchak, "Thomism and the Second Vatican Council," pp. 63-64.

25. Aquinas famously states in the first question of the *Summa theologiae* that the argument from authority is the weakest form of argument (*Summa theologiae* I.1, art. 8, *ad* 2).

hermeneutical reading of Aquinas places his work more as the culmination of patristic thought and theology, rather than in the later medieval scholasticism of the fourteenth and fifteenth centuries.[26] As we will see below, this is particularly important for understanding both Aquinas's theology of the church and his understanding of the nature of moral theology and the practice of the virtues.

Therefore, the rejection of neo-Thomism in the early days of the council did not necessarily entail the rejection of a more historically sensitive hermeneutic for the use of Thomistic principles to address the intellectual and spiritual needs of the church in the modern world. Although officially rejected in the first session, certain Thomistic notions were integrated into the theology of the council. For example, Cardinal Suenens, a Belgian bishop who led the "Suenens intervention" in the spring of 1962, steered the momentum of the council away from the more rigid neo-scholastic, institutional images of the church found in the earlier preparatory documents. This intervention seems to have had a twofold effect on subsequent developments at the council. First, it shifted the methodology and tone away from the Roman neo-Thomist system. Second, it placed discussion of the nature of the church squarely at the heart of the council's deliberations.[27] Suenens played a key role in the development of Schema XVII, which later became *Gaudium et spes,* and he and others from the French and Belgian schools of thought tended to be much more open to a more historically and contextually sensitive form of Thomism.[28] Thus, despite the initial rejection of Thomism, one

---

26. I follow Servais Pinckaers, O.P., on this point, insofar as he reads Aquinas in relation to the patristic masters before him and in distinction from the turn to nominalism in the fourteenth century (see *The Sources of Christian Ethics,* trans. Mary Thomas Noble, O.P. [Washington, D.C.: Catholic University of America Press, 1995], chapter 9, especially pp. 220 and 239).

27. Christoph Theobald refers to this as the "Belgian strategy," which was backed by Cardinal Montini (the future Pope Paul VI). He claims that "these two days in fact decided the fate of the Council: *the Church became its 'main subject matter'"* ("The Theological Options of Vatican II: Seeking an 'Internal' Principle of Interpretation," in *Vatican II: A Forgotten Future?* ed. Alberto Melloni and Christoph Theobald, trans. Paul Burns [London: SCM, 2005], pp. 87-108, p. 89).

28. Joseph A. Komonchak, "Vatican II and the Encounter Between Catholicism and Liberalism," in *Catholicism and Liberalism: Contributions to American Public Philosophy,* ed. R. Bruce Douglass and David Hollenbach (New York: Cambridge University Press, 1994), pp. 76-99, p. 88. McCool notes the development of a historically nuanced form of Thomism in dialogue with modern philosophy at the Higher Institute of Philosophy at Louvain, Belgium, in *The Neo-Thomists* (Milwaukee, Wis.: Marquette University Press, 2003), pp. 42-43.

may note a gradual and more subtle infusion of Thomistic principles into the texts of Vatican II, one that was more hermeneutical than rigidly deductive.

In these more subtle ways the insights of Aquinas (and of course many other great patristic and other theologians of the church) could therefore be put to use as a tool for "scrutinizing the signs of the times and of interpreting them in the light of the Gospel."[29] Yves Congar writes, for example, that "it is less that we should be repeating [Aquinas's] theses than that we should go to school with him, after which we should set to work with whatever strength we have, but in his spirit and relying on him."[30] But the initial rejection of neo-Thomism, combined with a more subtle infusion of Thomistic principles into the texts of Vatican II, makes the task of identifying Thomistic notions of the church and of the virtues in the conciliar documents a more delicate task.

What Is the Church? Or Who Are the Church?[31]

Both Aquinas and the texts of Vatican II draw on a plurality of images, metaphors, and concepts to describe the nature of the church. Indeed, given the architectonic quality of the ecclesiology implicit within Aquinas's work, the church cannot be reduced to a univocal reality, but is rather expressed through a multitude of images, metaphors, and analogical concepts.[32] Primary among these is the church as the *congregatio fidelium* — the gathered and worshiping congregation of the baptized faithful. For Aquinas the church is first and foremost a theological phenomenon, that is, an effect of grace. Its purpose is to convey God's saving grace to all human persons through the preaching of the Word and the administering of the sacraments. Since the primary effect of grace is the interior conversion or justification of the person, the church is expressed most prominently within the gathered

29. *Gaudium et spes,* §4.

30. Yves Congar, "La theologie au Concile: Le 'theologiser' du Concile," in *Situation et taches presents de la theologie* (Paris: Editiones du Cerf, 1967), pp. 51-56, p. 55.

31. The latter form of this question is taken directly from the title of Joseph Komonchak's monograph, *Who Are the Church?* (Milwaukee, Wis.: Marquette University Press, 2008).

32. Sabra lists the following six categories for describing the church throughout Aquinas's work: occasional symbols and similes (particularly in his biblical commentaries), *civitas, domus, populus, congregatio fidelium,* and *corpus mysticum* (*Thomas Aquinas's Vision of the Church,* p. 43).

and worshiping congregation of believers who have received this infused gift of grace. As George Sabra states it, Aquinas "views the church mainly in terms of grace and the effects of grace," which is "essentially the *congregatio fidelium.*"[33]

Since the gathered community of believers brings forth a people who are united under a common life and practice of worship, the earthly manifestation of the church is also expressed in the institution and the ministerial functions of the leaders of the church. These ministerial and institutional modalities of the church, however, exist to support the faith of the entire people of God.[34] While Aquinas uses a wide array of biblical and theological themes to express the reality and mystery of the church, these two aspects — (1) the congregation of believers and (2) the institutional structures along with their attendant ministerial functions — are foundational. At the same time, however, the institutional structures remain secondary insofar as they exist to support and to serve the faith of the people, the *congregatio* and its faith. Thus, the congregation of believers remains the most foundational notion for understanding the church in Aquinas. For example, Sabra indicates that *ecclesia* in Aquinas "could refer to the congregation of believers, the communion of grace which is united and ordered to God by faith, hope, and love," or the "visible institution, the means of grace."[35] Each of these is the result of the grace of Jesus Christ made available to humankind through the work of the Holy Spirit. The institutional and juridical expressions, however, are in service to the faith of the church as a communion of believers.

Aquinas presents a concise statement of his theology of the church in his commentary on the Nicene-Constantinople Creed, in which he writes the following:

> As in a person there is one soul and one body, yet a diversity of members, so the Catholic Church is one body and has different members. The soul which quickens this body is the Holy Ghost . . . He who says Church

33. Sabra, *Thomas Aquinas's Vision of the Church,* p. 189; see also p. 98.

34. Sabra writes that the term *populos,* or "a people," is "one of those names of the church which are widespread in the writings of Thomas," and has found significant resonance in *Lumen gentium* and postconciliar ecclesiology (*Thomas Aquinas's Vision of the Church,* p. 43). It is important to note, however, that Aquinas and the texts of Vatican II use the term somewhat differently. The primary referent of *populos* for Aquinas, when referring specifically to the church, is the laity, whereas in *Lumen gentium* the term refers to the entire people of God in all of their various canonical and ministerial roles and functions.

35. Sabra, *Thomas Aquinas's Vision of the Church,* p. 28.

says congregation; and he who says Holy Church says congregation of the faithful; and he who says Christian person says member of the Church . . . The Church is one, and this unity of the Church is grounded in three elements. It is grounded first in the oneness of faith . . . the oneness of hope . . . and the oneness in love.[36]

Aquinas's commentary witnesses to an intrinsic connection between the church as a theological phenomenon (the Holy Spirit as the "soul" of the church) and the church as a congregation of believers that is united in a visible structure ("the Church is one"), and is finally manifested in this earthly pilgrimage through the theological virtues of faith, hope, and love. *Ecclesia* is thus a space of encounter between divine gift and human receptivity that bears fruit in the life of holiness and virtue on this earthly journey of God's people toward the heavenly home, paradigmatically expressed in the theological virtues of faith, hope, and love.

This theological image of the church as a community constituted by grace enables one to view the institutions, laws, and ministerial roles and functions as important and necessary without reducing the church to its external, juridical, and structural forms. Instead, the juridical and institutional aspects of the church serve to strengthen the people of God in faith and the virtues that are the effects of grace. Thomas O'Meara writes, for example, that Aquinas's ecclesiology is a "social pneumatology,"[37] in which "the life of the virtues and charisms complemented the reduction of all real ecclesial ministry to the priest."[38] There is thus a recognition that all persons who are called to participate in Christ's salvific work via the grace of the Holy Spirit and the universal call to holiness are equally members of the people of God, even as there are distinctive roles and functions for those who serve as ministers in the church.[39] This tension between magisterial and lay roles, which can be described as one between the common priesthood of all believers and

36. From the *Devotissima expositio super symbolum apostolorum.* I have reproduced the text and translation, with slight emendation for inclusive language, from Congar's "The Idea of the Church in St. Thomas Aquinas," p. 99.

37. Thomas O'Meara, "Theology of Church," in *The Theology of Thomas Aquinas,* ed. Rik Van Nieuwenhove and Joseph Wawrykow (Notre Dame, Ind.: University of Notre Dame Press, 2010), pp. 303-25, p. 314.

38. O'Meara, "Theology of Church," p. 320.

39. See *Summa theologiae* III 183 for Aquinas's discussion of the various roles and ministries held within the church that enable it to manifest as a true unity in Christ exemplified in a diversity of functions.

the ordained, ministerial priesthood, is mitigated — though never overcome — insofar as one views the pilgrim church as a grace-inspired social organism constituted by the entire people of God.[40]

The emphasis thus far has been on the theological virtues as the effect of grace. This could indicate that the church has very little to say with regard to Christian *civic* virtue — that is, with regard to the pursuit of justice and the common good of one's political community. In this view, the pilgrim church is solely concerned with the more private or interior life of grace expressed via the theological virtues, or perhaps with the internal structures and functions of the church itself. But this would be an overly narrow way of reading Aquinas. Congar suggests that "to define the Church as a body having community of life with God is to conceive of it as humanity vitalized Godwards by the theological virtues, which have God as their object, and organized in the likeness of God *by the moral virtues.*"[41] In fact, he goes even further to claim that "the entire *Secunda Pars* of the *Summa Theologica* is ecclesiology"[42] insofar as it describes the return of the creature to God. Note that he does not claim that the *Secunda Pars* is ecclesiolog*ical,* but rather that it is ecclesiolog*y.* Thus, the image of God in the human person is only fully understood when it is brought to greater perfection as the Christian wayfarer grows in the life of virtue, including both the theological and cardinal virtues. This process of sanctification is led toward its completion by growing into the "the stature of the fullness of Christ" (Eph. 4:13; cf. *Summa theologiae* III 8.3). The pursuit of the good of the political community that is mediated by the cardinal or moral virtues — in particular by justice — is therefore cultivated along with the theological virtues of faith, hope, and love. The church thus becomes seen as the entire congregation of believers, supported by the juridical, canonical, and ministerial functions of the hierarchical church, and manifested by way of the theological and moral virtues. In this way the image of the church upholds the transcendent goal of the Christian life without denigrating the commitment to the common good of this earthly life along the way.

A necessary correlate of such an ecclesiology is that the church itself

---

40. This tension is evident, for example, in *Lumen gentium:* "Though they differ essentially and not only in degree, the common priesthood of the faithful and the ministerial or hierarchical priesthood are none the less interrelated; each in its own way shares in the one priesthood of Christ" (§10).

41. Congar, "The Idea of Church in St. Thomas Aquinas," p. 101, italics added.

42. Congar, "The Idea of Church," p. 102; see also Sabra, *Thomas Aquinas's Vision of the Church,* p. 27.

becomes "a visible unity, the unity of a common life of concrete humanity,"[43] in which a way of life is embedded and practiced. This emphasis on the common life of the people of God, in relationship with God, with each other, and with creation, has certain resonances with the *communio* ecclesiology that has become a predominant paradigm of postconciliar ecclesiology.[44] Therefore, the life of virtue is embodied and practiced within the deeper mystery of the church and God's providential plan for human history. The church as mystery provides a rich paradigm for holding together the eschatological, transcendent ends of the church with the immanent, practical aspects of daily Christian living, both within the church itself and within the cultural and political contexts in which Christians find themselves living. A Thomistic account of civic virtue articulates one way of living out the Christian commitment to justice within the life of the wayfarer *in statu viae*.

I have begun with a very general overview of the notion of church implicit within Aquinas's theology and its place in fostering the virtues. The search for a coherent ecclesiology within the texts of Vatican II remains much more complicated, in part because many of the debates regarding the ecclesiology of Vatican II have not yet been fully resolved. As noted above, following the Suenens intervention the nature of the church itself became the focal point of the entire council. It would appear natural to focus solely on *Lumen gentium* in searching for a theology of church in the documents. In fact, my use of the image of the pilgrim church is derived directly from the letter to the Hebrews and chapter VII of *Lumen gentium*. However, we will have a much richer appreciation of the church if we take a wider perspective when considering the event and texts of Vatican II. For example, Christoph Theobald notes that there is a certain "polycentric structure"[45] to the texts of Vatican II. This polycentric structure suggests the need for a manner of interpreting the conciliar documents through the "phenomenon of intertextuality and the ideal of 'textual *corpus*' which, despite its internal complexity and multiple forms of compromise, offers a *coherent vision*."[46]

---

43. Louis Bouyer, *Church of God: Body of Christ and Temple of the Spirit,* trans. Charles Underhill Quinn (San Francisco: Ignatius, 2011), p. 165.

44. See, for example, David Schindler's *Heart of the World, Center of the Church: Communio Ecclesiology, Liberalism, and Liberation* (Grand Rapids: Eerdmans, 1996).

45. Theobald, "The Theological Options of Vatican II," p. 92.

46. Christoph Theobald, "The Principle of Pastorality at Vatican II: Challenges of a Prospective Interpretation of the Council," lecture presented at *The Legacy of Vatican II,* Boston College, September 26, 2013, translated by Andrea Vicini, S.J. http://www.bc.edu/content/dam/files/schools/stm_sites/c21online/pdf/legacy-translation.pdf. Accessed March 20,

Theobald suggests that a coherent vision of the church at Vatican II may emerge from the principle of "pastorality." He derives the concept of pastorality from the impetus and intention behind the council articulated by Pope John XXIII in his opening speech of the council. John proclaims that "types of presentation [of the church's doctrine] must be introduced which are more in accord with a teaching authority which is primarily pastoral in character."[47] Pastorality may therefore become a hermeneutical lens for considering the unified theology and vision of the church within the entire corpus of the documents of Vatican II.

In searching for this unifying principle, Theobald asks the following question: "should its internal unity be found in an *understanding of the Church,* stretched between the Church's interior *(Lumen gentium)* and its exterior *(Gaudium et spes),* or rather in the *word of God (Dei verbum),* received by the Church in the world of the time thanks to a new relationship — defined as 'pastoral' — to the scriptures and to tradition?"[48] Theobald suggests that it is in the hermeneutics of reception and interpretation of the Word of God provided in *Dei verbum* that we may more accurately perceive the true nature of the church as it exists within God's plan of salvation history. Interpreting the texts through Theobald's lens of pastorality places an emphasis on the reception of the Word of God as the generative moment for the church, and therefore places *Lumen gentium* in a critical dialogue with *Dei verbum* and the other documents as more directly related to the discussion of ecclesiology. This approach helps to make sense of the various images of the church that are often presented as in tension with one another within the text of *Lumen gentium.* It enables us to avoid the sense that the text represents a "compromise of 'contradictory pluralism'" that would make it impossible to discover a unified vision of the church at Vatican II.[49]

Although *Dei verbum* (1965) was officially promulgated later than *Lumen gentium* (1964), the Theological Commission noted as early as 1964 that *De revelatione* (which would become *Dei verbum*) was "in a way the first of all

---

2014. Critical publication forthcoming in the proceedings of the conference. Used with the translator's permission.

47. John XXIII, *Gaudet mater ecclesia* (October 11, 1962), trans. Joseph A. Komonchak, http://jakomonchak.files.wordpress.com/2012/10/john-xxiii-opening-speech.pdf. Accessed April 28, 2014.

48. Theobald, "The Theological Options of Vatican II," p. 90.

49. Peter Hunermann, "The Ignored 'Text': On the Hermeneutics of the Second Vatican Council," in *Vatican II: A Forgotten Future?* ed. Alberto Melloni and Christoph Theobald (London: SCM, 2005), pp. 118-36, p. 128.

the Constitutions of this Council, so that its Preface introduces them all to a certain extent."[50] The preface to *Dei verbum* may therefore hold important insights into the overall meaning of the council and the church's role in salvation history. It begins: "*Hearing* the word of God reverently and *proclaiming* it confidently . . . this sacred synod wishes to set forth the authentic teaching on divine revelation and its transmission."[51] This suggests that a central function of the church in God's plan of salvation is first hearing or receiving the Word and then witnessing to and proclaiming it to the world. Many of the debates about the internal coherence of the texts of Vatican II and its ecclesiology revolve around how to understand the juridical-institutional image of the church that had dominated from the fourteenth until the early twentieth century. And in fact, Theobald observes that the statement of the Theological Commission noted above "was however to remain a dead letter due to a fact of reception, i.e. that the Constitution on the Church in practice took the premier place among all the council documents."[52] Therefore, the postconciliar debates, even up to the present day, tend to view "the postconciliar period rather from an institutional point of view."[53]

Viewed primarily from the institutional perspective, many of the most frequent ecclesiological debates of the postconciliar church, such as Pope Benedict XVI's distinction between a "hermeneutic of discontinuity and rupture" and a "hermeneutic of reform,"[54] or the claims that the texts are merely a "compromise of contradictory pluralism,"[55] seem intractable. A more holistic or intertextual approach to the ecclesiology of Vatican II combined with the principle of pastorality, however, allows us to see the church in both its mystical and historical dimensions in relation to its more essential role in the economy of salvation and God's self-revelation. What emerges is therefore a church that is brought into being first by hearing and receiving the Word of God, the very act of which constitutes the people of God or the congregation of the faithful, and that it exists primarily to witness to and proclaim the gospel. The pattern of the generation of the church is a

50. Cited by Theobald in "The Theological Options of Vatican II," p. 91.

51. *Dei verbum*, §1, italics added.

52. Theobald, "The Theological Options of Vatican II," p. 91.

53. Theobald, "The Theological Options of Vatican II," p. 91.

54. Benedict XVI, "A Proper Hermeneutic for the Second Vatican Council," in *Vatican II: Renewal within Tradition*, ed. Matthew L. Lamb and Matthew Levering (New York: Oxford University Press, 2008), pp. ix-xv. Original Latin text available as "Ad romanam curia ab omnia natalicia," *Acta Apostilicae Sedis* 98 (January 6, 2006): 40-53.

55. Hunermann, "The Ignored 'Text,'" p. 128.

dynamic movement of reception (of the Word), formation (into a people), and witness or proclamation (to the world).

We have already considered the first moment of listening or reception in *Dei verbum* §1. *Presbyterorum ordinis* describes this second movement when it states that "the people of God is formed into one in the first place by the word of the living God," and that "by this faith then the congregation of the faithful begins and grows."[56] This receptivity to God's Word is indeed constitutive of the church itself. Bouyer writes that "the Church, as the People of God 'fulfilling' their vocation, . . has no other function than receiving the Word and giving herself to it."[57] The existence of the church both as the congregation of the faithful and as a juridical-institutional-hierarchical structure serves no other purpose than the ongoing witness to and proclamation of the gospel and the offering of the sacraments. *Ad gentes* completes the third movement by representing the church as essentially missionary in nature. It describes the three stages of the formation and growth of the Christian community in chapter II on missionary work. These comprise (1) Christian witness, (2) preaching the gospel and assembling the people of God, and (3) forming the Christian community. This missionary aspect of the church's existence is inherently pastoral in outlook. Therefore, a holistic, intertextual, and pastoral reading of the texts of Vatican II enables us to view the church not as a "thing," but rather as a dynamic expression of God's grace at work in persons and in the world through revelation and its reception by the faithful, the formation and growth of the people of God, and their ongoing witness to and proclamation of the gospel.

The similarity between this intertextual and pastoral interpretation of Vatican II and the implicit ecclesiology of Aquinas may be found in the fact that the church is not a reified object in and of itself, but is rather a gathered congregation of faithful believers who are brought together first by listening to and receiving the Word of God, and whose essential mission is witness to and proclamation of the saving news of the gospel. This holistic vision of the church also provides a broader hermeneutical lens through which one may engage the text of *Lumen gentium* itself. *Lumen gentium* begins in chapter I by presenting the church first as a mystery and sacrament of salvation, "a people made one by the unity of the Father, the Son and the holy Spirit."[58] The document wisely begins by noting that the church as mystery

---

56. *Presbyterorum ordinis*, §4.
57. Bouyer, *Church of God*, p. 254.
58. *Lumen gentium*, §4.

transcends all of the images and metaphors that we may contemplate to come to a deeper understanding of its essential nature. Its very structure then unpacks the multiple layers of meaning bound up in the notion of the church as a mystery: the church is constituted by the people of God whom God has called and chosen in human history (chapter II), with a visible institutional and hierarchical structure (chapter III), where certain roles (laity, religious, the bishops and all those in orders) are defined yet where all are embraced equally by the universal call to holiness (chapters IV–VI). Commenting on this schema, Sabra writes that it is "quite clear that the New People of God [chapter II] embraces the *whole* church, and that" the "designation *populos,* as used by *Lumen Gentium,* is also meant to emphasize the pilgrim-status of the church and to bring to the fore an eschatological dimension of the church (e.g., 'messianic people')."[59] Thus, he finds traces of Aquinas's ecclesiological vision of the church as a people in *Lumen gentium.* The model of the pilgrim church that is presented in chapter VII both embraces this universal and all-inclusive notion of church as the entire people of God and highlights the fact that all Christians are marked by the paradoxical tension between a twofold commitment to the good of humankind on earth, and to an ultimate good that transcends every age in the kingdom of heaven.

The middle axiom between the church as mystery and the pilgrim church in *Lumen gentium* is the notion of the "people of God" (chapter II). Many of the debates over the meaning of the church at Vatican II revolve around how one interprets the significance of the people of God. On the one hand, Theobald writes, for example, that the primary way of proceeding at the council was oriented toward "placing the future of Christian life and of the ecclesial community in the hands of the *whole* people of God. Definitely, this is the main aim of the council."[60] Similarly, Hunermann writes that a distinguishing mark of Vatican II is the "transformations among the People of God, in the unfolding of their consciousness of having come of age."[61] Such interpretations would place the notion of the people of God as a central component of the ecclesiology of Vatican II as a counterbalance to the emphasis on institutional components of the church that dominated Catholic ecclesiology in the centuries prior to the council.

On the other hand, others have sought to downplay the importance of the people of God. Avery Cardinal Dulles claims, for example, that despite

---

59. Sabra, *Thomas Aquinas's Vision of the Church,* p. 48.
60. Theobald, "The Principle of Pastorality," p. 4.
61. Hunermann, "The Ignored 'Text,'" p. 130.

its usefulness for overcoming the ecclesial triumphalism of an earlier period "the People of God had its limitations," not least of which because he found, following the work of then Cardinal Ratzinger, "that it had only a meager basis in scripture and in the fathers."[62] He claims rather that "Chapter 3, which deals with the hierarchy, contains the most important doctrinal pronouncements of the entire council . . . its judgment seems to be definitive."[63] This downplaying of the role of the people of God therefore correlates with an emphasis on the institutional-juridical-hierarchical structures of the church. In defending his hermeneutic of "renewal within continuity" for interpreting Vatican II, Pope Benedict XVI seems to refer to the church as a subject that exists independently of the people of God themselves. He writes, for example, of "the one subject-Church that the Lord has given to us."[64]

Thus, we have arrived at the crux of the questions that I used to title this section: What is the church? Or who are the church? There is a constant temptation to make the church into a reified object rather than a congregation that exists where there are believing persons who constitute its existence. Thus, Komonchak writes that the image of the church as a subject itself is something "that one will not find in Augustine or Aquinas" because for them the church does not possess "a personhood of her own distinct from the persons of her members."[65] Therefore, "church" "will always refer us to a group of people, to 'real subjects,' "[66] rather than an object or subject that is distinguishable from the very people whose faith brings the church into being.

Arguably, the predominant trend since Vatican II has been to focus on *communio* ecclesiology, especially as this has been articulated and defended by the magisterium of the Catholic Church.[67] Additional support for seeing communion ecclesiology as a lens for interpreting the ecclesiology of Vatican II is provided by the influential work of Walter Kasper, who argues that

---

62. Avery Cardinal Dulles, S.J., "Nature, Mission, Structure of the Church," in Lamb and Levering, eds., *Vatican II: Renewal within Tradition*, pp. 25-36, p. 31.

63. Dulles, "Nature, Mission, Structure of the Church," p. 32.

64. Benedict XVI, "A Proper Hermeneutic for the Second Vatican Council," p. x.

65. Komonchak, *Who Are the Church?* p. 63.

66. Komonchak, *Who Are the Church?* p. 15.

67. Magisterial support for this model can be found in the final report of the 1985 extraordinary synod of bishops and the 1992 letter from the Congregation for the Doctrine of the Faith, "On Some Aspects of the Church Understood as Communion," http://www.vatican.va/roman_curia/congregations/cfaith/documents/rc_con_cfaith_doc_28051992_communionis-notio_en.html. Accessed August 23, 2013.

"one of the guiding ideas of the last council — perhaps *the* guiding idea — was therefore *communio* — communion."[68] Yet the one thing that all commentators can agree on is that, like all church models, *communio* is not a univocal concept. Rather, it entails many layers of meaning depending on the context in which it is used and who is using it.

Gerard Mannion, for example, sees all uses of *communio* ecclesiology as an effort to impose from the top down a centralized Vatican authority that harkens back more to the juridical-hierarchical model that had dominated ecclesiology from the fourteenth until the mid-twentieth century.[69] Others, however, find a much richer set of meanings within the concept of *communio* ecclesiology. I find Dennis Doyle's description to be complementary to my application of the pilgrim church model to Christian civic virtue. Doyle captures the essence of *communio* ecclesiology in the following:

> Communion ecclesiology . . . represents an attempt to move beyond the merely juridical and institutional understandings by emphasizing the mystical, sacramental, *and* historical dimensions of the Church. *It focuses on relationships,* whether among the persons of the Trinity, among human beings and God, among the members of the Communion of Saints, among members of a parish, or among the bishops dispersed throughout the world. It emphasizes the dynamic interplay between the Church universal and the local churches. Communion ecclesiology stresses that the Church is not simply the receiver of revelation, but as the Mystical Body of Christ is bound up with revelation itself.[70]

Doyle's interpretation of *communio* ecclesiology is congruent with the intertextual and pastoral lens of the church as a listening, formed, and witnessing community developed above. His interpretation focuses on relationships that have both a transcendent and an immanent dimension. His description finds within *communio* ecclesiology a space for both the transcendent-mystical and immanent-historical dimensions of the church. As such it is able to capture the twofold set of commitments expressed in the paradox of the Christian pilgrimage through this earthly existence.

The paradoxical tension between the mystical-transcendent and the

---

68. Walter Kasper, *Theology and Church* (New York: Crossroad, 1989), p. 149.

69. Gerard Mannion, *Ecclesiology and Postmodernity: Questions for the Church in Our Time* (Collegeville, Minn.: Liturgical, 2007), especially p. 44.

70. Dennis M. Doyle, *Communion Ecclesiology: Vision and Versions* (Maryknoll, N.Y.: Orbis, 2000), p. 12, italics added.

historical-immanent aspects of the pilgrim church serves an important function for guiding the development of a Thomistic account of civic virtue. First, by highlighting the eschatological dimension of the church it is understood as a theological reality that ultimately transcends the congregation of the faithful, its juridical and institutional manifestations and structures, and the life of virtue that the church serves to foster. In other words these three aspects of the church, essential as they are in human history, are ultimately subordinate to the kingdom in which "God [will] be all in all" (1 Cor. 15:28). As Sabra states it, understanding the church primarily as a theological phenomenon is a "conception of the church that 'explodes' the limits of the [historically] constituted church."[71]

Dennis Doyle suggests, for example, that there are two contrasting models of the church that scholars have highlighted since Vatican II. The first, more often associated with a more conservative approach, includes the church as the mystical body of Christ, the bride of Christ, and the communion of saints. The second, more often associated with a more liberal or progressive approach, includes the church as people of God, pilgrim church, and servant church.[72] Doyle finds "the contrast between the mystical and historical to express one of the greatest points of tension in Catholic ecclesiology today."[73] Although the image of the pilgrim church falls into Doyle's second, historical group, a more holistic use of the image of the pilgrim church demands that it be considered one biblical and theological way of referring to the one mysterious reality that is the church. Thus, a comprehensive image of the pilgrim church entails both transcendent-mystical and historical-communal components that is a particularly apt model for thinking about a political vision for a pilgrim church.

Therefore, the communion of the church as the gathered congregation of the faithful is essential for the image of the pilgrim church that frames a discussion of civic virtue. The church itself is not a "thing." Rather it is a communion of persons called by God to listen to the Word of God, formed by grace into a people to act as free and dignified subjects in pursuit of their heavenly home and of the common good of this earth. It is precisely this gathering of a pilgrim people (a *synagogue, congregatio,* or *ecclesia*) who "are brought into being through the sacraments and the virtues"[74] that forms

---

71. Sabra, *Thomas Aquinas's Vision of the Church,* p. 181.
72. Doyle, *Communion Ecclesiology,* p. 11.
73. Doyle, *Communion Ecclesiology,* p. 18.
74. *Lumen gentium,* §11.

the notion of church that guides my exploration of civic virtue in Aquinas's thought.

The manner in which the image of the pilgrim church holds together the eschatological and historical dimensions of the Christian life prevents the church from being reduced to a mere sociological phenomenon that is justified only insofar as it forms model citizens who serve the common good. In other words, it resists the tendency — particularly strong in some strands of liberal thought — to reduce the church to either personal faith or its instrumental value in public life. A Thomistic theory of civic virtue seeks rather to articulate a way of harmonizing the pursuit of the earthly common good with the ultimate common good in the life of the wayfarer without reducing Christian virtue to political expediency or ideology. This connection will be expressed in a distinctively Thomistic manner when dealing with the relationship between the twofold ends of the one ultimate good of the human person, and between the acquired and infused virtues in Chapter 2.

The church as a *public* space of encounter between human and divine agency vouchsafes the transcendent nature of each human person and safeguards persons from the totalizing pretensions on the part of the state and its laws. In other words, it enables Christians to desacralize politics and in the process to challenge the tendency for political authority and state sovereignty to totalize human existence. As Louis Bouyer states it, there is always a tendency for the state to move "toward pretensions that are religious, if not quasi-divine."[75] The church is thus one aspect of contemporary civil life that guards against the totalizing tendencies of the modern nation-state. As a public institution in an increasingly secular culture, the church creates a space for examining contemporary politics and policies in light of the ultimate ideals and goals that transcend our limited experience of time and history. The pilgrim church serves as a constant reminder that both the state's and the church's authority derive from their roles in fostering the good of their individual members and the common good.

While the image of the pilgrim church safeguards individuals from these external pretentions of power, it also helps to protect Christians against the temptation to turn their political ideals and values into political ideology. Recalling one's pilgrim status frees the Christian from the constant temptation to make the things of this world into ultimate goods, or to interpret one's political goals and ideologies as necessarily consistent with the will of God. In this regard the pilgrim church highlights the analogical relationship be-

75. Bouyer, *Church of God*, p. 512.

tween the earthly city and the heavenly city of the New Jerusalem (see Heb. 12:22; Rev. 21:2), as classically articulated by Augustine in *The City of God*. I apply this insight to a Thomistic approach to civic virtue when discussing the relationship between nature and grace in Chapter 5.

Upholding the image of the pilgrim church enables Christians to resist associating the kingdom of God with either an idealized state or an idealized church in its pursuit of justice and charity. On the one hand, the perfect justice of the kingdom thus remains a transcendent goal, fully realized only by God's grace and not by human effort alone. But on the other hand, the tethering of the sacramental and institutional life of the church to the practice of all the virtues ensures that Christians cannot quietly withdraw from the societies in which they seek the imperfect — though no less necessary — justice that can be attained in this life.

The image of the pilgrim church is therefore an apt model for situating many of the issues that I discuss regarding the development of a Thomistic theory of civic virtue. The model of the pilgrim church helps to frame the discussions that follow in later chapters regarding (1) the one, transcendent end of the human person, which can be considered under a twofold aspect: one natural, the other supernatural, (2) the relationship between nature and grace, and its implications for (3) the relationship between the acquired and the infused virtues in civic life and (4) the nature of the common good as an analogical concept linking God as the ultimate good of all creation with the temporal common good that is the goal of civic virtue and justice. The rest of this book is dedicated to developing these ideas historically, theologically, and systematically, while also demonstrating the continued usefulness of a Thomistic account of civic virtue for life in the democratic societies of the late modern world.

The Structure of This Book

After an historical introduction to civic virtue in Chapter 1, the project of constructing a contemporary Thomistic account of civic virtue within democratic regimes proceeds in two parts. In the first part, I examine the work of Thomas Aquinas and some of his medieval, scholastic interlocutors on the virtue of justice and correlative concepts from which I begin to construct a Thomistic account of civic virtue. Chapter 1 serves as a bridge from our contemporary location to the historical account of Aquinas on justice. It begins within the discourse of modern Catholic social thought to make the case that a retrieval of Thomistic notions of civic virtue is needed in the contemporary church. In this chapter I begin by noting three tendencies for interpreting modern Catholic social thought. The first is the neoconservative tendency, which interprets Catholic social thought through the lens of neoclassical, free market economics. The second tends to reject the modern nation-state entirely as inimical to authentic Christian virtue, and to propose the church as an alternative society within which the virtues may flourish. The third tends to endorse liberalism, but often at the expense of keeping Christian virtue and identity in the forefront when engaging in contemporary politics. The Thomistic account of civic virtue developed from the work of Aquinas is most congruent with the latter two tendencies, as it both affirms and critiques certain aspects of these approaches to political engagement. Ultimately, however, I reject entirely the first tendency as incongruent with Catholic social thought. I also note that each group witnesses to a certain ambivalence toward the modern nation-state that forms a common thread in contemporary Catholic political thought.

In the second part of Chapter 1 I trace the development of the Catholic Church's relationship with the modern nation-state between the French Revolution (1789-99) and Vatican II (1962-65) to demonstrate where this ambiguity toward the state and political authority originates. Post-Revolutionary France marks a crucial turning point for Catholic political thought as it is the first time that the church is confronted with a secular, liberal regime intent on removing the church's influence from the political realm. The two and a half centuries between the Revolution and Vatican II are a time of refinement and clarification of the Catholic Church's stance toward the modern nation-state. I claim that it is only possible to understand Catholic social and political thought by recognizing how it rejects the more doctrinaire forms of liberalism's emphasis on the absolute value of freedom (over and against the common good), while upholding more moderate forms of liberal freedom that support the authentic flourishing and natural rights of human persons.

Chapter 2 turns toward an exegetical examination of Aquinas's discussion of general justice considered within the historical and theological context of the thirteenth century. It traces early scholastic discussions on the virtue of justice and notes the ways in which Aquinas both inherited and developed a rich tradition of thought on the virtues vis-à-vis the political community and sought to harmonize these with the transcendent end of the human wayfarer. I note the ways in which Aquinas understood general justice as functioning at the level of the temporal, human community in seeking to build up the common good, while also maintaining an intrinsic connection to the transcendent ends of the church and of the Christian wayfarer, and to the theological virtues (especially charity). When read in the context of medieval Christendom, it becomes more apparent that Aquinas's goal was to create a space for considering the temporal and political implications of general justice as distinct from the purely theological appraisal of infused virtues by distinguishing, yet not completely severing, the twofold ends of the virtues vis-à-vis politics and eschatology.

In addition to building a conceptual framework from which to develop an account of civic virtue, I suggest in this chapter that in the late modern era our task is the exact opposite of the one that confronted Aquinas and his interlocutors. If the medieval scholastics undertook the task of considering the political implications of justice as distinct from a sole focus on infused virtue, a contemporary theological account of civic virtue in a secular, pluralistic culture must seek to demonstrate how insights into the nature of the common good understood from within a distinctively theological paradigm of civic virtue continue to have something essential to contribute to the temporal aims of the political community in a pluralistic, secular age.[76] Despite this important cultural and temporal divide between our world and Aquinas's, however, I argue that there is much to learn from his discussion of general justice for a modern retrieval and development of civic virtue, and for pursuing the temporal common good while bearing in mind its connection to the ultimate common good of creation, who is God.

In Chapter 3 I remain focused on the work of Aquinas, but I move beyond what he claims explicitly about general justice and its related concepts to construct a fuller picture of what a Thomistic notion of civic virtue entails. Here I explore the intrinsic connection between justice as a virtue of the will and the emotions — in Aquinas's language, the affections and the passions — that motivate acts of civic virtue. Hence I explore what it means to speak about "a passion for justice" within the terms operative in Aquinas's Christian anthropology and his understanding of the motivational structure of human acts. Second, I explore the essential connection between civic virtue and prudence, or practical reasoning. Prudence is truly at the heart of the kind of moral deliberation that is necessary for pursuing the particular goods that sustain a thriving political community and the flourishing of its mem-

---

76. The cultural shift between these two worldviews is commonly accredited to, or blame is laid on, what is broadly referred to as "modernity." Charles Taylor calls this process the "Great Disembedding," and he writes that "what makes modern humanism unprecedented, of course, is the idea that this flourishing involves no relation to anything higher" (*A Secular Age* [Cambridge, Mass.: Belknap Press of Harvard University Press, 2007], p. 151).

bers. As the virtue of the intellect that connects the affections of the will (the seat of civic virtue) with the passions and ends of the moral virtues, political prudence is essential for sustaining the kind of public deliberation that is needed to maintain a vibrant civil discourse in pursuit of the common good.

The consideration of prudence also tethers my account of civic virtue to discussions of natural law as the intellectual framework within which practical reasoning and political deliberation are practiced. I begin to explore this connection in Chapter 3, both in relation to Aquinas's discussion of prudence and natural law and in relation to John Courtney Murray's re-appropriation of natural law in the mid-twentieth century. With regard to Murray, I claim that his account of natural law exhibits an elitism that is at its heart inimical to the kind of democratic civic virtue that I want to develop. Chapter 3 thus articulates the intrinsic connections between a Thomistic conception of civic virtue, the passions, prudence, and natural law. I conclude Part I with a summary and review of the aspects of Thomistic civic virtue that have been developed in Chapters 2 and 3.

In Part II I move into the modern context and begin to construct an account of Thomistic civic virtue for the church and liberal societies today. Although my primary audience is the Roman Catholic ecclesial context, given that the intellectual paradigm of my account of civic virtue is grounded in natural law, these ideas are intended to resonate with all Christians and those of other religious or philosophical traditions, insofar as they present a rationally coherent theory of civic engagement. The discussion of natural law begun in Chapter 3 connects directly to Chapters 4 and 5, where I begin by considering the modern context and discussions of civic virtue vis-à-vis two intellectual paradigms — natural law and political philosophy, respectively. These two chapters provide a cultural and conceptual framework within which the construction of a Thomistic account of civic virtue and public rhetoric is undertaken more fully in Chapter 6.

In Chapter 4 I locate a Thomistic notion of civic virtue within the discourse of natural law in the Catholic tradition. In particular, I revisit the status of Henri de Lubac's influential thesis regarding the relationship between nature and grace as a foundation for thinking about natural law morality. I survey recent scholarship on de Lubac that is more critical of his tendency to collapse the distinction between nature and grace in favor of emphasizing the supernatural over the natural. Like several recent critical responses to de Lubac, I also want to uphold a stronger distinction between nature and grace as a foundation for natural law than his thesis seems to allow. However, in defining my stance within this contemporary debate I distance myself from both the elitism in Murray's account of natural law and a kind of epistemic moral superiority that emerges from some scholars who critique de Lubac's work. Some ways of upholding a stronger distinction between nature and grace are also coupled with a tendency to downplay the capacities of natural reason in a manner that moves toward a quasi-Jansenist denigration of natural reason. I suggest that amending de Lubac's thesis in favor of a greater distinction between nature and grace provides a theoretical paradigm in Catholic moral theology for considering how civic virtue might contribute to a broadly humanistic and democratic form of deliberation, while still allowing room for distinctively theological or religious claims to contribute to the common good amid a pluralistic culture.

Chapter 5 then places a Thomistic concept of civic virtue in dialogue with two strands of political philosophy that are particularly salient for democratic societies today — the liberal and the classical republican traditions of political thought. As the journalist and political commentator E. J. Dionne notes, democratic societies, especially the American one, have been marked by dual and sometimes conflicting commitments to the individualistic tenets of modern liberal thought and of the more communitarian tradition of classical republicanism.[77] In considering the work of liberal political philosophers such as John Rawls, William Galston, and others, I note that the fundamental commitments of liberal political philosophy make it difficult for secular, liberal theorists to identify the common good without reducing it to an amalgamation of individual goods or rights. This is one area where a theological construal of civic virtue continues to have an essential contribution to make to the democratic discourse regarding the goods of political life — in particular the ability to name and act on behalf of the common good. Catholic social thought in general, and a Thomist account of civic virtue in particular, require that the common good be a real, subsistent good that is capable of being grasped by the will of moral agents. It also must be cognized as an object capable of individual and communal deliberation that serves to highlight the goods to be pursued in democratic societies. To speak in the language that Aquinas himself utilizes, the common good must be capable of reducing the will from potency to act in pursuit of a flourishing community. In particular I challenge Rawls's insistence that liberalism maintains the priority of the right over the good. As an alternative, I engage William Galston's work in identifying the substantive goods that liberal po-

---

77. E. J. Dionne, *Our Divided Political Heart: The Battle for the American Ideal in an Age of Discontent* (New York: Bloomsbury, 2012), pp. 92-99.

litical institutions seek to instantiate and defend. I also suggest, however, that if Rawls's priority of the right over the good is reversed in favor of the priority of the good over the right, then something like Rawls's overlapping consensus may provide a helpful paradigm for thinking about how Christians and others may deliberate together in pursuit of the common good in late modern democratic societies.

The second strand of democratic political thought that I engage in Chapter 5 is represented by the tradition of classical republicanism. In this section I engage the work of the influential British political philosopher Philip Pettit. In his defense of modern republican notions of freedom and the common good, he reminds us that there is an ancient tradition of thought that construes the relationship between individual freedom and the commonweal in terms that are critical of liberalism's emphasis on negative freedom, and that are strikingly familiar to those that have been maintained in some strands of Thomistic thought. Both Augustine and Aquinas were familiar with Cicero and the Roman republican tradition, and both kept aspects of that tradition alive within their distinctively theological considerations of politics and civic virtue. Engaging Pettit indicates that a theological account of civic virtue may participate in constructive dialogue with other political philosophies operative within modern democratic societies that also construe the relationship between individual autonomy and the common good somewhat differently than most liberal thinkers. In fact, the balance — and sometimes the direct tension — between the emphasis on negative freedom (that is, the absence of external interference from others or from the state) in the liberal tradition and the intrinsic connection between autonomy and community in the republican tradition suggests that contemporary liberal politics is not entirely inimical to more robust notions of civic virtue and the common good. The account of rhetoric tethered to civic virtue that I subsequently develop in Chapter 6 seeks to harness this tension and direct it toward the common good by cultivating a robust discourse regarding the goods of liberal, democratic societies that enable the pursuit of individual and communal flourishing in democratic societies.

In Chapter 6 I apply the Thomistic notion of civic virtue to a consideration of how Christians are called to engage in public deliberation about the goods of democratic societies. Here I engage the work of James Davison Hunter in defining and critiquing the notion of the "culture wars" and propose that Christians rethink their predominant ways of engaging in culture and politics. Civic virtue suggests that Christians reframe public political discussions to move away from the conception that Christians must fight a "culture war" to save liberal, democratic culture from itself. I believe that the culture war mentality is disastrous for two reasons. The first is that it is spiritually destructive for those Christians who engage in it and for the church as a whole. The culture war mentality only serves to underwrite the modern theological error that tends to place temporal and political power above the transcendent aims of the church. Or stated in another way, it makes the church into a political instrument of a particular political end or ideology. The second reason is that the culture wars approach is bad politics. It tends to foster self-righteousness on the part of those who claim to speak for the moral core of the Western, democratic tradition (or of the church), and as a consequence it tends to foster resentment and stagnation in regard to public deliberation about the goods of liberal societies. Ultimately, engaging in the rhetoric of the culture wars only leads to a dissolution of moral meaning and value that is so essential for appreciating the ongoing validity of natural law reasoning and the vitality of democratic institutions.

As an alternative, a Thomistic account of civic virtue turns to a substantive engagement with Aristotelian rhetoric and some contemporary philosophers of rhetoric to develop a proactive model of Christian engagement in public deliberation about the common good. I engage the work of Eugene Garver, who highlights the ways in which Aristotle helps us to understand the nature of public deliberation in democratic societies. In particular, he underscores the intrinsic connection between reason or logic *(logos)*, character *(ethos)*, and emotion or passions *(pathos)* in public deliberation. Rhetoric seeks to integrate all three of these and to direct them toward the pursuit of practical deliberation and moral truth in the political community. What rhetoric provides for a pilgrim church is a deeper appreciation for the ways in which the logical rigor of the Catholic moral and natural law tradition are not our only tools in seeking the common good. Rhetoric provides a way to witness to the existence of the common good utilizing not only logic, but also by submitting our moral claims to the deliberation of the political community as a sign of trust and in an effort to build civic friendship. Such acts of humility lend greater authenticity and credibility to Christian moral witness and ultimately enable Christians to deliberate with others in a pluralistic society in pursuit of practical moral truth that will serve the common good of all members of the body politic.

Finally, in the conclusion, I tie together the image of the pilgrim church from Chapter 1 with the model of rhetoric developed in Chapter 6 by noting that they both focus on the central notion of public witness. The politics of a pilgrim church is united by its commitment to truthful and authentic witness, and the members of the pilgrim church witness to the truth of the gospel in the church's ecclesiological and political witness. I then provide some practical suggestions for considering how civic virtue might motivate new ways of engaging culture and politics. I draw on the examples provided by Sant'Egidio and the Focolare movement, two lay apostolates whose members are engaging in cultural dialogue in creative and constructive ways that are illuminative for understanding how a Thomistic theory of civic virtue might function in liberal, pluralistic cultures. Civic virtue provides a normative paradigm for all persons of good will, and for the members of a pilgrim church in particular, for seeking to enhance and support the common good.

CHAPTER 1

The Theological Challenge of Political Authority

Introduction

At the time I am writing, there is a general ambivalence among Christian theologians about political engagement in the modern nation-state system, a deep cynicism about the hopes for civil political discourse between rival camps of political ideologies, and a general anxiety about the future of Western culture as a whole. Are we on a steady decline toward the eroding of the moral core of Western civilization? And if so, what is the role of the church within that decline and the potential renewal of that moral core? Are we experiencing a particularly difficult period in our history, but one that will ultimately be overcome with a courageous political and cultural renewal? Or are we simply witnessing a particular manifestation of the wisdom from Ecclesiastes "that there is nothing new under the sun" (1:9), and that the struggle for justice in the earthly city has always been marred by sin and imperfection? Whichever way one answers these questions, almost no one — Christian or otherwise — believes that the deep ideological divides in our society today reflect an ideal, or even desirable, state of affairs. Financial uncertainty, continued wars and conflicts of culture and ideology, political rhetoric based on anger and hatred rather than dialogue and mutual trust, a lack of trust in the political process, self-interest (especially financial self-interest) above a sense of the common good — all of these are bemoaned by many in our political climate.

But the fact that there is an often-unarticulated sense of what we want to be as a people indicates that there are ideals of civic virtue that still call us to a more authentic expression of ourselves as a people. Even as we live in a pluralistic, secular age, many of our most cherished political ideals were formed within the crucible of a history that involves a complex tradition of theological and philosophical commitments that have contributed to the development of Western political thought. Therefore, understanding the historical forces that led to our current situation can help us to see the present in new ways, and most important, may help us to envision new ways of moving forward. The Thomistic account of civic virtue that I develop offers just such a hopeful way forward, first by looking back to a shared past, then by reevaluating our present situation, and finally by offering tools to look forward toward a common future in the ongoing pilgrimage through this life in search of the common good.

One source for a renewed hope may be found in the cultivation of civic virtue embodied in the members of the body politic of democratic societies.[1] I define civic virtue — following Aristotle's and Aquinas's discussion of general justice — as *a firm and stable disposition to direct the acts of the virtues toward the common good of one's society.* The goal of this chapter is to trace the reasons that civic virtue has been overlooked or underdeveloped within contemporary Catholic moral, political, and social thought, and to suggest that this notion can be re-appropriated, in particular with the help of Thomas Aquinas's moral and political thought. Moreover, this account proves fruitful for a theological understanding, on both a theoretical and a practical level, of the ways in which Christians are called to build up and enhance the common good within contemporary democratic societies, even while striving for a transcendent end beyond the social conditions of this life.

For Aquinas, each virtue is defined in relation to its object, and the object of civic virtue is the common good. The concept of the common good has been a remarkably flexible and influential ideal that has been upheld within the tradition of Catholic moral thought (though certainly other traditions recognize and defend it as well). Despite its endurance, there remains a certain amount of ambiguity when it comes to the ways in which the common good is defined and employed in political thought. Thus, it is

1. For the purposes of this study, I use Jacques Maritain's language and description of the "body politic" in *Man and the State* (Chicago: University of Chicago Press, 1951) interchangeably with what contemporary sociologists typically refer to as "civil society" — that is, the entire collection of persons, institutions, organizations, businesses, groups, and government agencies that make up a particular society. In addition, I intentionally try to avoid the use of the term "citizens" and favor instead the phrase "members of the body politic" to refer to those persons who embody civic virtue to include and recognize those who are not legally recognized citizens but who nonetheless contribute in essential ways to the common good of the body politic.

not always entirely clear what is meant when Catholic moral theologians or the magisterium of the church use the phrase. For example, the temporal common good can be considered analogically as related to the ultimate common good of the universe, who is God — the theological approach. It can be considered as a good that transcends individual human goods — the classical republican approach. It may be taken as the sum total of the goods possessed by a collection of individuals — the liberal approach. Or it can be defined as an instrumental good that secures the possibility for persons to pursue their own, individual ideals of the good or human flourishing — the neoconservative approach. Following Augustine's interpretation of Cicero in *The City of God,* I define the common good as a set of ideals or values that are embodied in a particular way of life within a community and that provide a meaningful context in which members of that community are enabled to engage in meaningful and collective endeavors. The common good is the collective value that a community places on particular ways of life, practices, ideals, and goods and is roughly equivalent to what Augustine calls a community's "common objects of love" (*De civitate Dei* XIV 28). I believe this definition to be an adequate representation both of what Aquinas means when he speaks of the object of general justice as the common good, and of the ways that the common good functions (or ideally functions) within late modern democratic societies.

Because I am a Roman Catholic moral theologian writing in America in the twenty-first century, my approach is focused on the Roman Catholic Church as a social-spiritual location for engaging in politics. At the same time I also engage directly with the political philosophies that have formed the institutions and practices of the democratic tradition. Thus, my approach is focused on the sources and histories that have formed both the Catholic and the liberal, democratic traditions of the West. While I focus primarily on the work of Thomas Aquinas and his interpreters within the tradition of Catholic social thought, I also engage a wide array of theological and political thinkers to construct a contemporary theological account of civic virtue. It is this notion of civic virtue that provides the normative core that holds together the interdisciplinary engagement in Part II of this book. The structure of this book mirrors the broader rhetorical goals of the work, in which I write as one conscious of my own tradition and its practices and resources, but in an attempt to engage in a rhetorical style that is fitting for the pluralistic context that defines political engagement in our day.

The claim that Western political culture has become increasingly polarized among competing and increasingly insular islands of ideological thought is hardly in need of defense, and the same kind of division can be found within the church as well.[2] In what follows I identify three tendencies among those who interpret the political implications of Catholic social thought. I offer these characterizations with full cognizance that doing so requires oversimplification of a tradition as wide and historically diverse as Catholic social and political thought. Bearing in mind that these are not hard and fast distinctions but rather tendencies, the following three trends in modern Catholic social thought remain helpful for situating the account of civic virtue that follows.

The first tendency consists of the neoconservative interpreters of the tradition of Catholic social thought. One encounters in these thinkers a distaste for state power in relation to economics because of a preference for free market capitalism and self-interest, combined with a relatively uncritical use of state power in national defense and military intervention. There is seemingly unflinching trust in what the twentieth-century Austrian economist Friedrich Hayek referred to as "spontaneous order."[3] They see any form of strong government as an impediment to industry and economic growth, and as a de facto hindrance to individual freedom and autonomy. The common good is best achieved — in fact, can only be achieved — by standing back and letting the forces of self-interest and the free market reach a just equilibrium.

A second tendency involves advocating for Christian political engagement outside the mechanisms of the modern nation-state. Frequently scholars who follow this trend focus on the Christian call to pacifism and nonviolence and on building local forms of community and political engagement. In their estimation, this allows Christians to avoid as much as possible the violence of the nation-state and the exclusionary forces of the capitalist economy. Despite the many ideological, theological, and practical differ-

---

2. Massimo Faggioli claims that this intra-ecclesial division is particularly acute in the American context, in part due to the fact that the two-party system limits the political loyalties and imaginations of American Catholics (see "The View from Abroad: The Shrinking Common Ground in the American Church," *America* 210, no. 6 [February 24, 2014]: 20-23, p. 22).

3. Hayek outlines this kind of spontaneous order in *Law, Legislation and Liberty* (Chicago: University of Chicago Press, 1973). For an excellent treatment of the development of late modern notions of market freedom and its relation to classical republican virtue and political thought, see Eric MacGilvray, *The Invention of Market Freedom* (New York: Cambridge University Press, 2011), especially chapters 4-5. The citation of Hayek regarding spontaneous order can be found on p. 145, note 54.

ences that divide these first two approaches to civic virtue, they both share a general lack of trust in the political institutions of the modern, democratic state (save for the use of military intervention advocated by those of the neoconservative tendency). For both of these schools of thought the nation-state system has proven unable to provide a public space for practicing even a limited sense of civic virtue in pursuit of the common good.

The third tendency sees the mechanism of the state as a necessary force for instituting justice within democratic societies and frequently lends theological or ecclesial support to democratic political institutions. While the first two groups reject — or at least denigrate — Christian involvement in the state, those who tend toward this more liberal approach face a different set of challenges. That is, the temptation for liberal political theology is a recurring tendency to place liberal politics before Christian and ecclesial identity. If left unchecked, this temptation leads to submerging distinctively theological claims in favor of a broad public consensus on liberal political aims amid a pluralistic society. Louis Bouyer refers to this as a doctrinaire form of "contemporary Progressivism" that leads to the "dissolution of *any* traditional sense."[4] This doctrinaire liberalism erodes the very tradition on which a robustly theological notion of civic virtue might be based.

A few examples will help to highlight my claims regarding these three tendencies in Catholic social thought. Michael Novak and George Weigel both exemplify the first tendency toward neoconservative interpretation of Catholic social thought. They both hold an exceptionally attenuated understanding of the role of civic virtue. The key problem with trying to square neoconservative political and economic thought with Aquinas and the tradition of Catholic social thought revolves around their understanding of what Novak calls "order unplanned"[5] and what Weigel calls "ordered liberty."[6] Novak, for example, claims that citizens in liberal societies do not (in fact, cannot) *intend* the common good, but that they can only discover it in the working out of their own economic self-interest. For Novak, practical reasoning yields choices that are based on an individual's estimation of the maximization of "self-interest *rightly* understood."[7] The common good

4. Louis Bouyer, *Church of God: Body of Christ and Temple of the Spirit,* trans. Charles Underhill Quinn (San Francisco: Ignatius, 2011), p. 159.

5. Michael Novak, *Free Persons and the Common Good* (New York: Madison, 1989), chapter 3: "Order Unplanned," pp. 75-109.

6. George Weigel, *Catholicism and the Renewal of American Democracy* (Mahwah, N.J.: Paulist, 1989), p. 9.

7. Picking up this concept from Tocqueville, he develops what he perceives to be the

is achieved for Novak through an amalgamation of individual choices. He writes that the liberal conception of the common good is that its "essence consists in mutual cooperation *apart from the common intention, aims, and purposes*" of individuals or of political authorities.[8] While thinkers such as James Madison, Lord Acton, and Alexis de Tocqueville are invoked to defend this conception of the common good, the theories that seem to be driving Novak's work, but which are never footnoted or invoked, are a particular interpretation of Adam Smith's invisible hand and Hayek's notion of spontaneous order. The belief that the common good can be achieved without directing the intentions of the members of the body politic toward it through some form of cooperation between individual wills and political authority is logically incoherent.

A Thomistic account of civic virtue demands that individuals direct their desires toward the pursuit of justice and the common good of one's community. The belief that the common good can be achieved without the direction of either the will of certain individuals or of some form of civil authority completely negates the insights of the tradition of Thomistic moral philosophy on which Catholic social thought has been developed. As Thomas Rourke notes, the society that Novak is describing is one "in which none intends . . . a particular good [and] is like a dead world."[9] The ultimate fault in Novak's line of reasoning comes from transposing many of the assumptions operative in contemporary neoclassical economics into the realm of Catholic political and moral thought. In the process he not only distorts the rich tradition of Catholic social thought, but he also completely eliminates the possibility of developing a Thomistic account of civic virtue. It is axiomatic in the neoconservative approach that the common good cannot in principle be the object of intentional acts of virtue.

Weigel's work also admits of similar faults in assuming that a version of Catholic moral and political philosophy can be developed out of an economic theory of free markets. To be fair, in his attempt to proclaim a "Catholic moment" for American Catholicism in the late 1980s and early 1990s, he does present a more robust conception of the moral tradition of the church than Novak. To do this, he argues that his vision of the church's contribution to public debates about civic virtue goes beyond the material concerns of

---

correct understanding of self-interest in chapter 2 of *Free Persons and the Common Good*, pp. 41-74.

8. Novak, *Free Persons and the Common Good*, p. 83, italics added.

9. Thomas R. Rourke, "Michael Novak and Yves R. Simon on the Common Good and Capitalism," *Review of Politics* 58, no. 2 (1996): 229-58, p. 244.

what he calls a bourgeois church. Such a church is "characterized by a self-ishness and radical individualism which has little or no concern for moral norms, or for the common good."[10] And yet his analysis of the moral contribution to be made to contemporary culture by the Catholic Church remains focused almost exclusively at the level of sexual morality. At the same time his approach lacks the resources necessary to account for or potentially overcome the social or moral problems that arise out of the kind of alienation and exclusion that is often fostered by the forces of an unfettered free market.

Nowhere is his selective interpretation of Catholic social thought more evident than in his commentary on Pope Benedict's encyclical, *Caritas in veritate* (June 29, 2009). In an article commenting on the encyclical Weigel suggests that the social justice claims made by Benedict XVI in the encyclical do not represent his true thoughts. Rather, they can be disregarded as ideological remarks inserted into the document by members of Pontifical Council for Justice and Peace. Benedict's true thoughts, according to Weigel, lie in his concern for the "life issues." Any remarks that he makes about the problems of exclusion, alienation, or disproportionate distribution of wealth in today's market economy are a remnant of those who still hold to the Marxist ideology that dominated socially conscious Catholicism and liberation theologians in the 1970s.[11] Such claims ignore the thoughts that Benedict has proclaimed publicly on these issues. For example, he has written that "democratic socialism has proved to be a healthy counterweight to radical liberal positions . . . On many points, democratic socialism has been and remains close to Catholic social doctrine, and it has at any rate made a considerable contribution to the creation of a social consciousness."[12] The neoconservative tendency can only be defended by such selective interpretation of the Catholic social tradition.

The refusal on the part of Novak to admit of any role for the virtue of justice or civic virtue in terms of intentional action aimed at the common good, and Weigel's narrowing of all political and moral analysis to reproductive or sexual issues represent significant attenuations of the theory and practice of civic virtue such as may be developed out of the work of Thomas Aquinas and the subsequent tradition of Catholic social thought. The desire

10. Weigel, *Catholicism and the Renewal of American Democracy,* p. 16.

11. See George Weigel, "*Caritas in Veritate* in Gold and Red: The Revenge of Justice and Peace (or So They May Think)," *National Review Online Edition* (July 7, 2009). Accessed January 3, 2014.

12. Benedict XVI, *Values in a Time of Upheaval,* trans. Brian McNeil (San Francisco: Ignatius, 2006), p. 144.

to fit the Catholic social tradition into the narrow confines of the neoconservative, extreme liberal (that is, laissez-faire economics) paradigm leads to a significant denigration of the full theological account of civic virtue that is particularly needed from Christians at this time.

The second tendency is more difficult to classify within the American political spectrum, but there is a similar distrust of the modern nation-state as in the first tendency. The rejection of the nation-state among this second trend is typically grounded either in a commitment to Christian pacifism or in a rejection of the capitalist market system. I am sympathetic to the concerns of this second tendency, insofar as they rightly point out the abusive use of violence and the tendency of capitalist markets to exclude and dominate those with the least access to power and capital. Thinkers such as Michael Baxter and William Cavanaugh both work as Catholic moral theologians to create a distinctive blend of the Christian pacifism advocated by John Howard Yoder (a Mennonite) and Stanley Hauerwas (a former Methodist who is now Anglican) with Alasdair MacIntyre's (a Roman Catholic) criticisms of capitalism and state power as inimical to practices that foster virtue.

William Cavanaugh's view on the role of the state vis-à-vis the church is evident in the title of the first chapter of his recent book, "Killing for the Telephone Company: Why the Nation-State Is Not the Keeper of the Common Good."[13] Cavanaugh argues that the modern nation-state does not qualify as a natural social institution (in the Aristotelian-Thomistic sense), but is rather a perversion of the traditional notion of political authority. Contrary to Jacques Maritain's analysis in *Man and the State*,[14] Cavanaugh suggests that the modern state is not simply the uppermost coordinating authority of what Maritain calls the "body politic" whose purpose is to coordinate the actions of the people toward the common good. In practice the state therefore absorbs the whole of society into itself, essentially violating the doctrine of subsidiarity and becoming a tyrannical or totalitarian state.[15] Basing his argument on examples of the failures of modern states to secure the common good, he argues that the liberal state is not to be understood as an example of the natural need for political authority. Rather, it is a construc-

13. William T. Cavanaugh, *Migrations of the Holy: God, State, and the Political Meaning of the Church* (Grand Rapids: Eerdmans, 2011), chapter 1.

14. Jacques Maritain describes these distinctions in chapter 1, "The People and the State," in *Man and the State*, pp. 1-27. For him, "The State is only that part of the body politic especially concerned with the maintenance of law, the promotion of the common welfare and public order, and the administration of public affairs" (p. 12).

15. Cavanaugh, *Migrations of the Holy*, pp. 24-33.

tion of nineteenth-century doctrinaire liberalism. This kind of doctrinaire liberalism for Cavanaugh is not simply an imperfect expression of the natural need for humans as social animals to live together under a common law (as Augustine or Aquinas might have understood). Rather, it is akin to a modern heresy that explicitly rejects the theological foundations of political authority. As such, Christians are to avoid participation in the modern state to the extent possible and focus on the local ecclesial and political communities within which the practice of the virtues remains a viable option.

Part of what is missing from a critique such as Cavanaugh's, however, is precisely the kind of distinctions that Maritain upholds in *Man and the State* between state, nation, and the body politic. By failing to distinguish between these levels of public and political culture, a critique of the power structures of the state (even when correct and necessary) becomes inseparable from rejection of the entire project of political authority and legitimacy. Thus, it seems that the only viable alternative is for Christians to turn away from the engagement with the political life of the state, and any other social institutions or practices bound up with it. In a recent article, co-written with Michael Baxter, Cavanaugh responds to the accusation that their work promotes disengagement with the state. They claim that they are not advocating withdrawal from the state, "any more than we could advocate withdrawal from the weather. At this point in history, nation-states are a fact of life; they are there, like the sun and the rain."[16] Instead, they "advocate for experiments in local, face-to-face community where democracy is not an empty slogan."[17] From the standpoint of civic virtue, however, the challenge to those who exhibit this second tendency is that they offer strong and incisive critiques of the injustice of the modern state, but provide very little normative content in regard to how one might faithfully engage in the civic and cultural milieu of democratic states. Despite protests to the contrary, the thrust of their work seems to suggest that Christians should try to avoid engagement with contemporary forms of political power in modern nation-states.

Given the liberal assumption that the state has a monopoly on coercive power and the total rejection of such power in this second tendency, very few venues are left for practical engagement in the higher levels of the body politic — or in the mechanisms of the state — by Christians. Even if one is sympathetic to the goal of fostering local forms of virtuous community, which I wholeheart-

---

16. William Cavanaugh and Michael Baxter, "Reply to 'A View from Abroad' by Massimo Faggioli," *America Magazine Online Edition* (March 31, 2014). Accessed April 11, 2014.

17. Cavanaugh and Baxter, "Reply to 'A View from Abroad.'"

edly support, there seems to be no logical reason that Christian engagement should stop short of the official mechanisms of state. Moreover, in such a context the church becomes an isolated, privileged locus of both orthodoxy and orthopraxy — of morality, politics, and liturgy — that is left uncorrupted by abusive forms of power. The price of such moral and spiritual purity, however, is the lessening of the force of precisely the kind of solidarity on which an authentic Christian humanism and a theory of civic virtue depends. As the sociologist James Davison Hunter states it, "Cavanaugh argues that many efforts to distinguish the public from the political fail because so much of the public is subsumed by the state — its laws, policies, and other instrumentalities."[18] Any viable theory of civic virtue, however, must remain cognizant of the kind of distinctions between state, nation, and body politic (Maritain), or between public culture and politics (Hunter). In the absence of these distinctions, Christians are left with little positive venues for the enactment of civic virtue in its fullest expression. Civic virtue as I am describing it becomes attenuated under such conditions, or is at least reduced to the public or political significance of acts of Christian virtue or worship that do not have direct political intent.

A similar lack of distinction between the various political aspects of society can be seen in Michael Baxter's criticisms of the modern state. In criticizing the work of Charles Curran and Michael and Kenneth Himes, Baxter writes that the desire for Catholics to provide an ethic for "the wider society" subverts the ecclesial dimension of Catholic social ethics. Ultimately, such efforts end up as a form of uncritical endorsement of the sovereign power of "the empire, the domain of the king, or the nation-state."[19] He claims that those who follow the work of John Courtney Murray in trying to engage the modern nation-state end up being co-opted by its all-encompassing power and its typical expressions of political rhetoric and divisiveness. For Baxter, this kind of engagement threatens the Christian identity of all those who engage in attempts to live out a commitment to Christian virtue in liberal, democratic states.

For example, in a recent commentary on Murray's work in *America Magazine* Baxter writes:

> For several decades Alasdair MacIntyre has been arguing on Thomistic-Aristotelian grounds — the same grounds on which Father Murray argued

---

18. James Davison Hunter, *To Change the World: The Irony, Tragedy, and Possibility of Christianity in the Late Modern World* (New York: Oxford University Press, 2010), p. 163.

19. Michael J. Baxter, "The Non-Catholic Character of the 'Public Church,'" *Modern Theology* 11, no. 2 (April 1995): 243-58, p. 257.

— that the natural law does not serve the modern state but subverts it, that the modern state must be resisted because it is corrosive to the practices and virtues necessary for genuine political community. Only small-scale, practice-based communities, MacIntyre argues, can support the kind of practical reasoning aimed at achieving the common good.[20]

On the one hand, it is certainly true that the natural law tradition calls for resistance to certain forms of injustice and coercive uses of power. On the other hand, one has to selectively read the postconciliar developments in the Catholic Church in relation to liberal political practices to claim that the only faithful response to liberalism is for Catholics to join small-scale communities of resistance to the state. A broader theological perspective is needed to make sense out of the complex forms of power that are exhibited in the cultural matrix of late modern democratic societies. And such a perspective must account for the complex history regarding the relationship between the Catholic Church and the modern nation-state system. I explore this history in the following section.

For both Cavanaugh and Baxter the modern nation-state presents an either-or choice between loyalty to the church and loyalty to the state, and they challenge Catholics to side decisively with the church. I remain sympathetic to their desire to place ecclesial identity ahead of political or national identity (or what is more likely today, partisan political identity).[21] Indeed, the image of the pilgrim church developed in the introduction insists that the purpose of the Christian wayfarer is to "seek first the kingdom of God" (Matt. 6:33). I also find myself in support of their efforts to sustain small, local communities of virtue. The problem, however, with their approach is that neither Cavanaugh nor Baxter is able to present a viable alternative to democratic states that does not seem to lead back either to some form of integration between church-state relationships or to an idealized, persecuted early church prior to Constantine's legalization of Christianity. Neither of these, however, presents a viable alternative or positive vision to guide Christian political engagement in the late modern context. A pilgrim church

20. Michael J. Baxter, "Murray's Mistake," *America* 209, no. 7, EBSCO*host*, Notre Dame, Ind., Notre Dame University Web. Accessed January 6, 2014.

21. I would add here that both Cavanaugh and Baxter have demonstrated a personal commitment to serving the poor and the most vulnerable in society, and in this they both provide important witnesses to Christian humility and virtue. My disagreement with them lies more in their *political* interpretation of the theological tradition, not in their commitment to service as an expression of Christian charity.

has more to offer pluralistic, democratic societies than rebukes of its pretensions toward violence and ideology, even as these are often necessary components of its prophetic dialogue with contemporary political institutions.

The third tendency might be broadly labeled liberal political theology. In this third trend, David Hollenbach comes closest to endorsing the vision of civic virtue and the pursuit of the common good that I develop in this book. For example, he claims that what we need in a modern, pluralistic, liberal, democratic state is the virtue of civility. He defines civility as "a personal virtue that leads citizens to seek to live together cooperatively."[22] Moreover, he is interested in providing a conception of the common good that challenges the thin notions of the good that are upheld in much liberal political thought. He believes that the Christian tradition possesses deeper theological resources than are often employed in liberal thought, and that these can make significant contributions to the contemporary discourses about democratic politics.

While I agree with many of his basic tenets, his work suggests that there is room to explore deeper theological resources for the Christian tradition for the ongoing development of civic virtue. Outside of a brief commentary on Augustine's and Aquinas's contributions to modern notions of the common good and the desacralization of politics,[23] when it comes to the actual analytic and/or prescriptive work of his text, much of the substantive work is done by social scientific data and liberal political thought. As I claim in Part I, liberal political thought has difficulty describing and working toward anything that might be construed as a common good that cannot be reduced to an instrumental good or a sum total of individual goods or rights. Despite all the talk of the common good in ecclesial and theological circles, a coherent and systematically developed language for seeking the common good remains a visible lacuna in much contemporary Catholic social thought. The Thomistic account of civic virtue that I develop throughout this work aims to contribute to the construction of just such a discourse and practice of working toward the common good.

I become more sympathetic with the claims of each of these three tendencies as we move from the first to the third. The downside is that my account of civic virtue is most susceptible to the challenges posed to this third group. A consistent temptation (even when not intended) within lib-

---

22. David Hollenbach, S.J., *The Common Good and Christian Ethics* (Cambridge: Cambridge University Press, 2002), p. 145.

23. Hollenbach, *The Common Good and Christian Ethics,* pp. 120-36.

eral political theology is to see the church, or Catholic social thought, as a utilitarian means of endorsing the ends and aims of the nation-state, or at the very least of one's partisan vision of the temporal common good. It becomes what sociologists would call a "functionalist" view of religion — that is, the church or theological notions of civic virtue become important not in and of themselves, but insofar as they contribute to other utilitarian ends. The aims of a pilgrim church proclaiming the gospel through history can never be conflated with the penultimate aims of the political community. In other words, theology must come before policy, no matter how passionately Christians pursue the common good. This is the fundamental theological problem posed by theological engagement in the political authority and apparatus of the state. How do we maintain the conviction that our primary aims are not political but rather eschatological and soteriological, while also striving toward the common good?

A Thomistic notion of civic virtue recognizes that the ultimate goals of the church transcend any earthly community, while at the same time it seeks to harmonize the ultimate end of the Christian wayfarer — friendship with God in charity — with the penultimate ends of the political community. The aims of justice and the common good remain important insofar as they are a primary way that Christians are called to live out love of neighbor. Yet we must always remain vigilant against a correlative temptation to hope for a utopian society this side of the eschaton. The pervasiveness of sin and human suffering leads to a more chastened, yet no less real, sense of hope for seeking the temporal common good. Before clarifying these theological points, however, there is an important question to be answered: How did these prevailing approaches to Catholic engagement in modern politics come to dominate our discourse? A brief turn to history will help to clarify this question.

Civic Virtue in Catholic Social Thought

Every culture is inevitably shaped by the stories that it tells and retells about its founding ideals, how they have been enacted — or ignored — in a people's history, and how the history of those ideals both informs its current practices and opens possibilities for greater fidelity to those ideals in the future. This is no less true of the pilgrim church than it is of any particular nation or political community. As the historian Eric Foner writes, history "is not simply a collection of facts, not a politically sanctioned listing of indisputable 'truths,' but an ongoing means of collective self-understanding about the nature of our society."[24] Thus, the telling of history is inextricably political, and therefore my account of civic virtue is tethered to an account of the history of the relationship between the church and political authority. Such a history must facilitate the accomplishment of two related tasks. First, it must show how the most salient features of a Thomistic account of civic virtue remain underdeveloped within contemporary Catholic social thought. Second, it must demonstrate why a recovery of this particular Thomistic notion of civic virtue enables us to address the problems that confront Christians and others living in modern, democratic societies with new insight for today. Such an account must infuse us with a greater sense of identity rooted in our shared history and ecclesiological tradition and, equally important, with renewed hope for the future.

In turning to history, Russell Hittinger and Emile Perreau-Saussine are correct to note that to understand modern Catholic social thought on the nature of political engagement it is necessary to understand the impact that the French Revolution continues to have on the Catholic Church's relationship with the modern nation-state.[25] To comprehend what a radical shift the French Revolution caused for the church it will be helpful to look a little more closely at the situation in Europe prior to 1789. After the principle of *cuius regio, eius religio* ("whose realm, his religion") was established by the Peace of Augsburg in 1555 and later extended throughout Europe by the Peace of Westphalia in 1648 it was the common practice for local princes and kingdoms to officially endorse the particular denomination of Christianity that they found to be most personally appealing, most politically expeditious, or some combination thereof.[26]

Thus, after the Protestant Reformation and the wars of religion in the sixteenth and seventeenth centuries signaled the end of medieval Chris-

---

24. Eric Foner, *Who Owns History? Rethinking the Past in a Changing World* (New York: Hill and Wang, 2002), p. 188.

25. See Russell Hittinger, "Introduction to Modern Catholicism," in *The Teachings of Modern Roman Catholicism on Law, Politics, and Human Nature,* ed. John Witte Jr. and Frank S. Alexander (New York: Columbia University Press, 2007), pp. 1-38, p. 2, and Emile Perreau-Saussine, *Catholicism and Democracy: An Essay in the History of Political Thought,* trans. Richard Rex (Princeton, N.J.: Princeton University Press, 2012), p. 4. Later he writes that "from the French Revolution to Vatican II, France played a decisive part in shaping the response of the Catholic Church to liberal democracy" (p. 116).

26. See John Witte Jr. and Joel A. Nichols, *Religion and the American Constitutional Experiment,* 3rd ed. (New York: Westview, 2010), p. 10.

tendom, both the Protestant churches and the Roman Catholic Church in Europe survived by aligning themselves with princes or kings who were willing to provide political support and protection. This is what Hittinger calls the *"ius patronus"* model, or the system of patronal privileges.[27] Perreau-Saussine refers to this model in pre-Revolutionary France as the tradition of "political Gallicanism."[28] Political Gallicanism as a Catholic political philosophy upheld a necessary distinction between the political and ecclesial powers. At the same time, however, it was built on a close cooperation between the two powers. Both were seen as necessary for upholding a just social order. Proponents of this political Gallicanism or *ius patronus* model expected Christian kings or princes to uphold the rights of the church. In response the church supported the political rights of the prince in his own affairs, and in turn this tended to infuse the political realm with a tinge of the sacred. Both the *ius patronus* model and political Gallicanism expected mutual cooperation between church and state.

Thus, according to Hittinger the "architects of the French Revolution of 1789 did not invent, but rather inherited, the principle that the Church, as a visible and temporal society, was the property of the state."[29] The novelty of the French Revolution was not the patronal status of the church in regard to civic authority, but rather that the civil authority was thoroughly infused with an Enlightenment political philosophy of *laïcité* — that is, a vision of secular government that was not just indifferent to religion, but hostile to religion in political life. Given the history of pre-Revolutionary France,[30] the revolutionaries were particularly hostile to the Roman Church, which they viewed as at odds with the ideals of equality, fraternity, and liberty.[31] This

27. Hittinger, "Introduction to Modern Catholicism," pp. 4, 8.

28. Perreau-Saussine describes it in the following manner: "This constituted 'political Gallicanism,' the doctrine of the French monarchy: the king of France held his kingdom from God alone and recognized no superior power on earth. Though as a Catholic he was a subject of the pope, as a sovereign he owed the papacy nothing" (*Catholicism and Democracy*, p. 15).

29. Hittinger, "Introduction to Modern Catholicism," p. 6.

30. King Louis XIV's (1638-1715) revocation of the Edict of Nantes (ratified in 1598), which permitted religious toleration of Protestant churches in France, was seen as a particularly problematic result of Gallicanism's close association between ecclesial and political authority (see Witte and Nichols, *Religion and the American Constitutional Experiment*, pp. 13-14).

31. The church's initial reaction to the Revolution is exemplified in Pope Pius VI's response to the *Civil Constitution of the Clergy* with the publication of his encyclical letter, *Charitas*, on April 13, 1791. In the letter, he declared the *Constitution* to be "composed of

more doctrinaire form of political liberalism is what many in the church came to label "laicism."[32] Laicism is a term for a doctrinaire philosophical position that views the secular realm as the only source of moral or political authority. Thus, laicism excludes the church and theological considerations from the political realm.

In the period following the Revolution, Catholic responses were typically divided into two camps. On the one hand was the conservative view represented by legitimism or integralism.[33] Integralism tended to seek a restoration of an intimate relationship between altar and throne in some form analogous to the Gallicanism of the French nationalized church.[34] Legitimism is quite similar. It supports integralism insofar as the church functions to *legitimate* the political authority and the two powers remain closely aligned. On the other hand there were those who advocated for a more liberal view. Liberal Catholics tended to view some of the advances of the French Revolution and the modern nation-state, especially those elements that endorsed equality and freedom, as reconcilable with and often even as necessary corollaries of Christian faith, the gospel, and natural law.[35]

---

principles derived from heresy," and pronounced any official member of the church who had sworn the oath of obedience to the *Constitution* to be immediately suspended from the exercise of his office. See Pius VI, "Charitas," in *The Papal Encyclicals: 1740-1878,* vol. 1, ed. Claudia Carlen, I.H.M. (Beloit, Kans.: McGrath, 1981), pp. 177-86, §11, 20. Subsequent references to papal encyclicals are from this same edition unless otherwise noted. The original Latin texts can be found in *Acta Sanctae Sedis,* 41 vols. (Rome: Typis Polyglottae Officiniae S.C. de Propaganda Fide, 1865-1908).

32. Perreau-Saussine, *Catholicism and Democracy,* p. 91. He contrasts this doctrinaire laicism with "laicity," a more moderate political liberalism that held the state unfit for determining the ultimate purpose of human life beyond the political.

33. Bouyer writes that "integralism perfected the false identity between routine and tradition by refusing to admit any development of tradition, which it confused with dissociating evolution" (*Church of God,* p. 158).

34. The most conservative strain of Catholic thought at the time was advocated by Joseph de Maistre, who was also joined by the likes of Louis de Bonald and Donoso Cortes (see Hittinger, "Introduction to Modern Catholicism," p. 8).

35. The most influential of this latter strand of liberal Catholic social thought can be found in the work of Felicite Robert de Lamennais, who, along with Henri Dominique Lacordaire and Charles de Montalembert, began to publish *L'Avenir,* a daily newspaper advocating separation of church and state and democratic political principles (see Michael Schuck, "Early Modern Roman Catholic Social Thought: 1740-1890," in *Modern Catholic Social Teaching: Commentaries and Interpretations,* ed. Kenneth R. Himes, O.F.M. [Washington, D.C.: Georgetown University Press, 2005], pp. 99-124, p. 108). One could also include Alexis de Tocqueville in this liberal camp as well, especially as he expresses his views in

In the nineteenth century the process of industrialization was radically altering the political landscape of Europe, and eventually all but the most recalcitrant conservative thinkers in the Catholic Church began to realize that the system of the *ius patronus* would need to be abandoned in favor of what Hittinger calls a "Gregorian ideal of liberty."[36] One thing, however, became completely clear following the growing popularity of socialist responses to the problems posed by industrialization in the nineteenth century: the church now had a battle to fight on two fronts. Liberalism, with its false notions of human liberty, had long been considered by the Roman magisterium to be the root cause of disturbance and revolution in the social order, not to mention the enemy of true religion. But now socialism came to be seen as the bastard offspring of liberalism. By casting off due deference to the God-given authority of the civil authorities (see Romans 13), in accepting a materialistic and atheistic conception of history, and in fomenting class struggle that led to such violent revolutions as those witnessed in the workers' revolutions of 1848, socialism was now perceived within the Roman magisterium to be an unacceptable alternative for socially conscious Catholics. Radical socialism turned out to be another form of laicism — that is, a political doctrine that excluded the church from the political realm.

In the years following the worker revolutions of 1848, and leading up to the publication of *Quanta cura* and its *Syllabus of Errors* by Pope Pius IX in 1864, liberalism and socialism would more and more come to be seen as the logical consequences of all the errors contained in what Pius referred to as the heresy of "modernism." Although precisely what defines modernism is not always clearly articulated, this led to what is commonly referred to as the "modernist controversy" of the late nineteenth and early twentieth centu-

---

Democracy in America, trans. Arthur Goldhammer (Washington, D.C.: Library of America, 2004).

In the early 1800s, Pope Gregory XVI (1831-46) represented the legitimist and restorationist hopes of the majority of Catholic opinion. In 1832 Gregory published *Mirari vos,* in which he condemned the doctrines of the separation of church and state and what he called "indifferentism," a theory of state neutrality on matters of religion that was circulating at the time.

36. This Gregorian ideal is a reference to the ecclesiastical and canonical reforms of Pope Gregory VII (1073-85), who settled the investiture controversy by reestablishing the power of Rome to install bishops over the power of local princes. In doing so, he initiated the early medieval reform that established the spiritual authority and superiority of the papacy and the church over the political authorities (see Hittinger, "Introduction to Modern Catholicism," p. 8, and Witte and Nichols, *Religion and the American Constitutional Experiment,* pp. 6-7).

ries in the Catholic Church. The negative poles that Catholic social thought needed to avoid had now been well established (militantly liberal laicism and socialism). However, it was much more difficult to put together a coherent system of thought on the positive political recommendations to be taken by Catholics in the nineteenth century. As Bouyer writes, "in limiting themselves to 'conserving,' 'protecting,' and 'defending,' the controlling agents of modern Catholicism were no longer able to guide, inspire, or elicit the living development of Catholic tradition in the whole body of the faithful."[37] It is precisely this ambivalence toward modern forms of political power and an ossified view of Catholic tradition, grounded in romanticized images of an integralist past, that contributed to a tendency to narrow the possibilities for cultivating civic virtue among Catholic thinkers at the time.

Meanwhile, in 1864 Pius IX published his encyclical *Quanta cura* along with its addendum, the *Syllabus of Errors*. In these two documents the pontiff took a decidedly reactionary stance to the movements of the age and the crisis of modernity that would have a lasting effect on Catholic thought and political involvement for many decades. In *Quanta cura* (December 8, 1864), Pius condemns the teachings of the modernists as contrary to natural and eternal law, and as enemies of the order and peace of human civilization and justice. He writes that "applying to civil society the impious and absurd principle of *naturalism,* as they call it, [they] dare to teach that 'the best constitution of civil society and (also) civil progress altogether require that human society be conducted and governed without regard being had to religion any more than if it did not exist; or at least, without any distinction being made between the true religion and false ones.' "[38] Thus does he attack the state-sponsored "indifferentism" of liberals such as Felicite de Lammenais. Likewise, proposition 80 of the *Syllabus of Errors* declares null and void the following: "The Roman Pontiff can,

---

37. Bouyer, *Church of God,* p. 159.

38. Pius IX, *"Quanta cura,"* in *Acta Sanctae Sedis* (Rome: Typis Polyglottae Officiniae S.C. de Propaganda Fide, 1867), pp. 160-67, §3. It is also worth noting that although much of the tone and conclusions of *Quanta cura* and the *Syllabus* are reactionary and overdrawn, there are elements that still seem prophetic. For example, Pius IX writes that when "the genuine notion itself of justice and human right is darkened and lost, . . . [then] the place of true justice and legitimate right is supplied by material force," and that "human society, when set loose from the bonds of religion and true justice, can have, in truth, no other end than the purpose of obtaining and amassing wealth, and that (society under such circumstances) follows no other law in its actions, except the unchastened desire of ministering to its own pleasures and interests" (§4).

and ought to, reconcile himself, and come to terms with progress, liberalism and modern civilization." Hittinger notes how the approach taken by Pius IX and later by Pius X, which he calls the "paper wars" method of attacking liberalism, was ultimately unsuccessful. It failed because "the bishops could not agree on any over-arching theory to unify [the various denouncements made in the *Syllabus*]."[39] Without a positive goal toward which Catholics (and others) can work together to create social and political harmony, it remains quite difficult — if not impossible — to cultivate any positive sense of civic virtue as a means of contributing to the common good. Reaction and rejection are not useful tools for building consensus and motivating action.

The pinnacle of the Catholic Church's reactionary stance to modern laicism or doctrinaire liberalism is typically understood to have been expressed in the ultramontanist ecclesiology that carried the day at Vatican I (1869-70). Its doctrine of papal infallibility is understood as the pinnacle of anti-liberal Catholic thought. Ironically, however, as Perreau-Saussine argues in his provocative thesis, Vatican I was both made possible by and served to underwrite a certain form of political liberalism. The split between church and the secular state, even if not initially desired by Catholics, had been in effect on the practical level for the previous one hundred years. Both the Civil Constitution on the Clergy (1790) and the Concordat between Napoleon I and the Catholic Church (1801) had each in their distinctive ways asserted French national control over the Catholic Church. While these secured a certain political recognition and support of the church, the cost of such support was the loss of the church's independence from the political regime in matters both spiritual and temporal. Ultimately, this was untenable for Catholics. On this point, even more reactionary Catholics like de Maistre could agree with more liberal Catholics such as Lammenais.

Alexis de Tocqueville writes the following commentary on the popular support among French Catholics for greater centralization of power in the pope and the ultramontanist position:

> It was not a matter of the pope seizing power over the faithful, but of the faithful themselves calling on the pope to become absolute master of the church. And this tendency was, if not universal, then widespread through

39. Russell Hittinger, "Two Modernities, Two Thomisms: Reflections on the Centenary of Pius X's Letter Against the Modernists," *Nova et Vetera* 5, no. 4 (2007): 843-80, pp. 849 and 855.

the Catholic world. The papal position we see today was not so much a *cause* as an *effect*.[40]

Once civil authorities had turned away from direct endorsement of Catholicism, Rome and the papacy remained "pretty much the only institution that could fill the void left by the state."[41]

While some have decried Vatican I's notion of papal authority as an endorsement of the worst possible form of integralism and caesaro-papism (and certainly some, such as de Maistre, hoped that it was), Perreau-Sassine sees in it an implicit endorsement of the older tradition of Gallicanism that respected the autonomy of the political and spiritual spheres of authority. He writes, "Not only did Catholics become ultramontanes, but their ultramontanism, paradoxically, ended up spiced with a distinct tang of liberalism."[42] This more moderate form of laicity, what he also refers to as "a positive conception of 'laicity'" in the documents of Vatican I,[43] recognizes a legitimate distinction between the political and spiritual spheres, precisely to reestablish the spiritual authority of the pope and the institutional church in spiritual matters. The net result was "a liberal ultramontanism that distinguished sharply between the theological and the political domains."[44]

Indeed, support for this liberal ultramontanism is at least implicitly contained in the documents of Vatican I. For example, the decrees recognize the legitimate autonomy of human reason and its capacity to investigate the nature of reality to discover both theoretical and practical truth.[45] The relative autonomy of reason likewise entails a distinction between the theological and political, or more generally between nature and grace. In general Perreau-Sassine's thesis seems correct insofar as he claims that there is an implicit endorsement of liberalism's concern to uphold the distinct sphere of the political authority apart from the church. At times, however, he seems

40. Personal correspondence from Tocqueville to Henry Reeve, October 7, 1856, in *Correspondence Anglaise,* in *Oeuvres Completes,* t. VI, part 1, p. 199, quoted in Perreau-Saussine, *Catholicism and Democracy,* p. 49.

41. Perreau-Saussine, *Catholicism and Democracy,* p. 22.

42. Perreau-Saussine, *Catholicism and Democracy,* p. 45.

43. Perreau-Saussine, *Catholicism and Democracy,* p. 141.

44. Perreau-Saussine, *Catholicism and Democracy,* p. 57.

45. See especially the decrees of Vatican I, session 3 (April 24, 1870), chapter 4, "On Faith and Reason." Latin text with English translation is available in *The Decrees of the Ecumenical Councils,* vol. 2, ed. Norman P. Tanner, S.J. (London: Sheed & Ward, 1990), pp. 802-16.

to overlook the fact that there is very little evidence that the council fathers at Vatican I *intended* to endorse political liberalism. Taking this view might contribute to a tendency to overlook the significant changes in the attitude of the magisterium toward the liberal nation-state system. In other words, Vatican II's Declaration on Religious Freedom *(Dignitatis humanae)* does contain an essentially new doctrine when compared with previous magisterial teaching. However, what Perreau-Saussine's analysis does help to highlight is how the period between Vatican I and Vatican II can be seen as the attempt to express more explicitly in theological terms the political implications of the kind of positive laicity, or moderate political liberalism, that was already implicit and practically in effect beginning with the ecclesiology developed at Vatican I. In addition, his assertion that Vatican I and Vatican II represent the two poles between which Catholic political thought with regard to the modern state vacillates is entirely correct. The endorsement of moderate liberalism with a strong critique of doctrinaire liberalism remains in the church's social doctrine up to the present time.

Within this historical context, the spark that finally lit the fires of Catholic social thought within the magisterium arrived with the election of Vincenzo Giacchino Raffaele Luigi Pecci to the papacy in 1878, where he took the name Leo XIII. Leo introduced new and more flexible methods of thinking in regard to political authority, the most important of which was his consideration of the possibility of Christian endorsement of democracy. He did this primarily through his rehabilitation of Thomistic moral, political, and legal thought, which he had learned from his Jesuit educators at La Civilita Cattolica.[46]

Leo was the first pope since the eighth century not to inherit the Papal States, which had been seized by Vittorio Emmanuele II in 1870.[47] One of the ways in which Leo took advantage of the social and political situation during his papacy was in his prolific use of the encyclical letter, nine of which deal directly with political issues. He also established the Pontifical Academy of St. Thomas Aquinas in Rome in 1879, and ushered in the official age of renewed attention to Thomistic Christian philosophy with the publication

46. La Civilita was founded by two neo-Thomist Jesuits, Matteo Liberatore and Luigi Taparelli. Hittinger, "Two Modernities, Two Thomisms," p. 859, and Paul Misner, *Social Catholicism in Europe: From the Onset of Industrialization to the First World War* (New York: Crossroad, 1991), p. 128.

47. Russell Hittinger, "Pope Leo XIII (1810-1903): Commentary," in *The Teachings of Modern Roman Catholicism on Law, Politics, and Human Nature,* ed. John Witte Jr. and Frank S. Alexander (New York: Columbia University Press, 2007), p. 40.

of *Aeterni Patris* in the same year. His acts in support of Thomism led to the establishment of the neo-scholasticism that came to dominate Catholic political philosophy in the late nineteenth and early twentieth centuries. One may note both positive and negative implications of this neo-scholastic revival for the ongoing relevance and development of civic virtue.

On the positive side, Leo's decisions in 1879 mark a significant move toward what Hittinger refers to as the "Leonine synthesis" of Catholic philosophy. Such a synthesis was desperately needed to address the political and social complexities of the nineteenth century. Leo inherited an unsystematic mess when it came to official Catholic thought in regard to social, moral, and political problems. He saw in Thomas Aquinas's method of moral reasoning a system of thought that maintained a connection between eternal and natural law, between metaphysical truths, revelation, and the principles of the Catholic faith, and the application of the first principles of natural law in historical, contingent circumstances. This latter point enabled him to incorporate the historical consciousness that dominates modern thought with the metaphysical principles that undergird natural law. He also began to envision an approach to civil authority and the state that allowed for various forms of government without the desire to return to the integralism that demanded a reunification of altar and throne.

Leo XIII's consistent application of these principles in regard to his thinking about the nature of political authority is evident in his subsequent encyclicals. He was able to develop a carefully nuanced position that recognizes the viability of certain historical developments in democratic statecraft without abandoning essential church teaching on morality and politics. None of this would be possible without recognizing a theological distinction between nature and grace that is expressed politically as a distinction between temporal and spiritual authority. He writes that "those who may be placed over the state may in certain cases be chosen by the will and decision of the multitude, without opposing or impugning the Catholic doctrine. And by this choice, in truth, the ruler is designated, but the rights of ruling are not thereby conferred. Nor is the authority delegated to him, but the person by whom it is to be exercised is determined upon."[48] Notice here that Leo is upholding a more substantive and natural foundation for the state

---

48. Leo XIII, *Diuturnum,* §6. Moreover, this is not an entirely new or radical position since similar arguments had been made by Cajetan, Bellarmine, and Suarez in the sixteenth-century Salamanca School (see Yves R. Simon, *Philosophy of Democratic Government* [Chicago: University of Chicago Press, 1951], pp. 158-76).

than many modern contract theories of state power advocate. The people are not delegating their power to those who rule, but are rather electing the persons through whom political authority is to be exercised. This is a subtle but important distinction. For both Aquinas and Leo the state has an ontological status rather than a purely contractual or contingent status.[49] When compared with the attitudes toward liberalism and democratic theories of political power in the thought of Pius VI or Gregory XVI, Leo's work represents the kind of development of doctrine that would lead to more direct endorsement of liberalism and democratic forms of government in later magisterial thought. Although certain strands of neo-Thomism were eventually abandoned at Vatican II (see the introduction), Leo helps to pave the way for a more substantive development of civic virtue.

The watershed moment, of course, for social Catholicism begins with the publication of *Rerum novarum* on May 15, 1891. In this document the convergence of several streams of thought and activity from all over Europe in the nineteenth century is evident. The concern for the working classes and the need for the church to take a stance on the side of the workers were highly influenced by the work of Catholic labor organizers, especially in Germany and Belgium. In the context of the labor movement Catholics began to become more open to the possibility of endorsing some of the more positive roles that the state could enact in civic affairs, particularly in the defense of the rights of the working classes. This was especially true as labor organizers became increasingly aware of the necessity for state intervention

49. Besides these historical and political trends, there are also linguistic and philosophical issues that often lie just below the more external, political manifestations of these tensions. In the original Latin of these encyclicals (from Pius VI to Leo XIII), the terms used to refer to the state are *res publica* and *civitas* (see *Acta Sanctae Sedis*). In the English translations provided by Carlen, O'Brien, and Shannon, these are both translated as "state" (in Carlen, moreover, "State" is always capitalized).

Jacques Maritain notes a similar linguistic difference when he writes that "the very word *State* only appeared in the course of modern history; the notion of the State was implicitly involved in the ancient concept of city ([Gk.], *polis*; [Lat.], *civitas*) which meant essentially body politic" (*Man and the State,* p. 14). The difficulty here lies in the fact that in the original context for these terms, *res publica* and *civitas* did not refer to anything like the modern nation-state, in either size or extent of centralized power. (Indeed, the modern state did not even exist in the original use of these terms.) The closest we can come to a comparison would be with the Roman republic, which did have extensive political power and a centralized form of republican government. This understanding of the state/*res publica* endures in the West through thinkers like Cicero and Justinian. Yet when these ideas were placed in the context of medieval Latin Christendom, the *civitas* was a much smaller, local urban context with more local forms of government.

in the protection of the rights of workers. The state was often the only civil authority with the power to effectively coerce the owners of capital to bring about more favorable conditions for the working classes.

The influence of these practical concerns is evident in Leo's thought when he writes that "the first duty, therefore, of the rulers of the State should be to make sure that the laws and institutions, the general character and administration of the commonwealth, shall be such as to produce of themselves public well-being and private prosperity."[50] If official Catholic teaching was to remain opposed to socialist revolutionary tactics for liberating the working classes, it needed to find an alternative solution to protect the rights of workers while still maintaining the principle of order and harmony within society. State protection of workers' rights, supported by the vibrant civic engagement of citizen advocacy, was the most effective means to achieve this aim. This of course entails at the very least an implicit recognition of the legitimate status of the liberal state.

Yet this endorsement of a positive role for the state remains mixed with a general uneasiness toward the potential for the over-extended use and abuse of totalitarian power by the centralized, liberal nation-state. Both Catholics and labor organizers in France experienced this during the Second and Third Republics (ca. 1848-52 and 1870-1940, respectively) and in Germany during Bismarck's *Kulturkampf* (ca. 1871-87). These liberal regimes were of the more doctrinaire variety that went beyond the separation of church and state. Instead, they sought to remove the power of the church within civil society. In practice, this kind of negative laicity sought to denigrate both the church's political influence and its claims to a spiritual authority that transcends the political order. The appeal to state power to protect individual rights had a shadow side when moderate political liberalism overstepped its bounds and became doctrinaire liberalism. This lesson would become even more poignant in relation to the totalitarian regimes of the early twentieth century.

The endorsement of subjective, individual rights that undergirds notions of labor rights could sometimes be interpreted as an endorsement of more individualist forms of social thought, a lessening of the ontological and substantial nature of the political community and state authority, and a decreased emphasis on the ways in which the common good is primary

---

50. *Rerum novarum,* in *Catholic Social Thought: The Documentary Heritage,* ed. David J. O'Brien and Thomas A. Shannon (Maryknoll, N.Y.: Orbis, 2004), §26. Leo also indicates that workers should have recourse to the laws of state in the protection of their rights (§13), and that the positive role for the state is to be found in the protection it offers to the most poor and vulnerable in society (§27).

to and essential for the securing of individual goods. This anxiety and ambiguity regarding the power and authority of the liberal state continues to contribute to ambiguity about the place of civic virtue in modern Catholic social thought. When combined with a philosophical bedrock of doctrinaire liberalism, the increasingly centralized power of the state threatened the legitimate autonomy of other social bodies, including the church. The lessons of post-Revolutionary France and Bismarck's *Kulturkampf* made this undeniably clear.

The principle that Leo used to dislodge and challenge the theory of the absolute authority and sovereignty of the totalitarian state was a combination of Thomistic personalism and the principle of subsidiarity. Leo writes that "man is older than the State, and he holds the right of providing for the life of his body prior to the formation of any State."[51] Political authority, therefore, is a natural and necessary element of the social nature of the human person. A full appreciation of Christian anthropology, however, is grounded in the deeper ontological nature of the human person, made in the image of God (see Gen. 1:26), and this nature is prior to and superior to the pretentions of the state's monopoly on coercive power. Thus, Leo's official endorsement of rights endowed on the very nature of the human person continued to underwrite the liberal state insofar as the modern state fulfills its legitimate purpose when it serves to protect the rights of individuals and of intermediate corporate bodies within society.[52] Natural rights were an assumed aspect of natural law, and as such were written into the created order itself — an order that no state, liberal or otherwise, has the right to derogate. Thus, Leo endorsed a legitimate role for state authority while also grounding this role in the deeper theological anthropology that transcends any particular state's authority.

On the one hand, these engagements with the theory and practice of rights, the philosophy of personalism, and subsidiarity represent important — even essential — developments in Catholic social thought. Subjective rights, personalism, and subsidiarity combined provide a powerful and

---

51. *Rerum novarum*, §6.

52. For example, Leo writes: "Particular societies, then, although they exist within the State, and are each a part of the State, nevertheless cannot be prohibited by the State absolutely and as such. For to enter into a 'society' of this kind is a natural right of man; and the State must protect natural rights, not destroy them" (*Rerum novarum*, §38). We can also witness here the full embrace of a doctrine of natural and inherent rights in the human person, a concept that was developed by Luigi Taparelli, S.J., among others (see *Saggio Teoretico di Dritto Naturale* [Rome: Edizioni "La Civilta Cattolica," 1949]).

flexible intellectual framework within which to circumscribe the potentially unlimited sovereignty of the modern, sovereign nation-state. They also provide a practical way for Christians to engage with the modern state without resorting to the tactics employed by those who advocated for a return to integralism or a Marxist or socialist solution. On the other hand, however, they lead to a lessening of the traditional Catholic understanding of the ontological, not merely contractual, pragmatic, or functional, status of the state or the political community. Hittinger writes that the "more thoughtful Catholic thinkers were not in doubt that this entailed a weakening and diffusion of political passion; but this was the price to be paid for curbing *l'integrisme* of the right and the left."[53] The move toward a Christian humanism and personalism and greater emphasis on the ontological status of other civic bodies within the state (articulated through the principle of subsidiarity) was necessary for the continued development of the Catholic social tradition. However, it also had the consequence of lessening individual commitment to civic engagement, and on the practical level contributed to a decreased appreciation for the role of civic virtue.

I argued above in support of Perreau-Saussine's thesis that the more centralized authority of the papacy and the Vatican was both a response to and an implicit endorsement of the growing power of the secular, liberal state. Indeed, in a certain sense ultramontanism can be seen as a necessary counterbalance to the centralized state that can also tend to reduce all social relations to that between individuals and the state. The "paradox here is that it is [a centralized, hierarchical] religious authority that can stave off authoritarian politics."[54] My argument for the continuing importance of civic virtue adds to this insight by noting that centralized ecclesiastical power is not enough by itself if it is not combined with the active engagement of the people. Civic virtue inspires the people to work as intermediate social agents between the centralized powers of both the state and the church. On this point, both classical republicans and liberal Catholics who endorse a positive form of laicity can agree. Without the virtue and engagement of the people in democratic life, there is a tendency to drift toward various forms of absolutism. Civic virtue, particularly as it is practiced within the pilgrim church, provides a distinctive counterbalance to the centralized power of both the pope and the state.[55]

53. Hittinger, "Introduction to Modern Catholicism," p. 30.
54. Perreau-Saussine, *Catholicism and Democracy*, p. 76.
55. Perreau-Saussine also notes the necessity of this more democratic form of balance

Following the death of Leo XIII in 1903, Pope Pius X issued *Pascendi dominicis gregis* (1907), in which he attacked the philosophical system of liberalism directly, calling modernism the "synthesis of all heresies."[56] In contrast to the practical and political liberalism of the more moderate forms of religious tolerance practiced in Belgium and the United States, Pius tended to correlate all forms of liberal thought with a practical agnosticism and materialism that in practice leads the way to atheism. Pius's reaction to liberalism represents the ongoing struggle within the church to distinguish between the doctrinaire liberalism that sought to replace the church's comprehensive moral vision with a secular, immanent version and a more positive laicity, or a moderate liberalism, that allows the church the freedom to pursue its own internal and social goals and to promote its vision of the ultimate goal of human life.

Pius returned to attempting to curb the work of liberal Catholics by means of two methods: the first was the return to list making and "paper wars," and the second was in taking direct legislative action against Catholic groups involved in social and political life.[57] The problem with this approach is that it provided neither a theoretical nor a practical foundation for a positive conception of the civic engagement of the people in search of the common good. In practice, it tended to foster more reactionary stances and the creation of a Catholic counterculture removed from the civic life of the people, or to force a practical choice between loyalty to the church and loyalty to the civic life of one's nation.

Following Pius, the papacy of Benedict XV (1914-22) witnessed the devastation wrought by World War I and the effects of the first communist revolution in Russia in 1917. Thus, in the period following World War I, Hittinger writes that the official thought of the Roman Catholic Church had become "adamantly antistatist."[58] This antistatist attitude contributed to a continued

---

of powers in both the church and political life. He writes, for example, that "the central authority of the pope, if it was not balanced by a Catholicism with deep local roots, could degenerate into hypercentralism and spiritual despotism" (*Catholicism and Democracy,* p. 69), and that "some citizens must devote themselves to the common good as judges, civil servants, or politicians. In the absence of virtue, democracies tend toward Caesarism" (p. 78).

56. Pius X, *Pascendi dominicis gregis,* §39.

57. He accomplished this goal by disbanding both the more integralist movement, the Opera dei Congressi, and the more liberal movement, the Lega Democratica Nazionale (see Misner, *Social Catholicism in Europe,* pp. 241, 286).

58. Hittinger, "Introduction to Modern Catholicism," p. 16.

tendency to overlook the positive aspects of classical and medieval civic virtue that had survived in the work of Aquinas and others in the Roman Catholic tradition. In this period, the root principles that could be used to foster a positive notion of civic virtue lay dormant within the tradition, even as the centralized power of the Vatican continued to exercise its counterweight and lend its implicit support to the liberal state.

In the same year that Pius XI was elected to the papacy in 1922, Benito Mussolini rose to power as the prime minister of Italy, and was later to rename himself the Duce of Fascism and Head of the Italian Government. Pius had realized by this time that the "paper wars" approach to modernity was not going to be effective. James Weisheipl writes that this led to a significant recognition that "legislation did not stimulate a return to the authentic thought and spirit of St. Thomas. Legislation rather led to the production of safe textbooks" characteristic of the neo-scholasticism and the manuals of the time.[59] The approach undertaken by the pope was to encourage Catholic Action in its various forms throughout Europe, especially in Italy and France.[60] Despite continued fear and hostility toward the state, social solidarity and civic virtue were kept alive in the kinds of intermediate civil institutions that were sustained by Catholic Action and similar popular movements.

When Pius published *Quadragesimo anno* on May 15, 1931, the fascist press immediately claimed that the Italian state had already achieved all the goals of the social order outlined by the encyclical. In fact, they argued that they had gone far beyond the demands of *Rerum novarum* and *Quadragesimo anno*.[61] There was no escaping, however, the critiques of the fascist state that were contained within the letter. The most striking of these appears in Pius's appropriation and development of the term "subsidiarity." The fascist Italian state had taken over control of all labor union activity and established a single, state-run trade union system. Thus, the challenge could not have gone unnoticed when Pius writes that "it is an injustice and at the same time a grave evil and a disturbance of right order to transfer to the larger and higher collectivity functions which can be performed and provided for by lesser

59. Quoted by Hittinger, "Two Modernities, Two Thomisms," p. 873.

60. In fact, Catholic Action in Italy had been so successful in its organizing efforts that by the time of Pius XI's pontificate, it had established throughout the mainland of Italy "banks, mutual benefit societies, peasant cooperatives, industrial trade unions, recreation and cultural associations, not to mention a flourishing press" (Hittinger, "Two Modernities, Two Thomisms," p. 7).

61. Hittinger, "Two Modernities, Two Thomisms," p. 138.

and subordinate bodies."[62] In the context of Catholic resistance to the new forms of totalitarian state power of the twentieth century, the principle of subsidiarity came to take on central importance. It upheld the necessity of a plurality of social institutions to support the health of the body politic and to act as a check on absolute state sovereignty. This twofold check on unlimited state sovereignty, expressed by the temporal and spiritual autonomy of the centralized papacy and the active civic engagement of the Catholic faithful, was thus kept alive at the time. Furthermore, Pius's explicit endorsement of such practices of civic virtue opened a wider, public space for Catholics within which forms of civic virtue could be cultivated and practiced. A more systematic approach to political authority and church-state relations was still desperately needed before a fully developed understanding of civic virtue could be undertaken.

Following the end of World War II and the rebuilding of Europe, the next watershed moment for Catholic social thought in regard to civic engagement arrives with Vatican II (1962-65). The documents from the council make two important shifts in the discourse that come to have a bearing on the further development of civic virtue during and after the council. The first is the endorsement of constitutional democracy as the most favorable form of government to respect the dignity and rights of the human person, a task explicitly undertaken in *Dignitatis humanae.* This affirmation of religious liberty confirms the commitment of the official teaching of the Catholic Church to rejecting an integralist solution and affirming the positive laicity that underwrites the distinction between church and state. This opens the way for a further consideration of civic virtue since healthy democratic forms of government depend on civic engagement from their citizenry.

The second move shifts the discourse away from the church-state problematic, and toward an analysis of the church's role in *society* and *culture* rather than in the state.[63] This second shift has a twofold effect on the sub-

---

62. Pius XI, *Quadragesimo anno,* §79. As an interesting historical aside, Oswald Nell-Breuning, the ghost writer of *Quadragesimo anno,* notes that there was some confusion on this point at the time, as many readers took certain elements of paragraphs 91-96, the only section of the encyclical written by the pope's hand, to be an endorsement of the state syndicalist system as the most favorable for the "peaceful collaboration of the classes" (§96). In contrast to this reading, Nell-Breuning reaffirms that the document is to be interpreted as "progressive, liberal, definitely democratic, against individualism and against statism; in short, correct" ("The Drafting of Quadragesimo Anno," in *Readings in Moral Theology,* no. 5 [Mahwah, N.J.: Paulist, 1986], p. 65).

63. As noted above, explicit considerations of a section within *Lumen gentium* on the

sequent development of civic virtue. First, it clearly affirms the faithful in their engagement in seeking to build up the common good of the particular societies in which they live and raises awareness of the global common good. Second, however, it left a great deal of ambiguity with regard to the church's attitude toward the role of the quintessentially modern form of political power — the liberal nation-state. A paradoxical, and often not well-articulated, twofold attitude remains toward the liberal state. The total rejection of doctrinaire, philosophical liberalism remains unchanged and in continuity with previous magisterial teachings.[64] At the same time, however, the Declaration on Religious Freedom, with its endorsement of positive laicity, or political liberalism, as the best defense of the dignity of the human person against totalitarian forms of power, clearly represents a development of doctrine in a new direction. Indeed, this twofold approach to modernity and liberalism remains in all levels of the church up to this day, and contributes to the distinctive approaches in the three tendencies noted above. In fact, a proper recognition of this distinction between official endorsement of political liberalism combined with rejection of doctrinaire liberalism is essential to understand the state of Catholic reflection on liberal politics in the modern world.

The Pastoral Constitution on the Church in the Modern World *(Gaudium et spes)* provides only a few general statements in regard to the political authority exercised by the modern state and the practice of civic virtue. The only concrete, practical endorsement of any kind of direct social or political engagement that is recommended by the document is in upholding the rights of labor unions to strike.[65] The same kind of abstraction and lack of specific detail can be found in the discussion on "The Life of the Political Community" in chapter IV of part I. The general notions of endorsing a juridical-political order that protects the basic rights of individuals, that the political community exists to promote the common good, and that a

---

church and the state were removed from the initial schema of the document. A similar shift can be found in Jacques Maritain's emphasis on "political society," or what many social scientists refer to as "civil society." See Jacques Maritain's discussion on "political society" in *Man and the State,* chapter 1, section IV.

64. This rejection is implied in the assertion in *Dignitatis humanae* that political freedom is not a replacement for the search for truth: "It is in accordance with their dignity that all human beings, because they are persons, that is, beings endowed with reason and free will and therefore bearing personal responsibility, are both impelled by their nature and bound by moral obligation to seek the truth, especially religious truth" (§2).

65. *Gaudium et spes,* §68.

positive system of law is necessary for the maintenance of justice and rights are all upheld, but very few concrete recommendations are provided. This general analysis is likely in keeping with the desire of the council fathers to respect the autonomy of local forms of political authority and an uneasiness with imposing a one-size-fits-all solution amid greater global awareness of political and cultural pluralism.[66]

The documents of Vatican II do not develop a more systematic reflection on the church's growing appreciation of and respect for the ancient philosophical and theological roots of the Catholic tradition that could be used to bolster an appreciation for modern expressions of civic virtue. In fact, John Courtney Murray considers this section of *Gaudium et spes* on the political community "uninspired and inadequate," and he bemoans the fact that "there is no mention of the cardinal political principle of the consent of the governed, which is as old as Aristotle and Cicero, and which was central to the political thought of the High Middle Ages."[67] I noted in the introduction that the initial schema of *Lumen gentium* also sought to address the question of the relationship between the church and the state, although it was rejected in part because it was based on a more reactionary integralism that the majority position at the council sought to disavow. Civic virtue is endorsed in a general manner in that citizens are encouraged to develop "a generous and loyal devotion to their country."[68] A more systematic reflection, drawing on the rich theological and philosophical resources of the Catholic tradition on political life and authority, is lacking from this and other documents of Vatican II.

What Vatican II did advance, however, is a more explicit recognition of its endorsement of political liberalism as the political solution most in keeping with its teaching on natural rights and the civil and legal separation of church and state. Perreau-Saussine writes that "there is something to be said for seeing Vatican II as marking the reconciliation of the Catholic Church with liberal Gallicanism. The council emphasized the political role of the laity, and showed that the church could be at ease with democracy

66. Indeed, this is one reason that the neo-scholastic version of Thomism was so adamantly rejected in the early session of the council. See Joseph A. Komonchak, "Thomism and the Second Vatican Council," in *Continuity and Plurality in Catholic Theology: Essays in Honor of Gerald A. McCool, S.J.*, ed. Anthony J. Cernera (Fairfield, Conn.: Sacred Heart University Press, 1998), pp. 53-73, p. 54.

67. John Courtney Murray, S.J., "The Issue of Church and State at Vatican Council II," *Theological Studies* 27, no. 4 (1966): 580-606, p. 602.

68. *Gaudium et spes*, §75.

and liberalism"[69] And it did so, as I argued in the introduction, by drawing on a theological approach to political philosophy that was informed in part by the work of Aquinas. This is true even if these sources were not always explicitly recognized at the council itself due to the rejection of the more rigid and ahistorical forms of neo-scholasticism that were found wanting in rejuvenating the life of the church or civil society.

These developments in the church's understanding of itself as an agent within the modern world at Vatican II had a twofold effect on the subsequent development of civic virtue. On the one hand, the growing awareness of the need to pursue a global common good grounded in the search for peace and human rights opened a wider conceptual space for Catholics to participate in their respective political communities on a multitude of levels. Simultaneous to this, however, the continued ambiguity with respect to the role of the political authority of the nation-state in pursuing this common good contributes to a residual ambivalence about modern statecraft and civic engagement that remains within the tradition of Catholic social thought up to this day.

Furthermore, it is possible to see how this ambiguity has had an impact on the ideological contours of each of the three tendencies outlined above. The neoconservative ideology easily grasps and then exploits the critical stance toward doctrinaire liberalism that is very much alive in the Catholic social tradition. It then all too easily combines this condemnation of doctrinaire liberalism and its implicit critique of the state with an uncritical and selective endorsement of free market liberalism, individual autonomy at best loosely tethered to the common good, and a largely uncritical use of violence to further the political and economic aims of the state. On the surface level these aims are endorsed under the guise of extending democracy, freedom, and human rights. However, the neoconservative approach ends up endorsing the worst facets of liberalism, precisely insofar as it takes an uncritical stance toward individual choice in the markets. Paradoxically, it ends up endorsing a more doctrinaire liberalism that rejects the right of any moral authority — either in the state or in the church — to criticize the free choice of individuals in economics while placing strict obligations in the realm of sexual ethics. Ultimately, it presents a morally incoherent view of the world, endorsing doctrinaire liberalism in economics but rejecting it in the realm of personal ethics, especially in matters pertaining to sexuality. While my account of civic virtue shares with the neoconservative position a concern with the need for economic growth to sustain the wellbeing of

69. Perreau-Saussine, *Catholicism and Democracy,* p. 125.

individuals and communities as one aspect of the common good, Thomistic civic virtue and Catholic social thought envision the connection and balance between markets, individual autonomy, and the common good in starkly different terms.

The second tendency that rejects the modern nation-state recognizes what is missing in the neoconservative paradigm. That is, that Catholic social thought consistently critiques the ideology of doctrinaire liberalism in all realms of social life, including both sexual ethics and economics. At the same time, however, this group overlooks the distinction between its endorsement of positive laicity made explicit at Vatican II and its rejection of doctrinaire liberalism. In response, it fails to make a distinction between better or worse forms of liberalism, and in the process rejects all liberal politics. In practice, those who follow this tendency in Catholic social thought seek to build up local forms of church and community while distancing themselves from direct engagement with the nation-state. They tend to focus on the ground-level end of subsidiarity by placing their emphasis on local politics. While their analyses are a helpful reminder of the corrupting tendency of power, it would strengthen the force of their negative critiques of state power if they provided a positive account of how Christian thought might engage the full scope of political authority at all subsidiary levels within the body politic. Harnessing the negative force of their critiques of violence by the nation-state while combining it with a positive account of civic virtue would further strengthen the kind of check on authoritarian forms of power that is cultivated by the practice of civic virtue among those in a pilgrim church. One thing those in this second group do exceptionally well, however, is remind those of us invested in liberal politics of our tendency to place political goals prior to Christian identity. Those who tend toward this second mode of engaging Catholic social thought provide an essential prophetic witness to the calling of the gospel to serve the poor regardless of one's political affiliations.

Finally, the third tendency downplays the aspects of Catholic social tradition that are more critical of doctrinaire liberalism. This approach may contribute to the tendency of liberal states toward all-encompassing pretensions over the facets of social life of the body politic. In practice, this can overshadow the centrality of theological and ecclesial commitments that supersede and transcend Christian civic virtue. If the second tendency focuses too exclusively on the lower end of subsidiarity, the liberal temptation is to focus too narrowly on the higher end, on the mechanisms of power at the highest level of state power. Two aspects of a Thomistic account of civic virtue provide a helpful corrective to these tendencies. First, the image of the pilgrim church focuses Christians first on the goals that transcend the earthly common good. It serves as a reminder for Christians to maintain the priority of theological commitments and ecclesial identities over political identities. Second, a democratic theory of civic virtue that requires the involvement of all members of the body politic in political deliberation can help to curb the tendency toward elitism or paternalism that is sometimes encountered in liberal political theology.

I have claimed in this chapter that certain historical forces have shaped the Catholic Church's reflection on the relationship between the church and the state in the modern world. While more ancient philosophical and theological teachings on the role of the people in self-government had always been part of the church's tradition, these tended to be downplayed as the forms of democratic government witnessed in the rise of the modern nation-state presented a whole new set of challenges for Catholic political thought. Specifically, the more doctrinaire forms of liberalism that emerged after the French Revolution created a more reactionary stance on the part of official magisterial teaching. With time, however, more moderate forms of liberalism came to be endorsed, especially in *Dignitatis humanae*'s assertion of the natural right to religious freedom as grounded in the dignity of the human person. Movements such as Catholic Action had kept practices of civic virtue alive even amid the modernist controversy, but postconciliar developments certainly open a wider space for the consideration of forms of civic engagement that are congruent with — indeed even demanded by — fidelity to the gospel. In Part I, I turn to consider the work of Thomas Aquinas on justice, civic virtue, and the common good within his thirteenth-century context. The goal of the following two chapters is to search deeper within the early scholastic tradition, with particular emphasis on Aquinas, for the theological roots of a conception of civic virtue that may continue to inspire ongoing development of civic virtue in our late modern context.

PART I

CHAPTER 2

Civic Virtue in Thomas Aquinas's Account of Justice

Introduction

As is often the case in the work of Thomas Aquinas, the concept of civic virtue can appear eminently simply and extremely complex at the same time. On the one hand, the working definition of civic virtue I have proposed derives from the concept of legal or general justice that Aquinas takes up, with slight modification, from Aristotle's *Nicomachean Ethics*. Civic virtue concerns the development of the will to direct all acts of virtue toward the common good of one's community. On the other hand, my account goes beyond and builds on what Aquinas has to say about general justice, and draws important conclusions from it for the church in the twenty-first century.

This suggests that the tasks in Part I are twofold. First, to best appreciate what Aquinas has to say about justice and its foundational role for an account of civic virtue, I examine his treatise on justice (*Summa theologiae* II-II 57-122) within the social, cultural, and intellectual trends of thirteenth-century Europe, within his own discussion of the virtues, and in relation to other virtues and concepts that are closely related to justice (such as the will, prudence, charity, and natural law). My primary aim is to outline the main contours of a Thomistic theory of civic virtue, although I try to note where substantive issues of interpretation within contemporary debates on Aquinas's corpus demand further defense in Part I in order to pick up and further defend these positions in Part II. My second task in Part I, which I take up more fully in the following chapter, is to extend some of the implications of Aquinas's discussion of justice that he himself does not explicitly make to begin to create a more robust picture of what a Thomistic account of civic virtue entails within modern democratic institutions and discourses.

For example, while Aquinas claims that as a virtue of the will justice does not have anything to do directly with the passions (*Summa theologiae* II-II 58.9), I find it necessary to explore what kind of emotional dispositions one might expect to find in the agent who possesses civic virtue (such as joy [*Summa theologiae* I-II 59.5] or compassion). Likewise, Aquinas's discussion of prudence in relation to general justice provides a promising — and more democratic — way forward beyond the kind of elitism that may be implied within certain interpretations of natural law (a theme that I explore more fully in Part II). In doing so, I develop an account of civic virtue beyond what Aquinas explicitly says regarding the role of emotions and passions, but I still want to ground my extension within Thomistic principles relating to the passions, prudence, and natural law reasoning.

To accomplish these tasks, I divide this chapter into two main parts. In the first I situate Aquinas's account of justice within the social and intellectual trends of his day. Second, I examine Aquinas's discussion of justice and interrelated concepts, focusing especially on his mature work in the *Summa theologiae*. In examining Aquinas's mature thought on justice, I note the ways in which I am picking up essential elements of Aquinas's thought in developing a Thomistic account of civic virtue, and I also note the places where his account is open to further clarification, correction, or development. When appropriate I hint at the ways that I develop these notions in Part II. This last task will make it possible to place Aquinas's work in dialogue with ongoing trends in Catholic social thought, ecclesiology, natural law, and contemporary political philosophy in Part II.

Justice among the Medieval Scholastics

Although Aristotelian discussions of the virtues were not unknown in the scholastics,[1] and other thinkers were highly influential on the development of medieval political thought (especially Cicero and Augustine), the translation of Aristotle's texts (particularly the *Nicomachean Ethics* and the *Politics*) into Latin facilitated the possibility of closer study of a wider array of Aristotle's works. In fact, Aquinas's teacher and mentor, Albert the Great, was

---

1. The version of the *Nicomachean Ethics* known as the *ethica vetus* can be traced back to at least the twelfth century (see Cary J. Nederman, *Medieval Aristotelianism and Its Limits: Classical Traditions in Moral and Political Philosophy, 12th-15th Centuries* [Brookfield, Vt.: Variorum, 1997], p. 55).

the first master to comment on the texts of Aristotle, and his full explication of the virtue of justice was never completed in his *Summa de bono*. Thus, one could say that Aquinas was in a unique position to contribute further to the development of the discussion of the virtue of justice, thereby opening the way to a greater appreciation of the role of civic virtue directed toward the immanent goods of the political community, while keeping such goods tethered to the transcendent ends of the pilgrim church and the Christian wayfarer.

It is important to note at the outset the distinction between the task presented to Aquinas in the thirteenth century and the task that presents itself to us in the twenty-first. Most — though not all — discussions of the virtues prior to Aquinas focused almost exclusively on the transcendent ends of the virtues made possible by grace. Thus, Aquinas and his contemporaries worked to resist a tendency to collapse natural virtues into the infused or theological forms of those virtues. One of their aims was to carve out a space for civic virtue vis-à-vis the political community. The early medieval trend might be said to "collapse up" toward a purely theological, transcendent analysis and discussion of the virtues. Within this cultural trend, however, Aquinas makes space for the political within the transcendent, by positing and defending a substantive nature-grace distinction. The naturalistic philosophy tethered to a robust metaphysics of "The Philosopher" was well suited for such a task. In our context, however, where the nature-grace distinction is not so much overlooked as systematically ignored (at least in the predominantly secular discourse that dominates our public culture), the opposite task is necessary. A theological account of civic virtue must extend the political to reconnect it to the transcendent, while simultaneously recognizing and respecting the autonomy and integrity of the political. This will eventually take us back into the debates over Henri de Lubac's discussion of nature and grace that still continue to define much of Catholic theology, and which have an often-unarticulated effect on moral theology (I consider this topic in Chapter 4). The predominant intellectual paradigm of late modern thought tends to collapse all forms of virtue into those available through the effort of natural human reason, thereby denying or ignoring the possibility of interaction between human reason and transcendent ends.[2]

2. The influence of Kant's distinction between the noumenal and the phenomenal is quite evident here, as is Hegel's emphasis on the political community of the state — what he calls *Sittlichkeit* — as the immanent space within which spirit, freedom, and ultimate truth are made available to human reason in history via dialectic (see *Elements of the Philosophy of Right,* ed. Allen W. Wood, trans. H. B. Nisbet [Cambridge: Cambridge University Press,

Scholastic reflection on morality and politics in the High Middle Ages was greatly influenced by one of the great systematic works that laid the foundation for the social and political unification of Europe that took place from the eleventh to the thirteenth centuries: Peter Lombard's *Sentences* (completed between 1145 and 1158).[3] The *Sentences* became the foundational text of medieval theology for (at least) the next two hundred years, and its influence was felt in all scholastic theology. Lombard's treatment of the virtues is almost exclusively focused on a theological construal of the virtues.[4] He did not make a clear distinction between the virtues as an effect of grace and grace itself, and thus all the virtues could be seen as various modalities expressing the central virtue of charity.[5] For him there was essentially no difference between the virtues and the actions of grace in the human soul, a point of which Aquinas himself was well aware, but which he also challenged (*Summa theologiae* I-II 110.4). Lombard writes that "grace is not incongru-

---

1991], §257-59, pp. 275-71). Charles Taylor traces the development of how Western culture has come to see all of reality as encompassed within this narrower view of reason, a world cut off from access to the divine or the transcendent in history, and fully responsible for its own destiny (see *A Secular Age* [Cambridge, Mass.: Belknap Press of Harvard University Press, 2007], especially chapter 3, "The Great Disembedding," pp. 146-58).

3. R. W. Southern, *Scholastic Humanism and the Unification of Europe,* vol. 2 (Cambridge, Mass.: Blackwell, 2001), pp. 140-46. Southern writes that Lombard's *Sententiae* "drove all competitors from the field, and became the first, the greatest, and (until, in the nineteenth century, when Thomas Aquinas was recognized as the scholastic theologian *par excellence*) the only universal textbook of theology which the schools ever produced . . . Peter Lombard's work may therefore be claimed as one of the great formative works of western intellectual history. It is certainly the humblest of all great works" (p. 145).

4. One should not get the impression, however, that Lombard's was the only influential reflection on the virtues in the scholastic period. Cary Nederman has demonstrated that familiarity with a generally Aristotelian analysis of the virtues would have been well known to all scholastics in the twelfth and thirteenth centuries. He provides evidence that Cicero and Boethius drew on Aristotle in their discussions of virtue, and that thinkers such as John of Salisbury (ca. 1115-80), Peter Abelard, Alan of Lille, and others were utilizing Aristotelian language of choice and the mean (*Medieval Aristotelianism and Its Limits,* pp. 55-75, and especially pp. 72-73).

5. On this point, Aquinas retained many of Lombard's central insights, while developing his own distinctions and contributions to the discourse. On this particular point, he still maintains that charity is the form of all the virtues (*Summa theologiae* II-II 23.8) and thus retains Lombard's (and Paul's) teaching on charity as the central virtue in the Christian life. But he also adds a distinction between grace as a created substance in the soul and as the principle of the infused virtues (*Summa theologiae* I-II 110.1-3). In doing so he distinguishes between grace and the virtues, which are an effect of grace.

ously called virtue," or that "grace itself is virtue."[6] Thus, in the *Sentences* virtue was understood primarily as the action of God in the human soul.

However, as scholastic masters began to apply their learning and knowledge to practical issues relating to the increasingly complicated and sophisticated political and legal unification of Europe, greater attention was also paid to the manner in which the virtues function as an essential element of a well-ordered society. This demanded greater sensitivity to the manner in which the virtues help one "to live well in this mortal life," as Augustine had stated it.[7] Thus, it became necessary to consider the difference between those virtues that function in the human person with regard to the ordering of political society, and those that function with regard to arriving at the state of eternal beatitude. In this cultural context theological discussions of the distinction and relationship between nature and grace — between the acquired virtues and the infused virtues — become much more salient for thinking about civic virtue.

What had not fully emerged, however, from these early scholastic discussions was an approach to justice that would provide a clear analysis of justice capable of distinguishing between justice as a cardinal virtue and justice functioning in relation to grace, or that would place the emphasis on what is due to another within a purely political setting. The primary definition of justice that Aquinas offers is that "justice is a constant and perpetual will rendering to each his right/due [*ius*]."[8] Aquinas's choice to use Justinian's definition of justice indicates a preference for a philosophical analysis of justice as a natural, acquired virtue, as opposed to a theological analysis of justice as an infused virtue and the gift of grace.[9] By opting for a prima facie

6. "Illa gratia virtus no incongrue nominator . . . ipsa gratia est vertus" (*Sententiae* Lib. IV, Dist. XXVII, c. 5).

7. "quibus in hac mortalitate bene vivitur" (Augustine, *De Trinitate* Lib. IV, c. 9, n. 12; quoted by Lombard, *Sententiae* Liber III, Dist. XXXIII, c. 1, n. 3).

8. "iustitia est constans et perpetua voluntas ius suum unicuique tribuens" (*Summa theologiae* II-II 58.1). My English translations of the *Summa* have been aided by the volume translated by the Fathers of the English Dominican Province, *Summa Theologica*, 5 vols. (Notre Dame, Ind.: Christian Classics, 1948), though I have made changes where they seemed to better capture the meaning of the original Latin. Latin excerpts are derived from the Leonine editions published between 1888 and 1906 (Rome: Typis Polyglottae Officiniae S.C. de Propaganda Fide), and can be found in full at www.corpusthomisticum.org/iopera .html or in any published critical edition.

9. This, in turn, implies that Aquinas, unlike Lombard, distinguished between grace and virtue since for Aquinas grace is the *cause* of the infused virtues in the soul not to be equated with the infused virtues themselves (*Summa theologiae* I-II 110.3). Moreover, his

philosophical analysis of justice, Aquinas is able to claim that "the justice which faith works in us . . . whereby the ungodly is justified" is distinct from the cardinal virtue of justice (*Summa theologiae* II-II 58.2). By dedicating a previous section of the *Summa theologiae* (I-II 109-14) to the treatise on grace Aquinas is able to make a clear distinction between his treatment of justice vis-à-vis the natural, political community and his treatment of grace and the infused virtues. This allows him to consider the natural virtue of justice within the broader teleological and transcendent aims of the wayfarer. In other words, he begins to carve out a conceptual space for a more robust conception of civic virtue.

These decisions about how to organize the structure of the *Summa theologiae* provided Aquinas a space in which to craft his own distinctive contribution to the discussion of justice. Perhaps the most important change that Aquinas made to Aristotle's discussion of justice in book V of the *Nicomachean Ethics* has to do with his decision to place justice in the will as the subject of the virtue. The concept of the will was entirely foreign to Aristotle. Placing justice in the will required Aquinas to harmonize the diverse range of sources from which he was drawing. On the one hand, Aristotle does not have a conception of a part of the soul that could be called the will. For him, the human soul consists of the intellect and the sensitive appetite, the latter of which includes the irascible and concupiscible faculties. Yet scholastic discussions, drawing on Augustine's emphasis on the will (*voluntas* or *liberum arbitrium*), combined with a general scholastic knowledge of the role of the will in Stoic philosophy (through Cicero and Augustine's comments in *Civitas Dei*), there was considerable argument about the role of the will in relation to the virtues. Since by definition all human action originates in the will (*Summa theologiae* I-II 8.1), some scholastics believed that all moral virtues belonged properly to the will as their subject.[10]

Aquinas, however, consistently defends his position that the virtue of justice resides in the will (along with charity and hope), which is the rational

---

analysis is simplified by upholding a clear distinction between acquired and infused virtues (*Summa theologiae* I-II 61-62, especially 62.1). I explore the implications of this distinction for civic virtue throughout the rest of the book, as its significance is wide ranging.

10. For example, Bonnie Kent writes that "all habits that are moral virtues properly so called, in their own right and without qualification, are habits of the will. In the later thirteenth and early fourteenth centuries, more than a dozen thinkers defended this view. Bonaventure, Henry of Ghent, Peter Olivi, Gonsalvus of Spain, and Duns Scotus were among them" (*Virtues of the Will: The Transformation of Ethics in the Late Thirteenth Century* [Washington, D.C.: Catholic University of America Press, 1995], p. 200).

appetite, while the other virtues perfect distinctive parts of the soul.[11] This is a position that he defends throughout his entire career, from his commentary on the *Sentences* all the way through to the *Summa theologiae*.[12] Moreover, he felt himself at liberty to make the claim that, even though Aristotle does not use the term in his moral psychology, Justinian's definition of justice (which mentions the will) is "about the same definition as that given by the Philosopher (*Nicomachean Ethics* V 5) who says that *justice is a habit whereby a man is said to be capable of doing just actions in accordance with his choice.*"[13] Aquinas explains his reasoning for making this interpretation in his commentary on the *Ethics*. In multiple places in his commentary he feels at liberty to extend the discussion of what Aristotle wrote, believing that he was simply drawing out the implications of Aristotle's work. In his commentary on the *Nicomachean Ethics* he writes that Aristotle "fittingly [*convenienter*] explained justice after the manner of a will."[14] Matthias Perkams indicates further that this association was facilitated by the "Latin translation *volunta iusta* of the Greek *boulontai ta dikaia*,"[15] thereby giving further weight to associating the notion of will with Aristotle's understanding of justice.

11. In his schema of the virtues in the human soul, each cardinal virtue fulfills the function of perfecting the part of which it is a subject. Thus, prudence perfects the intellect. Fortitude and temperance function to perfect the sensitive appetite of the human soul, which is broken down into the irascible and the concupiscible (*Summa theologiae* I 81.2). Fortitude perfects the irascible, and temperance the concupiscible parts of the sensitive appetite. The will, being the appetite that belongs properly to the intellect, is naturally desirous of the good as it is comprehended in the intellect (*Summa theologiae* I-II 8.1). The will is thus the seat of justice in the human soul since "the will moves the other powers of the soul to their acts" (*Summa theologiae* I-II 9.1), and justice is concerned primarily with external acts toward another (*Summa theologiae* II-II 57.1; 58.2; see also *Sententia libri ethicorum* Lib. 5, L. 1).

12. Aquinas makes this same argument about the location of justice in the will, drawing on the same quote from Anselm that is referenced by Lombard that "justice is rectitude of the will observed for its own sake" in his *Scriptum super Sententiarum* (Lib. 3, Dist. 33, Q. 2, A. 4, QC. 3) and in *Summa theologiae* (II-II 58.4).

13. "Et quasi est eadem definitio cum ea quam philosophus ponit, in V Ethic., dicens quod *iustitia est habitus secundum quem aliquis dicitur operativus secundum electionem iusti*" (*Summa theologiae* II-II 58.1).

14. "est considerandum, quod convenienter notificavit iustitiam per voluntatem" (*Sententia libri ethicorum* Lib. 5, L. 1, n. 5). English translation is taken from the translation by C. I. Litzinger, O.P., *Commentary on the Nicomachean Ethics, Volumes I-II* (Chicago: Henry Regnery, 1964).

15. Matthias Perkams, "Aquinas's Interpretation of the Aristotelian Virtue of Justice and his Doctrine of the Natural Law," in *Virtue Ethics in the Middle Ages: Commentaries on Aristotle's Nicomachean Ethics, 1200-1500,* ed. Istvan P. Bejczy (Leiden: Brill, 2008), pp. 131-50, p. 135.

This move to place justice in the will becomes important for developing an account of civic virtue since the definition of civic virtue includes the will to sustain and enhance the wellbeing of one's community by seeking the common good.

A second context in which Aquinas clarifies his own thought beyond what Aristotle says in the *Ethics* is in regard to the natural law, and this will also have important implications for the subsequent development of a Thomistic account of civic virtue. In the *Ethics* (book V, chapter 7; 1134b-1135a) Aristotle makes a distinction between natural and positive law, and maintains that natural law indicates that which is unchanging according to nature. When it comes to his normative analysis of law, however, natural law does very little work. He favors rather a regime-centered understanding of positive law, one that changes according to the circumstances as set up by each civil body.

Aquinas, on the other hand, inherits a much richer account of natural law from medieval jurists, from Augustine and the Stoics, and from his own biblical, theological, and philosophical analysis of law that he had developed earlier in his treatise on law (*Summa theologiae* I-II 90-108). This allowed him to move away from the regime-centered analysis of positive law as it is found in Aristotle, and to account for a greater normative role for natural law (as the reason's participation in the eternal law).[16] By making a slight modification (but one with far-reaching implications), Aquinas brought in a more normative sense of the natural law, thereby placing positive law in a dependent, derivative relation to the unchanging principles of natural law (which is further grounded in God's eternal law) in a way that Aristotle himself did not.

When considering Aquinas's discussion of justice for a modern context, it is helpful to keep in mind the ways in which he addresses some of the questions that emerged in scholastic discourse on the nature of justice. First of all, his emphasis on a philosophical analysis of justice that is focused primarily on relationships denoting a certain kind of equality between human persons allowed him to sidestep many of the problems associated with the Augustinian definition of justice (that Lombard had relied on). Augustine's definition had related to mercy and referred primarily to justice as justification through grace. This enabled Aquinas to provide an account of justice as a virtue that also addressed the needs of an increasingly unified and regulated European society.[17] Moreover, by tethering the virtue of justice closely to his account

16. See *Summa theologiae* I-II 93.2 and I-II 94.
17. For a richer account of the thirteenth-century context and development of these

of natural law, it became increasingly clear how essential the virtue of justice was in providing a foundation for social cohesion and a well-ordered society. He demonstrates this connection by showing how both the individual human mind and the positive laws of one's society have their foundations in natural law. And natural law, in turn, is a manifestation of human reason's participation in the eternal law through which God governs the whole of the created universe (through divine providence; see *Summa theologiae* I 22 and I-II 93.3). In making these distinctions, Aquinas carves out an analytical space to consider the importance of civic virtue for achieving the common good of the political community, while simultaneously recognizing that even the common good is subordinate to and remains tethered to the ultimate good and end of the universe.

General Justice and the Common Good: The Core of Civic Virtue

In *Summa theologiae* II-II 58.5, Aquinas distinguishes between general and specific justice, and he begins his treatment of the topic with general justice. It is immediately apparent that Aquinas's commentaries on the *Ethics* and, to a lesser extent, the *Politics,* were highly influential for his treatment of general and specific justice in the *Summa theologiae.* The distinction between general and specific justice is something that he maintained throughout his career, including a brief reference to the difference in his commentary on the *Sentences.*[18] His treatment in the *Summa theologiae,* however, shows significant development and maturity of thought in relation to general justice, even despite the brevity of his treatment. It is worth quoting this section at length to grasp the full import of what is being stated:

> Now it is evident that all who are included in a community stand in relation to that community as parts to a whole; while a part, as such, belongs to a whole, so that whatever is the good of the part can be directed to the good of the whole. It follows therefore that the good of any virtue, whether such virtue direct one in relation to himself, or in relation to certain other individual persons, is referable to the common good, to which justice directs: so that *all acts of virtue can pertain to justice, insofar as it*

---

notions, see Jean Porter, *Natural and Divine Law: Reclaiming the Tradition for Christian Ethics* (Grand Rapids: Eerdmans, 1999), especially chapter 1.

18. *Sententiae* Liber III, Dist. XXXIII, Q. 1, A. 1, qc. 3, ad. 3.

directs a person to the common good. It is in this sense that justice is called a general virtue. And since it belongs to the law to direct to the common good, as stated above (I-II 90.2), it follows that the justice which is in this way styled general, is called *legal justice,* because thereby a person is in harmony with the law which directs the acts of all the virtues to the common good. (*Summa theologiae* II-II 58.5)[19]

There is much to glean from this rich definition of general justice — indeed, it is the foundational text for developing a Thomistic account of civic virtue. First, general justice is distinguished from particular justice, which is in turn divided into its distributive and commutative species (*Summa theologiae* II-II 58.7-8; II-II 61). Even though particular justice is the primary sense of justice, and is worthy of its own independent study, it is beyond this current study of civic virtue to move into an analysis of commutative and distributive justice. Second, it seems that Aquinas uses both the terms "general *(generalis)* justice" and "legal *(legalis)* justice" interchangeably. He does, however, seem to prefer the former even though Aristotle favors the latter. It is likely that this reflects Aquinas's different understanding of the relationship between positive and natural law. For Aristotle, the general virtue that he calls legal justice could refer solely to following the written laws of one's community. Yet for Aquinas, this would not be enough to make one just, for laws themselves can be unjust.[20] The human mind is subject to a higher law through reason's participation in eternal law vis-à-vis natural law. Thus, the term "general justice" better captures the idea of what Aquinas means when he picks up the concept of legal justice from Aristotle and incorporates it into his own moral and political theory. General justice is not merely a propensity to follow the written laws of one's society — though it is that, when

19. "Manifestum est autem quod omnes qui sub communitate aliqua continentur comparantur ad communitatem sicut partes ad totum. Pars autem id quod est totius est, unde et quodlibet bonum partis est ordinabile in bonum totius. Secundum hoc igitur bonum cuiuslibet virtutis, sive ordinantis aliquem hominem ad seipsum sive ordinantis ipsum ad aliquas alias personas singulares, est referibile ad bonum commune, ad quod ordinat iustitia. Et secundum hoc actus omnium virtutum possunt ad iustitiam pertinere, secundum quod ordinat hominem ad bonum commune. Et quantum ad hoc iustitia dicitur virtus generalis. Et quia ad legem pertinet ordinare in bonum commune, ut supra habitum est, inde est quod talis iustitia, praedicto modo generalis, dicitur iustitia legalis, quia scilicet per eam homo concordat legi ordinanti actus omnium virtutum in bonum commune."

20. "Hence if the written law contains anything contrary to natural law, it is unjust and has no binding force.... Wherefore such documents are to be called not laws, but rather corruptions of law, as stated above (I-II 95.2)" (*Summa theologiae* II-I 60.5).

the laws are just — but rather a more deeply ingrained habit of following the dictates of natural law in pursuit of the common good.

Third, general justice is capable of directing all other acts of moral virtue, whether toward oneself or toward another person. This is so because general justice is seated in the will, which is the part of the human soul from which all external acts flow. Therefore, justice, like charity, can function architectonically to regulate acts relating to other virtues through the perfection of the will by orienting the will toward its proper ends. For example, Aquinas writes that "just as charity may be called a general virtue insofar is it directs the acts of all the virtues to the Divine good, so too is legal justice, insofar as it directs the acts of all the virtues to the common good" (*Summa theologiae* II-II 58.6).[21] Thus, justice and charity function analogously to perfect the will and to direct all other acts of the virtues in regard to their distinctive ends (the divine good for charity, and the temporal common good for justice). Here is one example of the way in which Aquinas creates a space for the necessity of pursuing the common good of the political community within the life of the wayfarer on the journey to the transcendent end of friendship with God. At the same time, however, he tethers the two ends to each other via his use of analogical comparison. (I explore the implications of analogical language more below.)

Fourth, and closely related to the previous point, the *terminus ad quem* of acts directed by general justice is the common good. "The common good" is a term frequently used in contemporary moral theology (especially Catholic social thought), but "the common good" often functions as a general term that can convey a wide array of ambiguous meanings.

It seems that when the phrase "the common good" is used by the majority of contemporary thinkers, whether in the context of Catholic social thought or in other, secular and/or political thinkers, it generally refers to a collection of individual goods that come to make up a whole of social goods or services that is instrumental to each individual's good. This view is made explicit in *Gaudium et spes,* which states that the common good is "the sum of those conditions of social life which allow social groups and their individual members relatively thorough and ready access to their own fulfillment."[22] Taking this definition as the definitive and final definition, however, would

---

21. "Sicut enim caritas potest dici virtus generalis inquantum ordinat actus omnium virtutum ad bonum divinum, ita etiam iustitia legalis inquantum ordinat actus omnium virtutum ad bonum commune."

22. *Gaudium et spes,* §26. Quoted from *The Basic Sixteen Documents of Vatican II: Constitutions, Decrees, Declarations,* ed. Austin Flannery, O.P. (Northport, N.Y.: Costello, 1996).

throw considerable confusion on the Thomist account of civic virtue. If the common good is to function as the object of civic virtue, it must be one good rather than an amalgamation of individual goods. This definition would require one to develop the will toward an aggregate of goods leading to a division of the object of civic virtue. Second, this definition tends to reduce the common good to an instrumental role involving more basic individual goods. The common good, even as it is made up of a set of interrelated concepts, must also be a single, unified good at least insofar as it is capable of attracting the will to become the object of particular acts of civic virtue.

A Thomistic account of the common good must assume that the common good is an independently existing good that transcends the sum total of individual goods in society. Aquinas states this explicitly when he writes that

> the common good of the realm and the particular good of the individual differ not only in respect of the many and the few, but also under a *formal aspect*. For the aspect of the common good differs from the aspect of the individual good, even as the aspect of the whole differs from that of its part. (*Summa theologiae* II-II 58.7, *ad* 2)[23]

Unfortunately, Aquinas never pursues a distinct set of questions on his understanding of the common good. Nor does he define exactly how the individual good differs in genus from the temporal common good. This formal distinction between the individual good and the common good is rarely recognized in Catholic social or political thought, and is a central tenet of a Thomistic account of civic virtue.

Since he does not develop a full, descriptive account of the common good, it is important to pay close attention to what Aquinas seems to mean by "the common good," as well as what he does not mean. First of all, Aquinas states earlier in the *Summa theologiae* that each virtue is defined and distinguished in relation to its object (*Summa theologiae* I-II 55.4). Thus, he states that "legal justice is a special virtue in respect of its essence, insofar as it regards the common good as its proper object" (*Summa theologiae* II-II 58.7, *ad* 2).[24] It is important to remember, therefore, that the common good is of

23. "bonum commune civitatis et bonum singulare unius personae non differunt solum secundum multum et paucum, sed secundum formalem differentiam, alia enim est ratio boni communis et boni singularis, sicut et alia est ratio totius et partis."

24. "Potest tamen quaelibet virtus, secundum quod a praedicta virtute, speciali quidem in essentia, generali autem secundum virtutem, ordinatur ad bonum commune, dici iustitia legalis."

a different genus than the individual good. To the extent that the common good can be considered as a good that transcends individual goods it can become the distinctive object of the general virtue of justice.

At this point it seems probable that Aquinas's understanding of general justice and the common good was deepened by his own reading of the *Politics*. For example, the purpose of law in Aristotle's thought has to do with making citizens good and happy through the instantiation of virtue (*Politics* VII.2 1325a7-11). Although Aquinas recognizes this pedagogical element of human law (*Summa theologiae* I-II 92.1, 95.3), he exhibits a clear preference for placing the emphasis of the purpose of law on the manner in which it serves, protects, and fosters the common good.[25] Hence, Aquinas's own discussion of general justice in the *Summa theologiae* is more heavily oriented toward the common good than is the discussion of justice in Aristotle's *Nicomachean Ethics*. In his commentary on the *Politics,* Aquinas places a strong emphasis on the life of the city as the most perfect good of all human societies and on the common good as the highest expression of the human good.[26]

The debate about which of these two ends of law is primary in Aquinas's

25. "Consequently, since the law is chiefly ordained to the common good, any other precept in regard to some individual work, must needs be devoid of the nature of a law, save insofar as it regards the common good. Therefore every law is ordained to the common good" (*Summa theologiae* I-II 90.2). For a more detailed defense of this particular claim, see Jean Porter's article, "The Common Good in Thomas Aquinas," in *In Search of the Common Good,* ed. Dennis P. McCann and Patrick D. Miller (New York: T&T Clark, 2005), pp. 94-120, especially p. 109. This places my account at odds with Robert George's insistence on defending the "perfectionistic tradition" (exemplified by Aristotle and Aquinas) in which the primary purpose of law is directed more toward providing a context for individuals to pursue virtue and moral perfection, as he argues in *Making Men Moral: Civil Liberties and Public Morality* (Oxford: Clarendon, 1993), chapter 1, pp. 19-47. His analysis of the purposes of law only tangentially mentions the common good (pp. 32 and 47), and, as noted among the trends of neoconservative political thought in the introduction, tends to focus on the social significance of sexuality and marriage (p. 45), while ignoring most other moral, political, and legal issues relating to the common good.

26. See the *Proemium* of Aquinas's *Sententia libri politicorum.* English translation can be found in "Commentary on the Politics," trans. Ernest L. Fortin and Peter D. O'Neill, in *Medieval Political Philosophy,* ed. Ralph Lerner and Muhsin Mahdi (New York: Free Press, 1963), pp. 297-334. One should also note that despite what many modern commentators eager to uphold the centrality of freedom or liberty have feared in recent literature on Aristotle and Aquinas, the common good is not a monolithic whole that is at best indifferent to, and at worst destructive of, the good of individuals. Rather, the common good is the highest good because it is the only thing capable of being ordered to "the satisfaction of all the needs of human life" (*Sententia libri politicorum, Proeumium*) for individuals as well as the whole.

thought has a long history, and seems to hinge on how one understands the role of the common good within the political community. In particular, whether or not the common good is understood to be an independently subsisting good, or whether it is seen as a place-marker for conditions that enable (or demand) a certain level of external virtue for citizens, has significant implications for how one understands the place of the common good in political life and the individual's pursuit of civic virtue. For example, the new natural law theorists exhibit a preference for understanding the political common good as a linguistic place-marker for individual goods and virtues. For them, the true purpose of law and the political community is reducible to these individual goods and virtues.[27] John Finnis writes, for example, that "the *specifically* political common good which is interdefined with the responsibilities of state government and law seems indeed to be an *instrumental* good or set of goods, albeit of preeminent complexity, scope, and dignity among instruments."[28] Such a claim indeed makes sense in light of the theory of natural law that Finnis describes in *Natural Law and Natural Rights,* in which the first principles of practical reasoning are reduced to basic individual goods.[29] It is difficult, however, to square this assertion with Aquinas's claim that the common good is a real, subsistent good that is of a different genus from the individual good. The full implications of such an account of the common good for civic virtue are expressed by Finnis

27. Germain Grisez writes, for example, that those who uphold a substantive and non-instrumental view of the common good "overlook limits on the competence of the state which have been clarified by recent Church teaching regarding the instrumental character of political society's common good" (*The Way of the Lord Jesus,* vol. 2, *Living a Christian Life* [Quincy, Ill.: Franciscan, 1993], p. 850). In a recent online exchange, Robert George also defends the common good as instrumental to other, more basic goods of individuals ("The Common Good: Instrumental but Not Just Contractual," *Public Discourse Blog* — http://www.thepublicdiscourse.com/2013/05/10166/, posted May 17, 2013). Accessed August 30, 2013.

28. John Finnis, "Public Good: The Specifically Political Common Good in Aquinas," in *Natural Law and Moral Inquiry: Ethics, Metaphysics, and Politics in the Work of Germain Grisez,* ed. Robert P. George (Washington, D.C.: Georgetown University Press, 1998), pp. 174-210, p. 191, italics added.

29. The one concession that Finnis allows is to the family as a natural social institution, which does seem to have its own ontological status in addition to that of individuals (see *Natural Law and Natural Rights* [Oxford: Clarendon, 1980], pp. 147-50). Elsewhere he writes that "families are noncontingent in the sense that they directly instantiate a basic human good" ("Public Good," p. 189). The same status, for reasons that are not entirely clear, is never afforded to the political community or to its more specific realm of authority within the legal apparatus of the state.

when he writes, "Aquinas's many statements that we are 'naturally political animals' . . . cannot be pressed into service as implying that the state or its common good is the object of a natural inclination or an intrinsic and basic good."[30] And yet, following Aquinas's analysis of the virtues, if general justice is a natural human virtue then it must be ordered by a natural inclination toward the common good. This inclination toward the common good is innate to human nature and an essential component of human flourishing. While Finnis's attitude may be understandable in response to the threat of state tyranny, something essential is lost in our understanding of the common good as a truly subsistent good in human life by such an instrumentalist approach. Something essential is lost in our understanding of the nature of the human person whose fulfillment can only be found in relation to others vis-à-vis the common good of one's community.

These concerns represented by Finnis and others, however, raise an important aspect of the common good that must be addressed in defending a more substantive notion of it. Does the subsistent, non-instrumental notion of the common good *necessarily* lead to a totalizing of the coercive power of the state over individual autonomy? To understand how this is not the case, one must balance the claims of Catholic social thought that uphold the endorsement of subjective human rights with the claim that natural human flourishing is only possible in relation to the common good.

Thus, even though Aquinas holds that the common good is a good that transcends the good of the individual and that no individual can seek her own good without also seeking the common good (*Summa theologiae* I-II 92.1, *ad* 3; II-II 47.10, *ad* 2), he does not mean by this that the individual good is justifiably overwritten by the primacy of the common good. The potential for the common good to overshadow individual rights and autonomy is a concern not just of moral theologians, but also of many liberal political theorists. For example, although he does not attack Aquinas or the concept of the common good directly, George Kateb vehemently defends individuality against any kind of insistence that the human person's true good or happiness can be found in any kind of essentially social existence. These "anti-individualist ideals" he lumps into one camp and pits them against democratic, rights-based individualism when he writes that

> nothing is worse than the horrors that do or would come from the un-
> qualified prestige of participation in sovereign politics, the societywide

30. Finnis, "Public Good," p. 191.

bond of community, the solidarity of the armed group, and the project of social self-realization. They are horrors in themselves and are auxiliaries to further horrors of statism. The remedies for the troubles must be found, at least in any democratic setting, within rights-based individualism and the aspiration to democratic individuality.[31]

In light of these liberal concerns, Aquinas's comment that "the common good [is] better than the good of the individual" (*Summa theologiae* II-II 47.10) could be taken to underwrite precisely such a fear that the common good may be used to justify the denigration of individual rights. This concern is only compounded for many contemporary thinkers by the fact that Aquinas himself has no account of individual, subjective, or natural human rights.[32] I return to this challenge below, but first I want to examine another way in which Aquinas defends a more robustly substantive account of the common good.

For a Thomistic account of civic virtue the common good is neither a sum of individual goods nor a merely instrumental good. But to appreciate how this is true we must first examine more closely the different ways in which Aquinas employs the concept of the common good. Throughout his work, rather than opting to develop a fully systematic, univocal account of the common good, Aquinas's discussion of the common good is best understood to function analogically.[33] Analogous language is used to draw

31. George Kateb, "Democratic Individuality and the Meaning of Rights," in *Liberalism and the Moral Life,* ed. Nancy L. Rosenblum (Cambridge, Mass.: Harvard University Press, 1989), pp. 183-206, p. 204. In relation to the discussion of the priority of the good over the right that I take up in Part II, Kateb writes that "the priority of the good over the right is the priority of the wrong over the right" (p. 202).

32. This is not to say that he does not uphold the importance of the human person's dignity as made in the image of God (*Summa theologiae* I. 93), on which Thomistic thinkers of the late nineteenth and early twentieth centuries could build a coherent theory of natural rights, or that the concept of rights was entirely foreign to medieval discussions of justice (see Brian Tierney, *The Idea of Natural Rights: Studies on Natural Rights, Natural Law, and Church Law, 1115-1625* [Atlanta, Ga.: Scholars, 1997]).

33. Although I am not aware of any place that Thomas himself makes this claim directly, it seems to be the best way to make sense of his discussion of the common good, and will be particularly helpful for articulating a rhetoric of the common good in Chapter 6. For example, Charles de Koninck comments in his essay, "On the Primacy of the Common Good: Against the Personalists" (1946), reprinted in *The Writings of Charles de Koninck,* ed. and trans. Ralph McInerny (Notre Dame, Ind.: Notre Dame University Press, 2008), that "the good of the particular [created nature] can be understood of the good which belongs to a cause by that similarity of analogy which 'principled' things (that is, which proceed from a

connections between two realities that are both alike and dissimilar. There-fore, analogous terms are inherently resistant to strict definitions. Thus, for example, Dennis McCann notes that one searches in vain for a "tight con-ceptual definition"[34] of the common good in Catholic social thought. Rather, it functions as a core concept that helps to elaborate certain "imperatives and virtues, as well as a basic moral vision"[35] that guides the pursuit of jus-tice across a wide array of cultural expressions. Indeed, the term's plasticity, endurance, and flexibility from Cicero to Augustine, through the medieval scholastics, and into contemporary Catholic social thought points to its fit-tingness for being taken as an analogous term.

As David Burrell has argued, analogy is most fitting for making judg-ments in regard to what are sometimes called the transcendentals — those essential qualities of being, such as truth, goodness, justice, beauty, unity, or oneness.[36] Since the *common* good explores the common element of the goodness of being or existence itself, it is fitting to draw analogous connec-tions between God as ultimate good of the universe and the common good as the highest good of the human community. Aquinas's use of analogies is a rich and complex concept, but for now my purpose is simply to claim that the language of analogy is well suited to discussions of the common good, and will provide helpful insights for discussing its function in moral delib-eration within late modern pluralistic, democratic contexts.

To begin, I note that Aquinas upholds (at least) two analogically related conceptions of the common good, one of which is grounded in a metaphys-ical analysis and the other grounded in the temporal good of the political communities. He applies these two conceptions with great flexibility and nuance in various contexts.[37] The metaphysical conception of the common

---

principle) have to their principle" (p. 76), and he later adds that "it is the created common good, of any order, which imitates most properly the absolute common good" (p. 78). Such imitation, it seems to me, can only be described via analogical language, particularly in reference to God as the uncreated common good of the entire universe.

34. Dennis P. McCann, "The Common Good in Catholic Social Teaching: A Case Study in Modernization," in McCann and Miller, eds., *In Search of the Common Good,* pp. 121-46, p. 122.

35. McCann, "The Common Good in Catholic Social Teaching," p. 123.

36. David Burrell, *Analogy and Philosophical Language* (New Haven, Conn.: Yale University Press, 1973), p. 22.

37. In the following analysis of the metaphysical participation in goodness I am in-debted to the discussion of the common good in Aquinas provided by M. S. Kempshall in *The Common Good in Late Medieval Political Thought* (Oxford: Clarendon, 1999), especially chapters 3-4.

good derives from his participation metaphysics of being, based on the following principles: that God is the ultimate good of the universe *(summum bonum)*;[38] and that all created beings participate in God's goodness[39] through a hierarchy of being,[40] in which all things are ordered to God as to their final end.[41] It therefore follows that God who is pure being *(esse ipsum)* and pure act can be considered as the ultimate common good for all of creation.[42] Additionally, although there is one hierarchy governing all of creation within God's providence, there are also distinct orders with their own distinctive ends operative within creation. Although each created nature has its own proper autonomous ends, they are still directed toward the ultimate end of all things in God. Thus all created natures are ordered by and participate in God's divine providence and wisdom.[43] This last point is espe-

38. "God is the supreme good simply" (*Summa theologiae* I 6.2).

39. Quoting Boethius's *De hebdomadibus,* Aquinas writes that "all things but God are good by participation" (*Summa theologiae* I 6.3, *sed contra*). See also *Summa theologiae* I 13.7 and I 45.3, *ad* 1.

40. "Therefore because there is one God, the Prince not only of all the angels but also of persons and all creatures; so there is one hierarchy, not only of all the angels, but also of all rational creatures, who can be participators of sacred things" (*Summa theologiae* I 108.1).

41. "He is not directed to anything else as to an end, but is Himself the last end of all things" (*Summa theologiae* I 6.3).

42. "Now it is manifest that the good of the part is for the good of the whole; hence everything, by its natural appetite and love, loves its own proper good on account of the common good [*bonum commune*] of the whole universe, which is God" (*Summa theologiae* I-II 109.3). Additionally, in his commentary on Romans 1:20, where he considers the possibility of pagan knowledge of the existence of God, he states that God is "the common good which is participated in by all" (*Expositio super Romanos* cap. 1, lec. 6). The notion of God as the common good of the whole universe is one that Aquinas expresses in his *Scriptum super Sententiarum* as well when he writes that there are two manners in which a good is said to be common. The first is by means of predication and the second is "according to participation in one and the same thing according to number; and this fellowship can be most fully in those things which pertain to the soul, in which they are found; because through itself it attains to that which is the common good of all things, which is God" (*Scriptum super Sententiarum* Lib. 4, Dist. 49, Q. 1, 1, 1, ad 3). Michael Sherwin's article is also helpful on this point ("St. Thomas and the Common Good: The Theological Perspective: An Invitation to Dialogue," *Angelicum* 70 [1993]: 307-28, p. 308, note 2).

43. For example, in the discussion quoted above from *Summa theologiae* I 108.1, Aquinas recognizes that there are distinct orders of angels and of humans, each with their own intrinsic ends, but which are also simultaneously ordered toward the ultimate end of God in the architectonic hierarchy in which all things participate via divine providence. On this point, Kempshall writes that "according to book XII of the *Metaphysics,* individual parts of a whole are ordered towards other parts in an intrinsic good but they are also ordered

cially pertinent with regard to the common good of the human community. The temporal common good can function as its own semi-autonomous end for political life by contributing to the perfection of human individuals, the human community, and the ordered whole of creation. At the same time, it is also ordered toward the higher end of God in the divine providence of which all created natures participate. This analogous understanding of the common good is precisely one of the key insights regarding the temporal common good offered by a Thomist theory of civic virtue. It also helps to explain in more precise philosophical terms how the members of a pilgrim church may pursue the genuine goods of the political community, which is ordered according to its own semi-autonomous ends, while remaining fixed on the ultimate goal that transcends the political order.

This analogical relationship between the temporal common good and God as the ultimate common good of creation presupposes a distinction between created nature and the order of grace. A lack of attention to this distinction leads to problematic conclusions when the properly political ends of the state are not distinguished from the eschatological aims of the church. For example, Robert Jenson also suggests that the common good "must be an intrinsically *analogous* term."[44] However, in his analysis he fails to recognize a distinction between properly terrestrial and political (penultimate) goods and the ultimate good toward which the pilgrim church journeys. Thus, he concludes that "all earthly polities perdure . . . by longing to be what the church in fact is, and therefore all political communities are ultimately parodies of the church itself."[45] While it may be true, as Louis Bouyer claims, that the state tends "to impose itself as the ultimate end (at least in this world) of every human activity, both individual and collective,"[46] Jenson's analysis fails to recognize the genuine created common good that is the goal of the political institutions of a society. This penultimate goal is distinct from the transcendent goal of the pilgrim church. Analogous language functions by recognizing both the similarities and the distinctions between the objects of consideration, and here we must recognize that the political common good, when properly pursued in human communities, contributes

---

towards the extrinsic good of the whole" (*The Common Good in Late Medieval Political Thought*, p. 100).

44. Robert W. Jenson, "The Triunity of Common Good," in McCann and Miller, eds., *In Search of the Common Good*, pp. 333-47, p. 341.

45. Jenson, "The Triunity of Common Good," p. 344.

46. Louis Bouyer, *Church of God: Body of Christ and Temple of the Holy Spirit*, trans. Charles Underhill Quinn (San Francisco: Ignatius, 2011), p. 511.

to the good and order of the whole of creation. Positive laicity or moderate liberalism recognizes precisely this distinction, whereas doctrinaire liberalism tends to impose the aims of the state as the ultimate good and goal of all human life. Without keeping these distinctions in mind one is inevitably led to the conclusion that the church and the state are intrinsically at odds with each other. But the practices of civic virtue by the members of a pilgrim church have the goal of facilitating the process of creating democratic institutions that leave space for the pursuit of ends that transcend the temporal community and the aims of the state.

Aquinas then tethers these metaphysical principles of being to the moral psychology of the desire for the good in the human person through his incorporation of Aristotle's doctrine that "the good is that at which all things aim" (*Nicomachean Ethics* I.1).[47] Aquinas adds to Aristotle's analysis by incorporating a biblical Christian anthropology in which the human person is made in the image of God. This enables him to have a more biblically based appreciation for the ways in which the human soul is able to participate in the being and goodness of God. The image of God in each human person is manifested in particular by the ability to reason and to act in pursuit of the ultimate good, and to rationally grasp and pursue the penultimate goods of the human community.[48] Thus, the choices that any one person makes with regard to her individual good and to the common good of the community have important implications for the manner in which the wayfarer moves toward union with God. A consequence of this for a Thomistic account of civic virtue is that even as one strives to enhance the imperfect, common good of human society, this can be done with an eye toward the higher end of union with God in such a way that the two aspects of the one ultimate end of the human person are harmonized in the will of the wayfarer.[49]

At least one difficulty emerges, however, when this metaphysical sche-

47. See also Kempshall's explication of these metaphysical principles and their relation to practical reason, which I am partially drawing on here, in *The Common Good in Late Medieval Political Thought*, pp. 81-84.

48. Craig A. Boyd provides a descriptive account of how Aquinas's participation metaphysics coupled with the doctrine of the human person as made in the image of God underscores the intrinsic connection between God's causality and the human person's capacity for reason in his article "Participation Metaphysics, the *Imago Dei* and Natural Law in Aquinas' Ethics," *New Blackfriars* 88 (May 2007): 274-87.

49. Aquinas discusses the possibility of simultaneously holding and pursuing two overlapping and hierarchically ordered goods in his analysis of intention, where he claims that it is possible to intend two ends in which "one is ordained to another (unus ad alium ordinetur)" within the same act of virtue (*Summa theologiae* I-II 12.3, *ad* 2).

mata of participation in God's goodness is applied to participation in the common good in the political context. For if, following the hierarchy of orders and ends that Aquinas picks up from Pseudo-Dionysius and Boethius, the wayfarer must move up through these orders in a hierarchy of goods in the ascent to God, it could seem that a certain kind of participation and submerging of the individual in the ends and ordering of the political community would be required to approach the perfection of life offered in the beatific vision.[50] The same problem emerges when considered from a more directly theological standpoint. The contemplation of perfect beatitude is experienced as something within the individual soul of the wayfarer called to friendship with God through sanctifying grace. Thus, for Aquinas eternal beatitude is a social phenomenon only accidentally insofar as there are many who are called into this communion (*Summa theologiae* I-II 4.8, *ad* 3). Fortunately Aquinas recognizes that analogous language has its limits, and that these limits must be respected, especially when talking about God. Therefore, even though Aquinas continues to use corporeal analogies about the manner in which the good of the individual parts of the body (that is, members of a community) are dependent on the health of the entire body (that is, the kingdom, state, or political community), he recognizes both the benefits and the limits of drawing out the analogy between the common good of the civic community and the infinite common good toward which all created beings strive in God. When it comes to the ultimate common good of the created universe, it is fitting for one to become absorbed into the infinite being of God in pure love and friendship. When it comes to the state, however, the analogy no longer applies. The person may not be totally subsumed into the political aims of the state or into the common good, no matter how just these ends may be, without doing violence to the freedom and rights of the human person.

Because Aquinas recognizes the limits of the uses of analogous language, the good toward which persons aim in directing their civic life is similar to, but does not directly correlate with, the ultimate good of beatitude with God. The former — the temporal common good — is a created good while the latter — the ultimate common good who is God — entirely transcends

---

50. Kempshall asks the question in the following manner: "Is the mediation of ends within the hierarchy of goodness so strict that the individual human being cannot attain his ultimate good in God without the good of human society? Or can the operation of the hierarchy of goodness be modified to make exception for the individual such that a human being can attain eternal beatitude directly, without the mediation of the human community?" (*The Common Good in Late Medieval Political Thought*, p. 86).

such predications as can be made of the temporal common good. Thus, in commenting on the *Nicomachean Ethics* I 1, Aquinas concludes by stating that

> we should note that [Aristotle] says political science is the most impor-
> tant, not simply, but in that division of practical sciences which are con-
> cerned with human things, the ultimate end of which political science
> considers. The ultimate end of the whole universe is considered in the-
> ology which is the most important without qualification. (*Sententia libri
> ethicorum* L. 1, n. 13)[51]

Combining this observation with Aquinas's comments above on the *Politics* about the common good as the highest good of human society, what emerges is a clear distinction between the common good as the end of human society and God as the common good and aim of all of creation. Thus, although there is an analogous relationship between the ultimate common good and the common good of human society, it would be a mistake to draw this con-nection too tightly and to assume that they function in the same manner. While it may be true that natural human flourishing is not possible without some form of participation in social life, and that the supernatural end of the human person entails a commitment to the good of others, it is not true that the temporal common good is an order into which each individual must be subsumed on order to participate in the process of beatification or diviniza-tion through which the soul is drawn close to God in friendship.[52]

Once this metaphysical-temporal distinction is established a further challenge emerges — that is, that Aquinas's conception of the temporal com-mon good may be seen as opposed to human freedom and autonomy. Here I pick up again the practical concern about individual autonomy raised by

51. "Sciendum est autem, quod politicam dicit esse principalissimam, non simpliciter, sed in genere activarum scientiarum, quae sunt circa res humanas, quarum ultimum finem politica considerat. Nam ultimum finem totius universi considerat scientia divina, quae est respectu omnium principalissima."

52. One practical way in which Aquinas defends this distinction is in his discussion of virginity. For him, virginity consecrated to God is of a higher order than carnal fruitfulness (*Summa theologiae* II-II 152.4, *ad* 3) since even though procreation is an essential good for the flourishing (indeed, for the continuation) of the human community, this does not mean that individuals cannot choose a celibate form of human life or have a vocation to single life. This is because the one who chooses celibacy for the sake of the kingdom of God (see Matt. 19:12) is considering a good of another genus than that of the temporal common good (and thus in such a case "the private good is better" than the common good).

Finnis and others. Aquinas provides a few helpful, practical examples that demonstrate that the individual cannot rightfully be subsumed within the whole of society. For example, he considers the possibility that the common good of the kingdom might best be furthered if someone in vowed religious life were to renounce his celibacy to engage in a marriage that would promote the common good of the kingdom. In such a case Aquinas argues that it would not be allowed for a prelate to dispense that person from his vows to marry (*Summa theologiae* II-II 88.11). He presents two reasons that this is so. The first is because the vow represents a spiritual sanctification of the individual to God, and spiritual goods are of a higher genus than human goods. Thus, any spiritual good is de facto higher than any human good (even if the latter be a common good). But the same argument against dispensing from the vow could be made on the basis of the fact that (under normal conditions) no act can be commanded against the free will of the individual.[53] For an act to be a truly human act it must flow from the free choice or judgment of the human will (*liberum arbitrium* or free judgment),[54] and if it be forced to do so it would be considered as having undergone violence (cf. *Summa theologiae* I-II 6.4). Therefore, the earthly common good of the kingdom or state cannot overwrite the will of the individual who has chosen to consecrate himself to virginity. Indeed, this was no mere abstract principle in Aquinas's own life. For he had to assert his own will in moving away from the Benedictines at Monte Cassino and in joining the Dominican friars against the wishes of his family.[55]

53. The rule would normally apply for free decisions and acts of individuals, but the limit case appears once someone begins to make free choices that harm the good of others or the common good, thereby contradicting the demands of justice. In such a case an individual would be restrained from acting, and even justly punished, against his own will (cf. *Summa theologiae* II-II 62 and 108, especially article 1).

54. See *Summa theologiae* I 83: *De libero arbitrio*. Note that despite the fact that we have become accustomed to translating *liberum arbitrium* as "free will," the Dominican fathers who translated the *Summa theologiae* suggest the translation of "free judgment," and Daniel Westberg proposes that it would be more accurately translated as "free choice" (see *Right Practical Reason: Aristotle, Action, and Prudence in Aquinas* [Oxford: Clarendon, 1994], p. 81). The term "free will" can seem to suggest a voluntarist understanding of the will, in which the will, rather than being reduced from potency to act by the object toward which it is attracted, is perceived as having a more radical freedom vis-à-vis its objects such that it seems to make arbitrary decisions amid a wide array of potential goods. The preference for "free judgment" is further underscored by the fact that some form of the noun *iudicium* or the verb *iudicare* occurs twenty-five times in Q. 83 alone.

55. Jean-Pierre Torrell, O.P., *Saint Thomas Aquinas*, vol. 1, *The Person and His Work*, rev.

At this point a fuller picture of the common good as the object of civic virtue begins to emerge. First, the common good is a good that is distinguishable either from individual goods in and of themselves or from an aggregate sum of individual goods or services. Nor is it merely an instrumental good. Second, although Aquinas uses language about the superiority of the common good in relation to the individual good, he does not believe that the individual good can be overwritten arbitrarily in favor of the common good. Although modern political discourse is right to speak about natural human rights and the autonomy of individual subjects as essential elements of a just society, Aquinas's moral and political thought on the common good cannot be dismissed simply because he does not use these terms. He clearly appreciates the importance of maintaining a space within which individuals can and must choose their own good insofar as it remains in harmony with the common good of the political community. Third, he recognizes the limits of human law insofar as it may tend to overextend its realm of authority by assuming too great of a role in proscribing vice or in prescribing every act of virtue.[56] Fourth, Aquinas's analysis demonstrates that the common good is a truly existent good in which individuals participate, not as a sum of individual goods or as a merely instrumental good, but as a form of the good that is truly available and rationally apprehensible to all members of a society. In addition, considering the common good of the political community as analogically related to God as the ultimate common good of creation provides a more substantive and robust role for the common good than is usually the case in Catholic social thought or contemporary political philosophy. This point is one of the most essential contributions that the Catholic tradition can and must continue to provide to public deliberation about the good in modern democratic societies.

Fifth, Aquinas's discussion of general justice highlights a necessarily intrinsic connection between the common good and political authority to sustain a Thomistic account of civic virtue. As Jean Porter notes, "Aquinas is the first scholastic to link legislative authority explicitly to the common good."[57] This in turn implies the existence of a duly appointed role for legisla-

---

ed., trans. Robert Royal (Washington, D.C.: Catholic University of America Press, 2005), pp. 8-12.

56. Aquinas notes that human, positive law is not meant to restrain every act of vice or to prescribe every act of virtue, but to safeguard against only those acts that harm the common good of the political community and to encourage those that sustain and enhance it (see *Summa theologiae* I-II 96.2-3).

57. Porter, "The Common Good in Thomas Aquinas," p. 109.

tors and those who frame and interpret laws. The manifestations of Catholic social thought and political theology that either seek to lessen the power of state in favor of free market economics or reject the modern nation-state entirely seem unable to fully appreciate this aspect of civic virtue. A firm commitment to a Thomistic form of civic virtue does not allow such a total rejection of political authority. Even if one remains highly critical of modern democracy and liberalism, Aquinas's work clearly indicates that issues of governmental structure and duly constituted authority cannot be ignored if Christians are to remain involved in cultivating civic virtue and seeking the common good.

The remainder of this chapter turns to consider some of the concepts related to justice in Aquinas's thought as they are essential to developing a Thomistic account of civic virtue. The list of related topics is not exhaustive but rather highlights the ways in which civic virtue functions vis-à-vis natural law, prudence, and the infused virtues. I begin by examining one aspect of what Aquinas calls the "parts" associated with the virtue of justice, the subjective part known as *epikeia*. A consideration of the role of *epikeia* in relation to general justice leads into a further exploration of the connection between civic virtue, natural law, and prudence. In the final section I consider the relationship between the theological virtues and general justice to explore how the infused form of the virtues functions within a distinctively theological account of civic virtue.

Epikeia, Natural Law, and Prudence

Epikeia is a very peculiar virtue that Aquinas picks up from Aristotle's discussion in the *Nicomachean Ethics* (V 10.1137b), and it has received relatively little attention in recent commentaries on Aquinas.[58] Despite its narrow range of application, it is helpful for an account of civic virtue insofar as it highlights the ways in which making practical judgments with the common good as the primary end requires a certain kind of interior disposition that directs such judgment. One of the ways that such a disposition manifests itself is in the virtue of *epikeia*. Thus, a brief consideration of *epikeia* leads

58. The most notable exception, though it is hardly recent, is Father Joseph Lawrence Riley's published doctoral dissertation, *The History, Nature, and Use of EPIKEIA in Moral Theology* (Washington, D.C.: Catholic University of America Press, 1948). See also Roger A. Couture, O.M.I., "The Use of *Epikeia* in Natural Law: Its Early Developments," *Eglise et Theologie* 4 (1973): 71-103.

nicely into considering the relationship between natural law and prudence in acts of civic virtue.

Epikeia represents a kind of interior, higher sense of the equality that justice seeks to preserve. It provides an agent with a sense for equality that she may draw on when a strict application of the written law would lead to an outcome that would harm the common good. In such a case a literal interpretation and application of a written law would be contrary to the intention of the lawgiver and of the purposes of human law itself. Aquinas describes *epikeia* as follows:

> since human actions, with which laws are concerned, are composed of contingent singulars and are innumerable in their diversity, it was not possible to lay down rules of law that would apply to every single case. Legislators in framing laws attend to what commonly happens: although if the law be applied to certain cases it will frustrate the equality of justice and be injurious to the common good, which the law has in view . . . In these and like cases it is bad to follow the law, and it is good to set aside the letter of the law and to follow the dictates of justice and the common good. This is the object of *epikeia* which we may call equity. (*Summa theologiae* II-II 120.1)

Aquinas provides two examples in which *epikeia* may legitimately be used to judge according to a higher rule than the written, human law.[59] The difficulty with interpreting this virtue, however, arises from Aristotle's comment, which Aquinas follows, that *epikeia* is both superior to justice itself and at the same time a part of legal justice.[60] How can it be both superior to and a

59. In the first instance he notes that in general it is just to return someone's property to him if it is put on deposit. However, it would be contrary to the common good to return a sword to a madman who had deposited it (*Summa theologiae* II-II 120.1). And in *Summa theologiae* I-II 96.6 he notes that if a magistrate has commanded that the doors of a besieged city be locked, it would be a legitimate application of *epikeia* to open the doors to allow soldiers who are being pursued by the enemy to enter since their wellbeing is essential for the common good and protection of the city. There is also considerable debate, particularly among the later scholastic commentators on Aquinas, as to whether or not *epikeia* applies to precepts of natural law, as distinct from positive law. Aquinas himself does not directly resolve this question, though it seems that he sees it only applying to human law where the common good would be harmed by a literal application, whereas the same virtue does not apply to natural or divine law (see Riley, *The History, Nature, and Use of EPIKEIA*, pp. 52-102).

60. "As the Philosopher states (*Ethic.* V, 10), *epikeia is better than a certain*, that is,

subjective part of legal justice? The resolution to this question will highlight the ways in which natural law and prudence function vis-à-vis practical judgments with respect to the common good for acts of civic virtue.

A further difficulty arises in considering the similarities and the differences between *epikeia* and *aequitas,* or "equity." For Aristotle, equity is a regard for the equality that justice seeks to establish that enables an agent to forgo a legitimate claim, even if under strict interpretation of the written law it is owed to him. Aquinas extends Aristotle's discussion to include a situation where a judge provides a lesser penalty than that which is called for under the law, if the lesser penalty will be sufficient for deterring the agent from sin.[61] Thus, both *aequitas* and *epikeia* function as a corrective to written law when contingencies arise that would result in an unjust outcome if a strictly literal application of the written law is followed. Similarly, both function as a means to grasp the higher purpose of law. They enable the agent to achieve the end of justice as fairness or equality, particularly when the letter of the law becomes a hindrance to justice itself. *Aequitas,* however, is broader than *epikeia* insofar as equity might be said to be necessary for appreciating the full range of justice, whereas *epikeia* is more closely associated with legal justice itself.

In his recognition that *epikeia* is closely connected with legal justice Aquinas implicitly suggests a connection between *epikeia,* natural law, and prudence. He states that *epikeia* is a subjective part of justice and that "legal justice is subject to the direction of *epikeia.* Hence *epikeia* is as it were a higher rule of human actions" (*Summa theologiae* II-II 120.2). Thus, a paradigmatic example of the possession of civic virtue (for one charged with interpretation and application of the law — that is, a judge) is the capacity to recognize when the letter of the law does not accurately represent the regard for fairness, equality, or the common good that it is intended to serve. In such an instance the judge is able to form a judgment according to a higher (objective) and more interior (subjective) sense of justice. The virtue of *epikeia* is a part of civic virtue that is particularly important for those who interpret the law within society, and this would apply especially to judges.

However, in moving beyond the judicial context, it seems that part of what enables the virtue of *epikeia* to achieve a great deal of its normative purchase for Aquinas is his understanding of the relationship between natural

---

legal, *justice,* which observes the letter of the law; yet since it is itself a kind of justice, it is not better than all justice" (*Summa theologiae* II-II 120.2, *ad* 2).

61. *Sententia libri ethicorum* Lib. V, Lect. XVI.

and positive law, and here is where it becomes illustrative for civic virtue. In Aristotle's treatment of *epikeia,* the only higher appeal that he can make is to the original intention of the lawgiver, but in Aquinas's treatment of the same virtue, he is able to draw on his deeper, normative analysis of natural law as a source for critically interpreting and applying the law. For Aquinas, *epikeia* applies primarily to human law (hence it is a subjective part of legal justice), and yet at the same time it is able to judge according to a higher law (hence it is simultaneously higher than legal justice). *Epikeia* thus seems to stand between natural law and positive law, and one who possesses this virtue is able to set aside the literal interpretation and application of positive law in certain circumstances precisely because of reason's capacity for exercising natural law. In other words, *epikeia* is an instance of the capacity for human reason to exercise the flexibility of natural law in concrete particulars. It is precisely this capacity to judge according to a higher standard than the laws of one's community that allows a judge to appropriately exemplify the use of reason according to the dictates of natural law.

The paradoxical nature of *epikeia* is further clarified if we turn to consider its relation to the potential parts of prudence. For Aquinas there are three such potential parts: "good counsel *(eubulia),* which concerns counsel, *synesis,* which concerns judgment in matters of ordinary occurrence, and *gnome,* which concerns judgment in matters of exception to the law" (*Summa theologiae* II-II 48.1). Since the primary act of prudence is judgment leading to the command of particular acts (*Summa theologiae* II-II 47.8), it follows that these potential parts have to do with forming proper judgment that will lead to the command and execution of moral acts. *Gnome* is related to *epikeia* as both concern contingencies where judgment is necessary to provide exceptions to the written law. Furthermore, since prudence perfects the practical intellect, *gnome* is a certain cognitive grasp of the higher purpose of the law within the intellect in situations where the letter of the law is deficient. Similarly, *synesis* is a cognitive grasp of the natural ends of human virtue in a wider, more general sense. Therefore, *synesis* and *gnome,* as parts of prudence residing in and perfecting the intellect, can be paired with *aequitas* and *epikeia* respectively as parts of justice residing in the will.[62] *Synesis,* as the habit of judging well in regard to practical matters (*Summa theologiae* II-II 51.3), is thus ordered toward the object of justice via the incli-

---

62. I am particularly indebted to the analysis provided by Riley for helping me to see this connection between the intellectual and appetitive aspects of practical reasoning in regard to justice and law (*The History, Nature, and Use of EPIKEIA,* p. 213).

nation of *aequitas,* while *gnome* is directed toward the more particular object of legal justice — that is, the common good — via the inclination of *epikeia.*

The above analysis explains the paradoxical nature of *epikeia* as both higher than legal justice and also a subjective part of legal justice. Whereas *synesis* and *aequitas* function for a lawgiver to create sound laws, *gnome* and *epikeia* serve as corrective parts of prudence and justice respectively that maintain the balance of fairness and equality that is an essential component of the common good and that law is intended to serve. Most important for a consideration of civic virtue, these parts of prudence and justice that function in particular ways for legislators and judges highlight the ways in which natural law and prudence function when making judgments with respect to the common good. Therefore, an account of civic virtue requires us to understand the relationship between natural law and prudence.

This connection between civic virtue and prudence is further underscored in Aquinas's discussion of the subjective part of prudence, which he calls political prudence. There is a direct correlation between political prudence and general or legal justice, as Aquinas writes that "just as every moral virtue that is directed to the common good is called *legal* justice, so the prudence that is directed to the common good is called *political* prudence, for the latter stands in the same relation to legal justice, as prudence simply so called to moral virtue" (*Summa theologiae* II-II 47.10, *ad* 1). Just as *epikeia* applies within a narrower range of contexts, so too does political prudence apply when deliberating or reasoning with regard to the pursuit of the common good. However, as *epikeia* applies primarily to a judge charged with applying the law, political prudence can apply to any citizen, regardless of her specific role or authority, who is called to judge and act with the common good as end. Prudence, although counted among the moral and intellectual virtues that perfect the agent interiorly, thus also functions exteriorly in relation to reason's deliberation vis-à-vis the common good, and in such cases it is called political prudence.

Aquinas further distinguishes between *regnative* prudence, which is found in the ruler of a city or a kingdom, and *political* prudence properly so called, which is in the subjects or citizens (*Summa theologiae* II-II 48.1). If we apply this distinction to a theory of civic virtue, then it seems that there is a distinctive kind of "civic prudence" (my term, not Aquinas's) that exists in one who holds a position of political authority, and this has some distinguishing qualities from the civic virtue required of every other citizen. I explore further some of the implications of this distinction between regnative prudence and political prudence in Chapter 4. For now we can note that civic virtue, as an orientation of the will toward the common good, is expressed as one aspect of reason's capacity for natural law reasoning regarding the good, and prudential reasoning seeks the most fitting means of achieving that good.

Civic Virtue and the Infused Virtues

Any Thomistic account of civic virtue must consider the relationship between the naturally acquired moral virtues and the infused theological virtues. It must also pay attention to the ways in which the cardinal virtues are affected by the new orientation to a higher end made possible by grace and the theological virtues. According to Paul in 1 Corinthians 13, the theological virtues of faith, hope, and charity are indispensable for the Christian wayfarer on the journey toward God. In his discussion of the necessity of the theological virtues, Aquinas maintains that persons are in need of revealed, interior principles so that human beings may act toward an end that transcends natural human happiness and natural reason. The theological virtues provide these necessary principles (*Summa theologiae* I-II 63.1). Unlike the natural cardinal virtues, these virtues are not acquired through human effort. Rather, they are infused into the human soul along with grace, the gifts of the Holy Spirit, and the beatitudes at the moment of conversion (*Summa theologiae* I-II 110.2-3). The intellect and will are provided with these new principles to orient them toward a higher end, and to heal the wounding caused by original sin and the disordered dispositions resulting from previously acquired vices. In light of these healing and elevating functions, faith makes possible revealed, supernatural knowledge of God in the intellect, hope resides in the will and provides the necessary encouragement to continue the arduous pilgrimage to an end that is impossible to attain through human power alone, and charity enables the will to love God above all else and to love all of creation in relation to God. One might conclude, therefore, that by healing and elevating the human soul the infusion of grace and theological virtues orient the powers of the soul toward God as last end and that this reorientation is sufficient to direct the acts of the already existing acquired virtues to this higher end. Indeed, several influential thinkers, including Duns Scotus (1265-1308), Cajetan (1469-1534), and Dom Odon Lottin (1880-1965) have held this position.[63]

---

63. Scotus makes this claim in his *Questiones in III Librum Sententiarum* d. 36, no. 28,

Aquinas, however, explicitly claims that to merit eternal life the human person is in need not only of the infused theological virtues, but also of infused cardinal virtues. Why? For Aquinas, the infusion of the theological virtues provides new, supernatural principles to human nature that enable a person to act toward the supernatural end of eternal happiness with God. However, the naturally acquired virtues remain grounded in the natural principles of the soul, which are not proportionate to the supernatural end. It is not enough that the theological virtues would transform the powers of the intellect and will solely in regard to acts of faith, hope, and charity, each of which have God as their object, while the naturally acquired virtues remain directed only toward their proper objects. Rather, the natural powers of the human person insofar as they are moved from potency to act via the acquired *habitus* of the cardinal virtues must also be elevated and transformed. In this way the entire being of the Christian wayfarer — even in relation to corporeal and earthly goods — may act with God as her object. This requires that even as the cardinal virtues maintain their proper orientation toward created, natural objects — and thus are still classified as cardinal virtues — they are also ordered toward a higher ultimate end. This new orientation transforms the nature of the acts of the cardinal virtues themselves. In other words, even in her earthly activities the Christian is made capable of ordering those activities toward God as last end such that the very nature of the act is transformed. My goal is to provide a clearer picture of the nature of this transformation with regard to civic virtue and the common good.

Aquinas is clear that the naturally acquired virtues are not "proportionate" to act toward God as final end. Therefore, "we need to receive from God other habits corresponding, in due proportion, to the theological virtues, which habits are to the theological virtues, what the moral and intellectual virtues are to the natural principles of virtue" (*Summa theologiae* I-II 63.3). Thus, the theological virtues come to function as new principles for the acts of the infused cardinal virtues, just as the natural inclinations functioning

---

quoted and translated by Romanus Cessario in *The Moral Virtues and Theological Ethics,* 2nd ed. (Notre Dame, Ind.: University of Notre Dame Press, 2009), p. 103. Cajetan defended such an opinion in his *Commentaria* on *Summa theologiae* I-II 63.3, quoted by Angela McKay Knobel, "Can Aquinas's Infused and Acquired Virtues Coexist in the Christian Life?" *Studies in Christian Ethics* 23, no. 4 (2010): 381-96, p. 389, note 24. Dom Odon Lottin defends similar claims in *Principes de Morale,* vol. 2 (Louvain: Editions de l'Abbaye du Mont Cesar, 1947), pp. 572-76, quoted by Michael Sherwin, "Infused Virtue and the Effects of Acquired Vice: A Test Case for the Thomistic Theory of Infused Cardinal Virtues," *The Thomist* 73 (2009): 29-52, p. 32.

through *synderesis* provide the principles for the acquired virtues. Or, as Sherwin states it, the "analogy, therefore, is as follows: natural principles are to the acquired virtues as the theological virtues are to the infused cardinal virtues."[64] The theological virtues become the principles not only of supernatural acts of faith, hope, and charity, but they also transform acts of prudence, temperance, justice, and fortitude as well. Although each cardinal virtue remains distinctive in its species and object, and thus is not reducible to charity, each of the infused moral virtues enables the agent to act with God as last end under the architectonic direction of charity. Such claims have direct implications for considering how acts of civic virtue function in the life of the Christian wayfarer, and I return to this below.

Aquinas further specifies that the infused forms of the moral virtues differ not only with respect to their principles (supernatural versus natural) and to their efficient cause (infusion versus acquired habits), but also with regard to their final cause, the mean that they seek, and their species. A basic principle of Aquinas's virtue theory is that each virtue is defined in its species according to the object of its distinctive acts (*Summa theologiae* I-II 54.2). When he discusses the distinctions between the acquired and infused moral virtues he notes that the proper material *(materia propria)* of the moral virtues remains the same. But the manner of relating to that material is altered such that the infused form takes on a different species from the acquired form. This is due both to its being ordered to a higher end and to the subsequent change in the manner in which the proper material object functions and the mean that is sought. Thus, he writes that acquired and infused moral virtues differ with respect not only to last end, but also "according to the relation *(ordinem)* to their proper object" (*Summa theologiae* I-II 63.4, *ad* 1). For these reasons, infused moral virtues are said to be of a different species from their acquired counterparts. Therefore, for Aquinas there are three distinctive species of virtue possible to the human person: acquired cardinal or moral virtues, infused theological virtues, and infused cardinal or moral virtues.[65]

This transformation of the ordering of the agent toward the material objects of the virtues also sets a new mean to be pursued by each infused form of the moral virtues. The one concrete example that Aquinas provides is in

---

64. Sherwin, "Infused Virtue and the Effects of Acquired Vice," p. 39.

65. William Mattison provides a similar description of the three types of virtue in his article "Can Christians Possess the Acquired Moral Virtues?" *The Thomist* 72 (2011): 558-85, p. 563.

regard to temperance. On the one hand, the material object of the acquired and infused forms of temperance remains identical — "the pleasurable good in regard to the concupiscible senses" (*Summa theologiae* I-II 63.4). On the other hand, however, acquired temperance functions along with prudence to judge the mean according to the standards of physical health appointed by human reason, whereas infused prudence judges the mean appointed by the divine rule or measure:

> in the consumption of food, the mean fixed by human reason is that food should not harm the health of the body, nor hinder the use of reason: whereas, according to the Divine rule, it behooves a person to "chastise his body, and bring it into subjection" (1 Cor. 9:27), by abstinence in food, drink and the like. It is therefore evident that infused and acquired temperance differ in species; and the same applies to the other virtues. (*Summa theologiae* I-II 63.4)

Thus, the infused forms of the moral virtues differ with respect to the last end, mean, and species, even as the matter remains the same. Furthermore, acquired and infused virtues are analogically related, as they are each analyzable according to the general patterns of virtue provided by Aristotle's virtue theory. The acquired virtues in Aquinas's moral theology become "subverted"[66] or "subalternated"[67] to a theological construal of infused virtue as the primary goal of the Christian moral life. Indeed, for Aquinas the only "strictly true virtue" is the infused form exercised in conjunction with and under the architectonic orientation of the will provided by charity (*Summa theologiae* II-II 23.7). In addition, Aquinas's discussion of infused temperance indicates that the naturally acquired virtues can only function in relation to prudence, which judges the mean and the most fitting manner of achieving the desired end. So too the infused moral virtues must also function congruently with infused prudence, which judges according to a divinely revealed rule and mean.

Infused prudence is a peculiar virtue because, as Aquinas himself recognizes, one need not be prudent or even particularly intelligent to be holy. Nor can those who are young be said to have cultivated the kind of experi-

---

66. Jean Porter, "The Subversion of Virtue: Acquired and Infused Virtues in the *Summa theologiae*," *Annual of the Society of Christian Ethics* (1992): 19-41.

67. Jacques Maritain discusses the subalternation of philosophy to theology in *An Essay on Christian Philosophy*, trans. Edward H. Flannery (New York: Philosophical Library, 1955), pp. 82-90.

ence and mature reflection necessary for prudential judgment. Yet holiness, which can be found in the simple and the young, clearly requires some capacity to judge and act rightly in regard to "matters necessary for salvation" (*Summa theologiae* II-II 47.14, *ad* 1). What this suggests is that for Aquinas, the infused forms of the virtues are present as supernatural principles in potency within all who are in a state of grace. It does not necessarily follow that in any given moment these will be fully cultivated such that they are present in act. As Sherwin states it, "the beginner [on the Christian journey] finds himself in the unique position of having virtues that he does not psychologically feel like he has."[68] Therefore, in *Summa theologiae* II-II 47.14, *ad* 3, Aquinas mentions that baptized children possess infused prudence in potency but not in act. He also adds that those in a state of grace practice wise effort *(industria)* with regard to things necessary for salvation, but may not be particularly prudent when it comes to ordering their own earthly affairs or those of others (*Summa theologiae* II-II 47.14, *ad* 1). This suggests that those with infused forms of the virtues are not yet fully perfected (indeed, they cannot be in this life). Rather, they continue to undergo struggle and growth into greater maturity vis-à-vis the infused virtues, much as Paul admonishes Christians to strive for "maturity, to the measure of the full stature of Christ" (Eph. 4:13). Just as one gains and strengthens the *habitus* of the acquired virtue through repeated acts, one may also grow in infused virtue by acting on these God-given principles. As Jean Porter indicates, in one with infused virtues, "this process should be understood in terms of the emergence of habits that were potentially there all along, rather than as the acquisition of virtues that did not exist in the subject before."[69] Thus, when Aquinas writes that "acts produced by an infused habit do not cause a habit, but strengthen the already existing habit" (*Summa theologiae* I-II 51.4, *ad* 3), he is indicating that infused habits are neither caused nor increased by acquired human habits, but rather are caused directly by God and increased by God as well, even as the person's efforts and *industria* function along with God's help in the growth in holiness.[70]

---

68. Sherwin, "Infused Virtue and the Effects of Acquired Vice," p. 46.

69. Porter, "The Subversion of Virtue," p. 37.

70. I do not have the space to deal with precisely how God's providential effects are reconciled with free human acts, but Aquinas provides further clues as to how this might function in his discussions of the human will as secondary efficient cause of human action in *Summa theologiae* I-II 10.4, and of operative and cooperative grace in *Summa theologiae* I-II 111.2. Porter writes that "this is not a process of mindless, as it were, automatic obedience to divine promptings. The justified individual attains genuine wisdom in and through her loving

One central question remains that Aquinas does not resolve. He never fully explains what occurs with the status of the acquired virtues after one receives the infused forms. Noting this lack of development, scholars have explored two basic possibilities: either (1) the acquired forms of the cardinal virtues remain and coexist with the infused forms in the life of the justified Christian, or (2) the infused cardinal virtues replace the acquired virtues in the Christian life. The problem in resolving this relationship arises from the fact that in the texts where Aquinas deals with the infused cardinal virtues he provides very few clues as to how one might understand the relationship between the acquired and infused forms. A number of scholars have argued for the first option, defending some form of what Angela McKay Knobel calls the "coexistence theory."[71] But recently McKay and others have defended the merits of the second position, claiming that the acquired virtues cannot coexist with the infused forms of the virtues in the Christian. It will be necessary to provide some clarity on this particular issue before considering the implications of infused general justice for a theological account of civic virtue.

It is difficult to imagine how an agent could act toward one material object while making use of both an infused and an acquired form of a particular virtue. Therefore, the second position seems the most plausible consequence of Aquinas's theory of infused virtues. Knobel and William Mattison have recently articulated why they believe the coexistence theory to be logically impossible. Mattison provides a concise summary of the argument: "To assert that persons continue to possess and act on the acquired cardinal virtues would be to assert that such persons (not only possess two last ends . . . but)

---

efforts to do God's will, and this wisdom is reflected in her ongoing reflections on how to best live the life of Christian virtue" ("The Subversion of Virtue," p. 37).

71. Knobel, "Can Aquinas's Infused and Acquired Virtues Coexist?" p. 382. She also provides a helpful list of recent scholars who have defended this position, including Denis Bradley, Thomas Osborne, Andrew Dell'Olio, Anthony Falanga, and Bonnie Kent (p. 382, note 2). Among recent scholarship, Sherwin seems to indicate a belief that acquired and infused virtues coexist ("Infused Virtue and the Effects of Acquired Vice," p. 49), and Jennifer Herdt defends a version of the coexistence theory in her discussion of Aquinas in *Putting on Virtue: The Legacy of the Splendid Vices* (Chicago: University of Chicago Press, 2008), pp. 87-88. Additionally, Josef Pieper seems to believe that, following Aquinas's discussion of the "fuller prudence" made possible by one who has both *industria* with regard to things necessary for salvation and for the things of this earthly life in *Summa theologiae* I-II 47.14, *ad* 1, that this creates a "graced unity" between the acquired and infused forms of the virtues. See *The Four Cardinal Virtues: Prudence, Justice, Fortitude, Temperance* (Notre Dame, Ind.: University of Notre Dame Press, 1966), p. 14.

would have to perform actions concerning the very same activity based upon two distinct rules, namely, the rule of human reason and the divine rule."[72] There is both a logical and an existential claim behind the force of this argument. Indeed, the coexistence of both the acquired and infused forms would create a "compartmentalized person . . . a fragmented virtuous life . . . [and] a competitive account of divine and human agency."[73] A person with acquired and infused virtues would need to be able to move back and forth between two kinds of virtue depending on whether she is acting solely toward the natural end of human life or toward her ultimate end. This would create a divided psychological structure within the soul in which grace does not seem to be perfecting nature but rather acting alongside of or parallel to it.[74]

But if one is to defend a theory in which the justified Christian possesses only the infused forms of the virtues, then there are several features of the psychology and action of such a person that must be addressed. Unfortunately, these are features that Aquinas neither addresses nor provides many clues as to how this might function (aside from the quote describing infused temperance mentioned above). Both Mattison and Knobel argue for a version of infused virtues in which whatever acquired virtues exist at the moment of conversion are either "taken up" or "transformed" into the infused cardinal virtues.[75] This might be called the transformation theory as opposed to the coexistence theory. The challenge for the transformation theory, and the divide between the natural and supernatural principles of human action that it requires, must therefore account for the continuity of the human personality before and after conversion. It demands an account that "would preserve both the complete gratuity of [grace and infused virtues] and the continuity and integrity of the individual's personality."[76]

A satisfactory answer can be developed from what Aquinas indicates regarding the dispositions that remain after the moment of conversion. He

72. Mattison, "Can Christians Possess the Acquired Moral Virtues?" p. 566.

73. Mattison, "Can Christians Possess the Acquired Moral Virtues?" p. 585.

74. Mattison, "Can Christians Possess the Acquired Moral Virtues?" p. 582.

75. Mattison, "Can Christians Possess the Acquired Moral Virtues?" p. 567; and Knobel, "Can Aquinas's Infused and Acquired Virtues Coexist?" p. 396. Knobel also provides a helpful list of those who have argued for some version of this transformation thesis, including Etienne Gilson, Terrence Irwin, and John Inglis (p. 382, note 2). Servais Pinckaers similarly argues for the transformation of acquired virtues, but he also claims that the infused forms are added to the acquired forms in "The Place of Philosophy in Moral Theology," in *The Pinckaers' Reader*, ed. John Berkman and Craig Steven Titus (Washington, D.C.: Catholic University of America Press, 2005), pp. 64-73, p. 67.

76. Porter, "The Subversion of Virtue," p. 38.

writes that "one may experience difficulty in performing actions proper to the *habitus* of the infused moral virtues because of certain contrary dispositions surviving from previous acts" (*Summa theologiae* I-II 65.3, *ad* 2).[77] In the *Disputed Questions on the Virtues* he claims that

> acquired virtue prevails in this, that the struggle is felt less, and this is due to how this type of virtue is caused, by which is repeated acts: for one loosens the custom of obeying such passions when one becomes accustomed to resisting them and that is why one is troubled by them less. But infused virtue prevails in this, that although such passions are felt, they in no way dominate. (*De virtutibus* 1.10, *ad* 14)

The infused form of the virtue removes whatever acquired vice might exist at the moment of conversion, but it does not remove the "custom of obeying such passions." That is, it does not remove the acquired negative dispositions that remain embodied in the disordered passions. Although Aquinas states this in primarily negative language, it may be stated conversely in more positive terms. That is, previously acquired, well-ordered dispositions will also persist insofar as they are taken up and transformed into the infused virtues, and these will be further strengthened by grace and made capable of meritorious action with God as final end. Indeed, Aquinas suggests in at least one place that the cultivation of acquired virtues may dispose one to receive the infused virtues in the first place. He writes that "our actions dispose to the increase of charity and the infused virtues, in the way that charity is obtained from the outset. A person who does what is in his power prepares himself so that he might receive charity from God" (*De virtutibus* art. 11, *corpus*).[78] He is very careful in his wording here, as he does not indicate that acquired habits are an efficient cause of infused virtue, as if human persons somehow make themselves worthy to receive grace. Rather, the existence of acquired virtues, expressed as well-ordered desires and dispositions, makes it less likely that one will experience resistance to the effects of grace acting on

---

77. See also *Quaestiones disputates de virtutibus: De virtutibus in communis* 5.2, *ad* 2.

78. Aquinas also claims, in an often cited passage, that the acquired virtues may become meritorious by the "mediation" of the infused virtues (*De virtutibus* 1.10, *ad* 4). But as Knobel notes "its cash value remains unclear" ("Relating Aquinas's Infused and Acquired Virtues: Some Problematic Texts for a Common Interpretation," *Nova et Vetera* 9, no. 2 [2011]: 411-31, p. 430, note 46). There is certainly more to be said about these claims, and further study is warranted, but this takes us beyond the purposes of relating the significance of infused virtue for a Thomistic account of civic virtue.

the intellect and will. This is not to say that miraculous conversions cannot occur to those steeped in vice, but it does indicate that the dispositions from previously acquired virtues and vices remain in effect after conversion. The existence of these dispositions provides the necessary continuity between the former personality and the character of the converted Christian.

Such growth in the infused forms of the cardinal virtues is made possible by the manner in which the theological virtues function as the new principles of the infused moral virtues as noted above. This growth is further subsumed under the architectonic orientation of the will provided by charity. I noted above that in *Summa theologiae* II-II 23.7 Aquinas indicates that full virtue requires charity, but a longer quotation is in order to better understand the relationship between charity and the infused form of the moral virtues in general, and civic virtue in particular:

> If, on the other hand, this particular good be a true good, for instance preserving the well-being of the state *(conservatio civitatis)* or the like, it will indeed be a true virtue, imperfect, however, unless it be referred to the final and perfect good. Accordingly no strictly true virtue is possible without charity.

Thus, the good of the political community or the state — that is, the common good — remains a truly existent good, even as the most perfect form of civic virtue is that in which acts on behalf of the common good are also directed to the final and perfect good. Here is where the cash value of the analogical relationship between God as ultimate common good of creation and the terrestrial common good, and between acquired and infused civic virtue, becomes evident. Infused civic virtue enables the Christian wayfarer to order acts of civic virtue to a higher end, and according to a different mean, while still referring them to the object of the community's common good. The object of public deliberation on the common good remains the same, while a Christian will approach this object in a slightly different manner than one with the acquired form of civic virtue. Note as well that a justified Christian does not necessarily possess a greater capacity to reason and act toward the common good than a non-Christian. Civic virtue may remain dormant and in potency in a Christian, while the same virtue may be a highly developed acquired habit in a non-Christian who has practiced *industria* with regard to the pursuit of the common good.

One of the ways that Christians will approach the common good in a distinctive manner is through charity "informing" acts of civic virtue, as charity is said to increase in the soul of the wayfarer, insofar as the subject comes to partake of the perfection of charity that inheres more and more in the soul (*Summa theologiae* II-II 24.5). This growth in the participation of charity in which God is loved above all else, and all things are loved as God loves them, extends to desiring the highest good for oneself, one's neighbors, and even to the point of love of one's enemies (*Summa theologiae* II-II 25). If, following the logic provided above, it is not possible to attain the good of one's self or of any individual without also protecting the common good of the realm, then it follows that such increase in charity likewise will increase the desire to serve and enhance the common good of one's community. Aquinas's doctrine of the interdependence of the virtues requires that growth in charity, rather than leading to denigration of the penultimate good of human persons insofar as it can be attained in this life, provides greater desire to love others that is expressed in one way by commitment to justice and the common good. Both charity and infused civic virtue function architectonically in the will to orient the agent toward God and the civil common good, and this relationship is best expressed analogically. That is, just as the terrestrial common good is the highest good of the political community and is also ordered to God as the ultimate common good of creation, so too does civic virtue aim at the highest human good while also being ordered to God via charity. One way that Aquinas expresses this analogical relationship between love and infused justice is to claim that "faith in Christ does not void the order of justice, but strengthens it" (*Summa theologiae* II-II 104.6).

We are now in a position to draw some conclusions from what Aquinas says about infused moral virtue and apply them directly to an account of civic virtue. First, following Aquinas's logic that "the same applies to the other virtues" as it does to his example of temperance, there is therefore an infused form of civic virtue. Second, the proper object of civic virtue — that is, the common good of the political community — remains the same in both the acquired and infused forms. Third, even as the object remains the same the common good is understood to be further oriented toward the final end of all things in God. This enables the person in possession of infused civic virtue to act toward the common good while simultaneously acting with God as last end within an ordered hierarchy of ends. Fourth, the mean sought with regard to the common good in infused acts of civic virtue is distinct from the mean sought in acquired acts of civic virtue. These last two points lead to the conclusion that the species of infused civic virtue differs from that of the acquired form. Similarly, this different mean entails a distinctive form of prudential reasoning, an aspect of civic virtue that is implied in the notion of political or civic prudence discussed above. Sixth, one in a state of sanctifying grace will always be acting on the infused form of civic virtue, even as the dispositions from previously acquired virtue or vice with regard to the common good may still dispose one either positively or negatively toward the common good. Seventh, growth in the moral and spiritual life of the Christian wayfarer will always include an element of greater desire to act for the good of others and to enhance the common good for all. This is a correlative component of growth in charity. This conclusion follows from the analogical conception of the common good and acquired virtues discussed above. As one grows in greater knowledge of and love toward the ultimate common good of creation (through faith and charity), there is a desire to pursue the good of all individuals insofar as any one individual's wellbeing is intrinsically tethered to the wellbeing of the community, represented through the terrestrial or political common good.

Perhaps the most difficult question that emerges from this analysis is precisely how the kind of political prudence demanded by a Thomistic account of infused civic virtue functions as a different species of virtue that seeks a different mean and different final end from naturally acquired civic virtue. This challenge is only increased by the conditions of pluralism in late modern culture. Does the account of infused civic virtue and infused political prudence defended here entail a claim of Christian epistemic superiority in public deliberation about the common good? Fortunately, the language of analogy enables both comparison and distinction between acquired and infused civic virtue, such that the contours of natural justice remain consistent even as those within a pilgrim church will articulate a distinctive approach to pursuing the common good. It enables Christians to practice civic virtue as directed toward a higher end and judged according to the divine rule provided in Scripture and the collective reflection on justice and the common good developed within the tradition of Christian social ethics. One may claim that distinctive, and perhaps even essential, insights emerge from this tradition without claiming epistemic superiority over non-Christians. It is precisely in such public deliberation that the insights developed within Catholic social ethics are brought to bear on the ways in which Christians work with all people of good will to pursue justice and the common good. I develop an account of Christian engagement in public deliberation regarding the common good motivated by civic virtue in Chapter 6.

CHAPTER 3

A Passion for Justice

Blessed are those who hunger and thirst for justice.

Matthew 5:6

Introduction

I turn now to consider two aspects of Aquinas's thought on justice that call for further development. The first concerns the relationship between the passions and justice, and the second develops his discussion of political prudence. With respect to justice and the passions I claim that well-ordered passions are an essential component of civic virtue as they draw the attention of the will toward injustice and spur greater fervor to protect and enhance the common good. The second aspect that I develop concerns the implications of political prudence. Under this second heading, there are two related aspects of Aquinas's account of political prudence to consider. On the one hand, Aquinas's insight into the distinctive kind of virtue required of those who govern is correct, even as the details of what this entails will need to be modified slightly to be congruent with contemporary democratic politics. On the other hand, however, one may identify the seeds of a kind of paternalistic elitism — one that comes to the fore in the work of John Courtney Murray — that is more directly inimical to democratic politics. At the end of the second section below I claim that there are aspects of the church's tradition of natural law that contain the necessary resources for overcoming the tendency toward political paternalism. I take up a more developed defense of this claim in Part II.

Engaging the Passions

One of the distinctive features of pursuing justice and the common good is that it demands a capacity for both detached, rational deliberation and passionate commitment. On the one hand, John Courtney Murray claims that it is characteristic of public debates concerning justice that they occur in the "coolness and dryness that characterizes good argument among informed and responsible [persons]."[1] On the other hand, Murray does admit one passion in the city — the passion for justice[2] — and it is common for individuals to speak of a "passion for justice." Bryan Massingale, for example, notes that most Western, rationalistic accounts of justice "render justice abstract and sterile."[3] Reflecting on his own experience with the pursuit of justice in the African American community, he notes that "justice is a pathos, a desire, a longing, a yearning . . . indeed a *passion* . . . before it is a concept or a definition."[4] He concludes with the claim that "I have come to believe that it is the standard accounts that are lacking and deficient,"[5] rather than those that begin from the passionate commitments of individuals and groups. Indeed, most people who become engaged in civic life are moved by some passionate commitment to a good that they value enough to dedicate their time, energy, and resources to civic or political engagement, often at great personal sacrifice. In this section I develop further the implications of Aquinas's discussion of the passions to demonstrate that civic virtue requires both rational deliberation and passionate commitment, and to claim that well-ordered passions are an essential aid to the cultivation of civic virtue.

Aquinas holds consistently throughout his career that "justice is not about the passions" because of "the subject of justice — that is, the will — whose movements are not passions" (*Summa theologiae* II-II 58.9).[6] The preceding chapter outlined the natural inclination toward justice found in the intellectual appetite or the will, and this remains normative in all of what follows. My purpose here is to further develop the manner in

---

1. John Courtney Murray, *We Hold These Truths: Catholic Reflections on the American Experiment* (New York: Sheed & Ward, 1960), p. 7.

2. Murray, *We Hold These Truths*, p. 8.

3. Bryan Massingale, *Racial Justice and the Catholic Church* (Maryknoll, N.Y.: Orbis, 2010), p. 130.

4. Massingale, *Racial Justice and the Catholic Church*, p. 131.

5. Massingale, *Racial Justice and the Catholic Church*, p. 131.

6. See also *Scriptum super Sententiarum* Dist. 33, Q. 2, A. 4, q. 3.

which well-ordered passions support and strengthen the will in acts of civic virtue.

If one pauses to look deeper into the moral psychology of the human soul as it is presented by Aquinas, further connections between general justice and the passions exist than may immediately be apparent. Indeed, Aquinas himself declares that

> legal justice which is directed to the common good, is more capable of extending to the internal passions whereby one is disposed in some way or other in himself, than particular justice which is directed to the good of another individual. (*Summa theologiae* II-II 58.9, *ad* 3)

Although justice is not directly related to the passions, Aquinas recognizes that there is something distinctive about general justice in which the person is oriented interiorly toward the common good.

Unfortunately, Aquinas never explains in greater detail how legal justice may be extended to the internal passions. This lack of development provides an opportunity to advance an analysis of some of the ways in which civic virtue demands passionate commitment. Such commitment entails a capacity to wisely recognize, discern, and channel the force of one's passions into fitting choices and actions on behalf of the common good. It is possible to infer from what Aquinas does claim to conclude that passions such as anger and compassion can be effectively harnessed to strengthen the will to protect the common good and to provide part of the motivational structure of acts of civic virtue.

Aquinas distinguishes between two types of human desires or appetites that motivate human action — passions and affections. The passions are the *embodied* movements of attraction or aversion that one experiences in response to external stimuli (such as goods or objects) or to internal stimuli (such as thoughts, emotions, or *phantasms*).[7] He describes passions as desires that are passively undergone by the person and that cause a "corporeal transmutation" (*Summa theologiae* I-II 22.3). Affections, on the other hand, are *spiritual* (that is, non-embodied) movements experienced in the will, or the intellectual appetite. The term "passion" derives from the Latin verb *passio,* which refers to something being undergone (as in the root of the

---

7. Aquinas describes the *phantasia* as the impressions that remain in the intellect's memory from the sensory organs' encounter with an external object of knowledge (see *Summa theologiae* I 84.6, *ad* 2).

English term "passive"). Strictly speaking, for Aquinas, only the corporeal matter of the bodily organs can undergo a passion. He writes that

> a passion is properly to be found where there is corporeal transmutation. This corporeal transmutation is found in the sensitive appetite . . . Now there is no need for corporeal transmutation in the act of the rational appetite [that is, the will], because this appetite is not exercised by means of a corporeal organ. (*Summa theologiae* I-II 22.3)

Hence the passions are experienced only in the embodied appetites, which Aquinas refers to as the sensitive appetites.

Aquinas further divides the sensitive appetites into the concupiscible and irascible appetites. The concupiscible appetite responds to the love of pleasure derived from external goods (such as food, drink, sex, money, etc.), and is brought into harmony with the rule of reason by the virtue of temperance. The irascible appetite responds to fear or anger (in Latin, *ira*) and is harmonized with reason through the virtue of fortitude or courage (*Summa theologiae* I-II 62.1). Thus, there are two basic kinds of passion for Aquinas. The first are the *embodied passions of attraction* for external goods that constitute the concupiscible appetite, and the second are the *embodied passions of aversion* to fearful or difficult situations that constitute the irascible appetite. In other words, passions are the natural inclinations of attraction and aversion that undergird the embodied component of human motivation and action, and are brought into harmony with reason and will through the proper exercise of temperance and courage (which likewise work congruently with justice and prudence, as I explain below).

Aquinas indicates that passions can disrupt practical reasoning in two ways, both of which represent unwise responses to the passions as they are engaged by reason and will. He asserts that the will can be led astray from "authentic" or "virtuous" goods (in Latin, *bonum honestum; Summa theologiae* I 5.6) through an improper response to a bodily sensation of attraction or aversion. Aquinas discusses the effects of the passions on practical reason in two places in the *Summa theologiae* (see I-II 24.3, *ad* 1, and 61.2). He indicates that passions can disrupt practical reasoning in two ways:

> First, by the passions inciting to something against reason; and then the passions need a curb, which we call *temperance*. Second, by the passions diverting us from following the dictate of reason, through fear of danger or hard work for example, and then a person needs to be strengthened

for that which reason dictates, lest he turn back. And to this end there is *fortitude.* (*Summa theologiae* I-II 61.2)[8]

On the one hand, the concupiscible passions of attraction can interfere at the beginning stages of prudential reasoning by drawing the attention of the will and intellect toward false goods. On the other hand, the irascible passions of aversion can interfere with the latter stages of practical reasoning by arresting the execution of an act.

The goal when exercising right reason or prudence is not the subjugation or eradication of the passions, but rather the harmonization of passions with reason. Aquinas's goal is to provide an account of the ways in which the passions are brought into harmony with reason, or under what Aristotle refers to as the "political rule" of reason.[9] Because of this he explicitly rejects the Stoic doctrine that all passions are evil, insisting instead that "passions are not called 'diseases' or 'disturbances' of the soul, except when they are not moderated by reason" (*Summa theologiae* I-II 24.2). This assertion reflects Aquinas's belief that the body and its sensual desires reflect the divine wisdom and order of the person as a composite of matter (body) and form (soul). In fact, the passions themselves are an expression of the natural inclinations that provide the initial ordering toward the proper objects of the virtues of temperance and courage. Although the desires of the body are often taken as the source of sin and disorder,[10] it is not the body and/or its passions themselves that are the root of disordered desire or sin. Rather, the goodness or malice of a particular act is determined by the manner in which the intellect and the will assess and respond to these desires to channel them into particular choices and acts.

Therefore, to make a normative moral decision about a particular act

8. See also *Summa theologiae* I-II 24.3, *ad* 1. Similar comments are reiterated in relation to sin in *Summa theologiae* I-II 77.1.

9. Aquinas draws on Aristotle's distinction between *despotic* and *political* rule (*Politics* I 3) to claim that the passions do not follow a despotic rule in the same way that the movements of the corporeal body follow the command of the soul without any capacity for rebellion. Rather, since the passions are capable of disobeying reason — due to either sin or ignorance — they must be brought under the *political rule* of reason. In the analogy the passions are free just as subjects who must be persuaded to follow the command of reason are free, rather than slaves who must be forced to follow reason without any autonomy on their part (see *Summa theologiae* I-II 58.2).

10. Jacques Le Goff, for example, describes a "rout of the body" in the development of early Christian thought in *L'imaginaire medieval* (Paris: Gallimard, 1985), 123; cited by Peter Brown in *The Body and Society: Men, Women and Sexual Renunciation in Early Christianity* (New York: Columbia University Press, 1988), p. 441.

concerning a sensible good the object must also be cognized through the intellect and will. The passions themselves simply link observable and sensible phenomena to one's internal states. However, prior to responding to these passions one must first become aware of, and then develop a proper capacity to respond to, these internal states. To take a more mundane example, the smells of a favorite food from childhood and one's family tend to produce immediate and strong emotional responses, not only of desire for the comfort of the food itself but also for the nostalgia of childhood (for me, my mother's apple crisp elicits strong responses). A quick and mindless response to such sensual cues can lead to a large helping of apple crisp, a ruined dinner, and an upset stomach. But if I know that Thanksgiving dinner is about to be served, or that it is a day of fasting, I may (hopefully) refrain from indulging that passionate response to pursue other more important, but perhaps less intensely desired, goods (turkey and stuffing, fasting in preparation for prayer, etc.).

For this reason Aquinas asserts that for humans as rational creatures "the inclination of nature . . . does not suffice" (*Summa theologiae* II-II 47.7, *ad* 3) for the execution of free choices and acts. Commenting on this aspect of practical reasoning, Jean Porter claims that the moral virtues are "underdetermined" by the natural inclinations that are ordered toward their final object, and Paul Wadell writes that they are "underdeveloped."[11] The further specification, determination, and development of the natural inclinations of the passions toward authentic goods is provided by rational deliberation and in particular by prudence. This further determination and ordering of the natural inclinations is provided by the process of practical reasoning that perfects the intellect through prudence, and is accompanied by movements or affections of the will at each stage.

Aquinas defines prudence as "right reason in action" (*Summa theologiae* II-II 47.2).[12] A simple way to summarize the stages of prudence is provided by the phrase "see, judge, act."[13] For the will to be reduced from potency to

11. See Jean Porter, *Nature as Reason: A Thomistic Theory of the Natural Law* (Grand Rapids: Eerdmans, 2005), pp. 126-27, and Paul Wadell, *The Primacy of Love* (New York: Paulist, 1992), pp. 106-24.

12. For a more in-depth analysis of practical reasoning, see Daniel Westberg, *Right Practical Reason: Aristotle, Action, and Prudence in Aquinas* (New York: Clarendon, 1994). My understanding of prudence in relation to intellect and will as related to Aquinas's discussion of these powers in *Summa theologiae* I-II 12-17 is deeply indebted to Westberg's analysis.

13. This tripartite model of prudential reasoning has found its way into the methodology common in Catholic social thought and can be traced back to Pope John XXIII's description in *Mater et magistra* (§236).

act, an object must first be presented to it in the intellect and the intention formed in the will to pursue that particular good. This is the first stage of *seeing (apprehensio)* in the intellect accompanied by intention *(intentio)* in the will (*Summa theologiae* I-II 12). In the second stage a judgment *(iudicium)* is formed with regard to the most fitting means to achieve the desired goal or outcome, and the will provides consent (*consensus; Summa theologiae* I-II 14).[14] Finally, prudence terminates in *action* in which the intellect commands (*imperium* or *praecipere*) and the will makes use *(usus)* of the intellect by applying the judgment and command of the intellect directly to action (*Summa theologiae* I-II 16-17).[15] Later in the *Summa theologiae* Aquinas applies a similar threefold process to prudence and uses the terms "counsel," "judgment," and "command" (*consiliare, iudicare,* and *praecipere; Summa theologiae* II-II 47.8).

The preceding analysis of intellect and will can be applied to the role of the passions in acts of civic virtue. The passions provide an impetus to the process of practical reasoning in the first stage of seeing or counsel. The immediacy of the passions as passive, embodied responses has the capacity to draw the attention of intellect and will so that the passions themselves may be brought under the political rule of reason. A particular passion is then further cognized through the intellect in the stages of prudence. First, one becomes mindful of a particular passion and the context in which it arises (the smell of apple crisp, hearing a story on the news that arouses anger at injustice, etc.). Second, if one takes a "sacred pause"[16] without immediately acting on the passion, then the intellect is able to deliberate about the initial inclination by asking something like the following question: What good am I being drawn toward by this attraction, or what evil to be avoided is indicated by this aversion? This inquiry into the nature of the passion concludes with a judgment. Finally, the intellect commands the will to execute or avoid the particular good or act toward which the initial order of the passion inclined. Prudence is therefore "dependent on right appetite,"[17] including both the intellectual and sensitive appetites.

---

14. This stage may or may not be accompanied by a longer process of deliberation that precedes the judgment, and is described in *Summa theologiae* I-II 14-15.

15. For a very helpful flow chart that diagrams this process, see Westberg, *Right Practical Reason,* p. 131.

16. I am borrowing this phrase from the psychologist and Buddhist teacher Tara Brach, who describes the idea of the "sacred pause" in *Radical Acceptance: Embracing Your Life with the Heart of a Buddha* (New York: Bantam, 2004), pp. 49-72.

17. Westberg, *Right Practical Reason,* p. 188.

On the one hand, everything created is good in and of itself, and is therefore capable of inclining one toward virtue. But it is the role of the intellect to judge of each created object whether the attainment of it and the means employed in its attainment will lead to the flourishing of the agent and the common good (the latter of which is cognized through civic virtue). Commenting on the tendency to interpret Aquinas through late medieval voluntarist notions of the primacy of the will over the intellect, Daniel Westberg writes that "the relation between intellect and passion is often set up as one of inherent opposition, with the will as arbiter. This is not the model used by St. Thomas."[18] Rather, the goal for Aquinas is to order the passions to work in harmony with intellect and will to act freely in pursuit of goods that will lead to true human flourishing — in this life and in the next. For him, intellect is primary as it judges and commands while the will provides consent and enacts the command through its power to initiate action in the other parts of the body and soul. Aquinas refers to such goods that are apprehended in the intellect and desired via the appetites as "appetible goods" (in Latin, *boni appetabili; Summa theologiae* I-II 9.1).[19] The passions function well when they help to align the *boni appetabili* with the pursuit of *boni honesti*. This analysis can then be applied more directly to justice and civic virtue.

Despite Aquinas's initial distinction between justice and passions, he notes that acts of justice result in a certain kind of joy that is experienced in both the will and the sensitive appetites. For example, in *Summa theologiae* I-II 59.5 Aquinas asks "whether there can be moral virtue without passion." In the *Sed contra* he claims that " 'no person is just who rejoices not in just deeds,' as stated in *Ethic.* i. 8. But joy is a passion. Therefore justice cannot be without passion, and still less can the other virtues be" (*Summa theologiae* I-II 59.5). In the *corpus* he clarifies that this joy is not strictly speaking a passion experienced in the body, but rather a strong affection of the will. He continues by stating that

> if this joy be increased through the perfection of justice, *it will overflow into the sensitive appetite* insofar as the lower powers follow the movement of the higher . . . Wherefore by reason of this kind of overflow, *the more perfect a virtue is, the more does it cause passion.* (*Summa theologiae* I-II 59.5, italics added)

18. Westberg, *Right Practical Reason,* p. 204.
19. See also Aristotle, *De anima* III 10.

Here Aquinas claims not only that it is possible for passions to accompany an act of justice, but he adds that the more perfect a virtue is the more intensely will the passions aid the will insofar as the passions and the affections are aligned in the pursuit of true goods.

Aquinas is therefore suggesting that passions can also have an indirectly positive effect on the will by making the choice of the good easier and more enjoyable. In *De veritate* he writes the following:

> when by a judgment of reason the will chooses anything it does so more promptly and easily if in addition a passion is aroused in the lower part, since the lower appetitive power is closely connected with changes in the body. Thus Augustine says: "The movement of mercy is of service to reason when compassion [*misericordia*] is shown in such a way that justice is preserved." And this is what the Philosopher also says in Book III of the *Ethics,* bringing in the verse of Homer: "Stir up your courage and rage," because when a person is virtuous with the virtue courage the passion of anger following upon the choice of virtue makes for greater alacrity in the act. (26.7)

Elsewhere Aquinas adds that a properly ordered passion can help to make an appropriate action appear more fitting or attractive to the intellect,[20] and that the virtuous person typically experiences passions functioning in harmony with reason (*Summa theologiae* I-II 59.2).[21] Indeed, this convergence of reason, virtue, affection, and passion leading to the correct choice of the common good as a truly appetible good is precisely the desired outcome of an act of civic virtue.

Aquinas provides some additional clues regarding the nature of the relationship between justice and the passions in his treatments of anger and compassion. He indicates that anger is frequently an appropriate response to injustice, and that it can be harnessed in the defense of the common good.

---

20. "According to a passion of the sensitive appetite a person is changed to a certain disposition. Wherefore according as a person is affected by a passion, something seems fitting, which does not seem so when he is not so affected" (*Summa theologiae* I-II 9.2).

21. Several recent commentaries on Aquinas's discussion of the passions note the importance of this supportive role provided by well-ordered passions in the psychology of human action. See, for example, Nicholas Lombardo, O.P., *The Logic of Desire: Aquinas on Emotion* (Washington, D.C.: Catholic University of America Press, 2011), p. 171, and Robert Miner, *Thomas Aquinas on the Passions: A Study of Summa Theologiae 1a2ae 22-48* (New York: Cambridge University Press, 2009), p. 297.

For example, anger as a response to a harm done to one's self, to others, or to the common good of one's community motivates acts of retributive justice or vengeance. The purpose of such anger and retribution is to restore the balance of equality to the community (see *Summa theologiae* I-II 46.7). A passion can therefore inspire seeking restitution after a wrongdoing has been committed. In fact, the Latin word for retribution is *contrapassum*. The term itself implies fighting back against *(contra)* the suffering caused by injustice (*passum* is the accusative supine form of *patior,* which means "to suffer"). Anger at the unjust suffering of one's self or another is therefore capable of being harnessed to motivate acts of retributive justice aimed at restoring the balance and equality required to uphold the common good.

Anger (in Latin, *ira*) is etymologically related to the *ira*scible appetite. Therefore, the inclination of anger is further ordered by courage. As noted above, fear tends to cause the will to deviate from the intellect's prudential judgment and command about what is to be done by arresting the execution of the act. Anger may provide a necessary counterforce to overcome the fear or resistance to engage in a difficult task that may prevent one from taking the risk to confront injustice. As is clear from those exemplars of civic virtue who have taken a stand against injustice, such as Nazi resisters, Martin Luther King Jr., or Nelson Mandela, this is often done at great cost to those involved, even to the point of imprisonment and death. Such heroic and sustained commitment to civic virtue might never be possible without harnessing anger and directing it toward the common good through courage, justice, and prudence.

While it is easy to admire the exemplary civic virtue of those mentioned above, a more mundane form of civic virtue is also required of all members of the body politic to maintain the balance of power in democratic government. The consistent willingness to uphold the common good of one's society in political life likewise requires a correlative possession of courage, civic virtue, and practical reasoning. In fact, I would argue that exemplary models of civic virtue are only possible because those persons had cultivated a more daily kind of commitment to the common good. Such a mundane commitment only becomes heroic under certain historical conditions of injustice. Moreover, the kind of critical patriotism that is an element of civic virtue may often require citizens to bravely call their leaders to account when they veer from pursuing the common good. This is one area in particular where a Thomistic account of civic virtue converges with the tradition of classical republicanism, and I explore this congruence further in Chapters 5 and 6.

Likewise, compassion *(compassio)*, meaning literally to "suffer with," may also support the will in its commitment to enhance the common good. For example, in his discussion of mercy Aquinas writes that "mercy is compassion for another's suffering . . . [and] one is saddened by or feels the pain of another's distress insofar as one looks upon another's suffering as one's own" (*Summa theologiae* II-II 30.2). This, he says, can happen in two ways: either through a kind of union of affection by which one makes another's suffering one's own, or through a fear that a similar evil may befall oneself. Both of these ways of describing compassion are closely related to more recent discussions of solidarity in Catholic social thought.

Christopher Vogt notes that general justice may be a helpful paradigm for cultivating a commitment to compassion and solidarity.[22] He writes that "to be compassionate is to develop the capacity to be moved by another's suffering in such a way that one shares in the other's pain and is moved to relieve it . . . compassion entails first of all developing a particular way of 'seeing' — that is, a way that has a strong affective dimension to it."[23] Vogt highlights an essential dimension of compassion in relation to the Thomistic analysis of human action provided above. The practice of compassion forms one into a particular way of seeing and knowing *(apprehensio),* and then engaging the world because it entails a concrete commitment to desiring and pursuing the good of another as if it were one's own.

When one recognizes and cultivates compassion along with solidarity as a commitment to the good of others, this has a direct impact on the ways that one knows or understands whether particular persons or groups are being excluded from the common good. This knowledge in turn influences the judgments and choices that one makes. Vogt describes this process as follows: "solidarity as an activity engaged alongside the oppressed is inseparable from the idea of solidarity as a process of knowing."[24] Compassion combined with solidarity thus have an epistemic quality, as they draw one's attention to the suffering of others. When injustice is perceived, anger nat-

22. Christopher Vogt, "Fostering a Catholic Commitment to the Common Good: An Approach Rooted in Virtue Ethics," *Theological Studies* 68 (2007): 394-417, p. 400.

23. Vogt, "Fostering a Catholic Commitment to the Common Good," p. 406. Although Vogt uses the term "affective" here, I take him to be using this in a wider sense that encompasses all emotions, and thus covers not just affections but also passions. For more on the modern attenuation of the language used to describe emotion as compared with Aquinas and other earlier analyses, see the introduction to Miner's *Thomas Aquinas on the Passions* (especially p. 3).

24. Vogt, "Fostering a Catholic Commitment to the Common Good," p. 404.

urally arises and is then moderated by courage working in congruence with prudence to act on behalf of the good of others and the common good. There is perhaps no better way to describe the way in which the passions can provide the initial impetus toward acts of civic virtue.

Massingale describes the ways in which practices of compassion and solidarity are essential for the formation of relationships across racial boundaries that lead to greater racial justice. He suggests that this process may proceed in three stages: lament, compassion, and then solidarity that is expressed as transformative love. Practices of lament follow on a mutual recognition between those who have been excluded and those who have benefited from racial inequality in society. As all parties lament the reality of inequality, a foundation is laid for recognizing how exclusion of any one group of persons from the common good is harmful to all. This leads logically into a sense of compassion. The process does not stop here, however. The internal logic of this *pathos* must be followed further into transformative love. Massingale writes that

> loving and committed relationships give one the visceral outrage, courage, strength, and motivation to break free from "rewards of conformity" that keep most whites complacent with white privilege. Transformative love, or compassion, empowers them for authentic solidarity.[25]

Massingale's analysis provides a concrete example of how compassion and solidarity engage the passions and order them toward greater racial harmony as part of a commitment to Christian civic virtue.

The late John Paul II has also developed a notion of solidarity. He describes it as both rationally available to all people and as a distinctively Christian virtue. As such, it is a fitting model of one particular virtue that highlights both the close relationship between the passions and justice and between acquired and infused forms of these virtues. John Paul writes that solidarity arises out of the recognition of mutual interdependence between persons that leads to a moral commitment. He defines this commitment as "a firm and persevering determination to commit oneself to the common good."[26] Solidarity is in theory perfectly capable of being rationally grasped and practiced by all human persons who recognize the interdependent na-

---

25. Massingale, *Racial Justice and the Catholic Church*, p. 120.

26. *Sollicitudo rei socialis*, §38, quoted from *Catholic Social Thought: The Documentary Heritage*, ed. David J. O'Brien and Thomas A. Shannon (Maryknoll, N.Y.: Orbis, 1992).

ture of the global community. At the same time, however, John Paul suggests that it can be cultivated as a distinctively Christian virtue.

John Paul notes that this distinctively Christian form of solidarity is aided by divine grace and informed by the theological virtue of charity. He writes that in the "light of faith, solidarity seeks to go beyond itself, to take on the *specifically Christian* dimension of total gratuity, forgiveness, and reconciliation . . . even to the ultimate [sacrifice]; to lay down one's life for the brethren (cf. 1 John 3:16)."[27] Although Aquinas does not use the term "solidarity," a similar connection can be found in his discussion of benevolence *(benevolentia)* as a component of charity (see *Summa theologiae* II-II 27.2). Benevolence entails a commitment to the good of others, and is capable of being practiced by any rational person. At the same time, however, when it is informed by charity it is lived out by Christians as a response to grace, and hence as an infused form of solidarity. As infused virtues under the architectonic direction of charity benevolence and solidarity are ordered to God as the ultimate good, while they also tether that good to a commitment to seeking the good of others vis-à-vis defending the temporal or civil common good.

These examples of anger and compassion provide further evidence that civic virtue demands both a capacity for rational deliberation and passionate commitment. Anger engages the natural inclinations of the body as a response to injustice and can be cognized to increase the stability of the will's commitment to the common good. Solidarity and compassion invite one to place one's body amid the suffering of others, and likewise enhance one's commitment to serve the good of others as if it were one's own. In the following section, I return to the component of rational deliberation in civic virtue and consider the implications of Aquinas's discussion of political prudence.

Political Prudence Revisited

Two implications of Aquinas's treatment of political prudence call for further development. First, he maintains that there is a certain kind of political prudence required of those who govern that he refers to as "legislative" prudence *(legum positivum; Summa theologiae* II-II 47.12) or "regnative" prudence *(regnativa; Summa theologiae* II-II 48.1). I want to affirm this basic insight and to consider further its implications for democratic forms of gov-

27. *Sollicitudo rei socialis,* §40, italics in original.

ernment. Second, the implications of this legislative or regnative prudence lead into a discussion of the kind of prudence required of those citizens who do not hold political office. Here Aquinas could have done more to develop a robust account of the role that the civic virtue of ordinary citizens plays in forestalling a certain kind of paternalistic elitism on the part of those who govern. An account of civic virtue for late modern democratic forms of government requires a more well-developed explanation of the active role of the members of the body politic in holding those who govern accountable to the common good.

First, I want to affirm that there is a distinctive kind of civic virtue that is expected from those who hold positions of political authority. In the *Politics* III 4 (1276b 16) Aristotle considers whether the good citizen must also be a good person in possession of the fullness of virtue, and Aquinas's commentary on this section is illuminative. Both Aristotle and Aquinas hold that good citizens need only to possess the virtues that would enable them to adequately support the good of the community. When it comes to the ruler, however, Aquinas, commenting on Aristotle, writes that

> a person is not said to be a good ruler unless he is good as a result of possessing the moral virtues and unless he is prudent. For it is said in Book VI of the *Ethics* that politics is a particular function of prudence. Hence the politician, that is to say, the head of a government regime, must be prudent and, consequently, must be a good person. (*Sententia libri politicorum* III, L. 3, no. 5)

Thus, a Thomistic account of civic virtue insists that there is a distinctive kind of political prudence working congruently with the moral virtues that is expected from those who hold public office. Moreover, those who hold public office are called on to exercise judgment on behalf of the community in a manner that the rest of the body politic is not called on to make. These areas of judgment falling under the exercise of regnative prudence regard the formulation, interpretation, and application of laws as they direct actions toward the common good and/or deter or punish actions that may harm it. Thus, Aquinas is correct to insist that those who govern are held to a higher standard of prudential reasoning and moral virtue when it comes to the common good, and thus are expected to be exemplars of civic virtue.

On the other hand, regnative prudence may be interpreted to underwrite a certain kind of elitism that is antithetical to the spirit of republican and democratic forms of government. I want to defend two paradoxical claims about the problems of elitism. First, it must be noted that those who hold positions of authority in government already occupy positions of elite power. Whether one is born into a princely ruling family, or has the means to generate the kind of financial and popular support necessary to win an election, governing implies access to elite forms of power that are not available to the majority of the population. As the Christian sociologist James Davison Hunter indicates, "elites operate in well-developed networks and powerful institutions," and they do so from the centers of power within those networks and institutions.[28] Politicians are clearly part of one elite infrastructure of power and cultural influence, and this is precisely why they are expected to demonstrate a higher degree of political prudence and moral virtue than the average citizen (all counterexamples notwithstanding).

Thus, there is a certain unavoidable elitism intrinsic to the nature of the power vested in those with authority to create, interpret, and apply the laws of a society. At the same time, however, it is possible to recognize the elite cultural status of politicians while also avoiding a kind of paternalistic elitism in which those who govern seek to impose legal norms on the rest of the population without the consent or involvement of those who are governed. In her analysis of political authority, Jean Porter claims that the authority and efficacy of contemporary political systems rests partly on the extent to which they are tethered to the "*sensus communis* — not in every respect, but at least to a considerable degree."[29] The alternative to a paternalistic elitism therefore entails a kind of public deliberation in which civic officials and members of a community cooperate in the working out of the middle axioms of the principles of natural law through a shared practice of political reasoning. Indeed, one of the goals of modern republican and democratic forms of government and deliberation about the good ensure that within the natural inequalities of power that exist in any society there are also resources for members of the body politic to participate in the construction of a political culture and its legal regulations.

The implications of a more paternalistic form of elitism can be witnessed in the work of John Courtney Murray and in his understanding of the manner in which natural law reasoning functions to order society. For Murray,

---

28. James Davison Hunter, *To Change the World: The Irony, Tragedy, and Possibility of Christianity in the Late Modern World* (New York: Oxford University Press, 2010), p. 41.

29. Jean Porter, *Ministers of the Law: A Natural Law Theory of Legal Authority* (Grand Rapids: Eerdmans, 2010), p. 165.

the application of the first principles of natural law to the contingencies of history in working out public policy is the work of the wise person *(sapientis)*.[30] In her analysis of Murray's work on the natural law, Porter indicates that Murray provides for very little role for intermediate norms between the first principles of natural law and their conclusions in practical reasoning. These intermediate norms enable members of the community to deliberate together effectively about the good in moving from the general first principles of natural law to specific precepts. Rather, "the perceptions and judgments of the wise appear to function as a substitute for the discernment of intermediate norms in Murray's thought."[31] One of the essential ingredients, however, of democratic deliberation about the good is the continual need for vigilance and moral discernment on the part of the members of the body politic. Therefore, a necessary function of civic virtue is to work out the middle axioms or norms of natural law precisely through argument, persuasion, deliberation, and rhetoric. This essential modality of civic virtue can only be practiced by all members of a community if they have access to involvement in the working out of those middle axioms through public deliberation. If the application of the natural law is left entirely to the elite leadership of a community, then it becomes all too easy for "an ideology which sustains the power relations of society" to be covered over "with a veneer of reasonableness."[32] As Hunter states it, under such conditions even "democratic justifications are not much more than a veneer over a will to power."[33] A contemporary Thomistic account of civic virtue develops a notion of political prudence that encourages the engagement of the members of a community to avoid this kind of political paternalism and elitism that may turn quickly to tyranny or the arbitrary use of power.

This tendency toward paternalistic elitism can be seen as one way of interpreting Aquinas's discussion of political prudence. For example, he maintains that

30. See, for example, Murray, *We Hold These Truths,* pp. 88, 111, and 118. These comments are perhaps mitigated slightly by his suggestion at the end of the book regarding the necessity of "popular sharing in the formation of the collective will, as expressed in legislation or in executive policy" (p. 334). However, I am not aware of any place that Murray develops this notion further.

31. Jean Porter, "In the Wake of a Doctrine: A Reassessment of the Doctrine of the Natural Law as Developed in *We Hold These Truths,*" in *John Courtney Murray and the Growth of Tradition,* ed. Todd Whitmore and J. Hooper (Kansas City, Mo.: Sheed & Ward, 1996), p. 31.

32. Porter, "In the Wake of a Doctrine," p. 37.

33. Hunter, *To Change the World,* p. 106.

the common good of the state cannot flourish, unless the citizens be virtuous, at least those whose business it is to govern. But it is enough for the good of the community that the other citizens be so far virtuous that they obey the commands of their rulers. (*Summa theologiae* I-II 92.1, *ad* 3)[34]

On the one hand, I affirm a general distinction between the requisite virtues of those who govern and those who do not. On the other hand, this distinction should not be used to underwrite a kind of elitism that downplays the necessity for all citizens to participate in the kind of public deliberation that the possession of political prudence makes possible. In other words, Aquinas correctly notes that the common good is best served when those who hold public office possess certain kinds of virtues such as honesty and a demonstrated capacity to enact prudent decisions with regard to legislation. In developing an account of civic virtue for democratic societies, however, the exercise of regnative prudence is supported and frequently challenged by the civic virtue of those engaged citizens who hold those who rule accountable. Thus, civic virtue requires more of citizens than merely a capacity to obey the command of the rulers.

The preceding analysis is also supported by drawing an analogy from the political realm to the ecclesiology of a pilgrim church. Positions of leadership, authority, and power in the church exist to support the congregation of the faithful on their pilgrimage to the heavenly city by the preaching of the Word, administering of the sacraments, and support for the cultivation of the virtues. The church as a theological reality, an effect of grace, provides a wider perspective on the nature of the church that enables the hierarchical and institutional structures (and the power they represent) to be understood in terms of the theological aims they serve, rather than as the essence of the church itself. Similarly, if human persons are understood as political animals and political society is understood as a natural human reality (not merely a social construct), this also provides a wider perspective in which those vested with political authority are understood in relation to the authentically political aims they serve in upholding the common good, rather than as the essence of society itself. The image of a pilgrim church provides a counterbalance to the political ideologies that can develop in either the church or

34. Aquinas applies this same logic to his discussion of political prudence as a subjective part of prudence when he writes that "some kind of rectitude with regard to political authority is required in [the citizens], so that they may direct themselves in obeying their rulers; and to this belongs that species of prudence which is called political" (*Summa theologiae* II-II 50.2).

in politics, because it holds out the ultimate goal of an end that transcends any temporal community while also upholding the common goods of those communities as important but penultimate goods.

If a paternalist role for those who govern is rejected, then it falls to the proper exercise of political prudence among a healthy body politic to order the political community toward authentic human goods. This political prudence is to be practiced by the members of a community as they work out the middle norms of natural law in response to the needs of the culture. In other words, within the daily deliberations and choices of individuals and groups within society there is a need for ongoing discernment with regard to whether particular choices and actions contribute to the common good. This is a more republican-democratic and less elitist approach to the application of the principles of the natural law than the one that Murray develops. Developing a modern, constructive account of civic virtue and its application within democratic and republican forms of deliberation and rhetoric is the goal of Part II.

PART II

CHAPTER 4

Civic Virtue and Natural Law

Introduction

In the following two chapters I begin to place the account of civic virtue developed in Part I in dialogue with two strands of thought operative within the ecclesial (Roman Catholic) and political (Western, democratic) contexts for which I write — natural law and political philosophy. In the previous chapter I argued that political prudence must account for two aspects of public deliberation about the common good: (1) the role of passions in practical reasoning, and (2) a democratic form of participation in public deliberation that curbs the tendency toward paternalistic elitism on the part of those who govern. In this chapter I continue to develop these two aspects of civic virtue in dialogue with central thinkers in the Catholic natural law tradition. First, I consider the status of the question among recent scholarship regarding the influential thesis of Henri de Lubac on the relationship between nature and grace, and his rejection of a putative state of "pure nature" in the work of Aquinas. While this may seem like a minor exegetical question to be taken up primarily by historians, the implications of how one construes the relationship between nature and grace has far-reaching implications for theology, ethics, and Christian political engagement. In what follows I defend a twofold response to de Lubac. First, I defend his rejection of the notion of pure nature. Second, however, I also argue for a stronger distinction between nature and grace than de Lubac's work seems to allow. I argue that upholding this distinction is not only a more accurate interpretation of Aquinas, but also creates some theological and conceptual breathing room for recognizing a public space for Christian engagement in rational deliberation about the natural, penultimate goods of the political community. This distinction is the best defense against the perennial temptations toward integralism that arise in political theology. In the following section, I continue to defend this distinction between nature and grace as a way to provide an alternative to the forms of elitism that arise in the accounts of natural law articulated by John Courtney Murray and more recently by Steven Long. My goal in this chapter is to provide a theoretical foundation within the natural law tradition for the development of an account of public deliberation that is congruent with a Thomistic theory of civic virtue in the final chapter.

Reevaluating de Lubac on Nature and Grace

The relationship between nature and grace bears directly on the role of the pilgrim church vis-à-vis the pursuit of the temporal common good in the political life of a people. I noted in Chapter 2 that Aquinas upholds a stronger distinction between nature and grace than Peter Lombard and other early scholastics to articulate a manner in which justice functions to order the penultimate good of a political community. My defense of this reading of Aquinas calls for rethinking de Lubac's thesis regarding the relationship between nature and grace. This reappraisal is necessary because de Lubac's work has influenced the interpretation of Aquinas on this point, and also because his construal of nature and grace has been highly influential in the political thought of the postconciliar church.[1] I claim that de Lubac was correct to reject a notion of pure nature in Aquinas, but I also argue for a stronger distinction between nature and grace than de Lubac's work seems to allow. Such a distinction is foundational for understanding how natural law morality functions as a guide for Christians interested in cooperating in public deliberation about the good in the democratic, pluralistic cultures of late modernity.

A central concept and fitting starting point for understanding Aquinas on the relationship between nature and grace is in his discussion of the natural desire for God. Aquinas leaves us with two sets of seemingly contradictory texts. On the one hand, Aquinas states clearly that "every intellect by nature desires the vision of the divine substance" (*Summa contra gentiles* III

---

1. Although a full defense of this claim is beyond the scope of this study, de Lubac's work has influenced the work of Pope John Paul II (who appointed de Lubac to the college of cardinals in 1983), Pope Benedict XVI, Hans Urs von Balthasar, and David Schindler, among others. Jon Milbank also draws on de Lubac's work to defend his own idiosyncratic version of postmodern integralist political theology in *The Suspended Middle: Henri de Lubac and the Debate Concerning the Supernatural* (Grand Rapids: Eerdmans, 2005).

57),[2] and that "final and perfect happiness can consist in nothing else than the vision of the Divine Essence . . . [since] for perfect happiness the intellect needs to reach the very Essence of the First Cause" (*Summa theologiae* I-II 3.8). Thus, the human intellect and will remain unsatisfied until coming to rest in the contemplation of God's Trinitarian essence in the beatific vision. Furthermore, he claims that "a natural desire cannot be in vain" (*Compendium theologiae* I 104).[3] Thus it appears that humans have one, final end — direct contemplation of the divine essence in the beatific vision — along with a natural desire for that end. If this were the whole picture, then this end must be understood to be implanted within the ontological contours of created human nature and it would seem that all humans are naturally capable of achieving this end.

In a second set of texts, however, Aquinas states clearly that no person can achieve this ultimate end by her natural faculties or capacities alone. He writes that

> every knowledge that is according to the mode of created substance, falls short of the vision of the Divine Essence, which infinitely surpasses all created substance. Consequently, neither the human person, nor any creature, can attain final happiness by his natural powers. (*Summa theologiae* I-II 5.5)

Thus, the human person is in need of additional help — that is, grace — to achieve his final end. Following Aquinas's logic, every rational creature naturally desires to see the divine essence, no natural desire can be in vain, and yet human nature itself is insufficient to attain its own end. These claims seem prima facie incompatible, and here one encounters the paradox and challenge of interpreting Aquinas on these points. If human nature is incapable of reaching its final end by its own natural powers, in what sense can the desire for God be *natural*?

The picture is further complicated by the fact that Aquinas posits one end of happiness for the human person — which is the beatific vision — but he also qualifies this by stating consistently that the single end of the human person can be analyzed under a "twofold aspect" *(duplex est).*[4] Although I

---

2. "Omnis intellectus naturaliter desiderat divinae substantiae visionem."

3. See also *Summa contra gentiles* III 51: "it is impossible for a natural desire to be incapable of fulfillment."

4. See *Summa theologiae* I 23.1, 62.1; I-II 62.1; *De veritate* 14.2.

discussed this twofold distinction in Chapter 2, it bears consideration again for it has direct implications for the relationship between nature and grace and natural law reasoning with regard to the civic good. For Aquinas, there is an imperfect, natural happiness that can be had in this life through the exercise of the person's natural faculties, and in particular through the acquisition and perfection of the cardinal virtues. At the same time there is the perfect, ultimate happiness that can only be found in the next life, in the end that transcends all human powers.

Unfortunately, Aquinas does not directly take up the question of the relationship between nature and grace in a manner that would provide a more systematic or definitive solution to the paradox inherent in his treatment of the twofold end of human nature.[5] He simply leaves us with a paradox, albeit one that he felt was rationally defensible in the light of faith. In his commentary on Aquinas regarding these points, de Lubac also employs the concept of paradox to describe the condition of the created rational creature called to an end that transcends her natural capacities. He describes this paradox in the following manner:

> The desire to see [God] is in us, it constitutes us, and yet it comes to us as a completely free gift. Such paradoxes should not surprise us, for they arise in every mystery; they are the hallmark of a truth that is beyond our depth.[6]

This depth, he concludes, can only be understood in the light of faith. For de Lubac, only with faith does a person understand her true spiritual nature and the destiny to which she is called.

The notion of paradox can be analogically compared to the status of the members of a pilgrim church vis-à-vis the terrestrial common good. While I agree with de Lubac that the transcendent calling of the human person indeed presents a paradox, he seems to resolve this paradox too heavily in favor of seeing a direct desire for God implanted within the ontological structure

---

5. Jean-Pierre Torrell, O.P., writes that "Thomas never wrote a monograph on nature and grace. . . . Right away he considers them in their relations, as though, at least when dealing with man, the one could not be defined without the other" ("Nature and Grace in Thomas Aquinas," in *Surnaturel: A Controversy at the Heart of Twentieth-Century Thomistic Thought,* ed. Serge-Thomas Bonino, O.P., trans. Robert Williams [Ave Maria, Fla.: Sapientia, 2009], pp. 155-88, p. 155).

6. Henri de Lubac, *The Mystery of the Supernatural,* trans. Rosemary Sheed (New York: Crossroad, 1998), p. 167.

of human nature. In his attempt to refute later commentators on Aquinas who posit a pure nature within Aquinas's thought, he resolves the paradox by seemingly collapsing everything up toward the supernatural. As Guy Mansini states it, in de Lubac's thesis "everything ends up on the theological bank of the divide," as "there is no divide, because there is nothing really and truly to divide the supernatural from."[7] In other words, de Lubac's solution leaves little tools for Christians to think about the pursuit of the temporal common good as a penultimate, created, natural good that has inherent worth, even as persons are paradoxically called to an end that transcends the terrestrial good. Moreover, it fails to provide adequate tools for negating the various forms of integralism that seem to recur in discussions of natural law. The ecclesiology of the people of God on pilgrimage through this life entails a distinction between nature and grace to avoid political integralism and to recognize the authentic — albeit penultimate and limited — value of the goods of civic life.

According to de Lubac, the late medieval commentators — in particular Cardinal Cajetan (1469-1534) — tended to interpret Aquinas as if they believed there were such a thing as a "pure nature" *(natura pura)* divorced from the supernatural economy of grace, and they did so precisely to defend the total gratuity of God's gift of grace. In doing so, according to de Lubac, they began to posit a "modern theory of a spiritual nature . . . with a 'purely natural' finality, [that] was born and developed in the intellectual context of a watered-down idea of what finality is."[8] This kind of natural finality he believes "to be verbal and irrelevant"[9] for Aquinas himself. He continues by claiming that a supernatural finality thus comes to be "considered as something fairly extrinsic: not a destiny inscribed in a man's very nature, directing him from within, and which he could not ontologically escape, but a mere destination given him from outside when he was already in existence."[10] In other words, nature and grace become seen as a two-tiered system where grace does not seem to touch the essential nature of the human being, but rather becomes a superstructure added on to an already self-sufficient human nature.

Once taken to the extreme of positing a pure nature, de Lubac believes that the desire for God is no longer natural and innate, but is a foreign de-

---

7. Guy Mansini, O.S.B., "Henri de Lubac, the Natural Desire to See God, and Pure Nature," *Gregorianium* 83, no. 1 (2002): 89-109, p. 97.

8. De Lubac, *The Mystery of the Supernatural*, p. 68.

9. De Lubac, *The Mystery of the Supernatural*, p. 67.

10. De Lubac, *The Mystery of the Supernatural*, pp. 68-69.

sire that must be superimposed on an already self-sufficient will. In short, grace and all that comes with it — eternal life, trust in divine providence, the sacraments, revelation, the theological virtues, and the infused cardinal virtues — become unnecessary for the satisfaction of human desires. For de Lubac, what began as a necessary and carefully nuanced philosophical and theological *distinction* in Aquinas between nature and grace becomes for the later commentators "a complete divorce."[11]

A recent wave of critical scholarship has begun to reconsider de Lubac's thesis.[12] Some of these scholars question whether de Lubac's correctives to the neo-scholastic interpretation of Aquinas's corpus may elide a necessary distinction between nature and grace. They claim that by subsuming nature into grace, or "supernaturalizing the natural," de Lubac's solution to the paradox of the human person seems to indicate that grace will flow naturally out of a spiritualized human nature. According to this logic, the character of grace as unmerited gift is lost if it seems to emerge naturally from within the contours of an already-graced human nature. As David Braine states the problem, de Lubac's solution to the paradox makes it seem that "grace is an

---

11. De Lubac, *The Mystery of the Supernatural,* p. 35.

12. See, for example, the following, non-exhaustive list: Bernard Mulcahy, O.P., *Aquinas's Notion of Pure Nature and the Christian Integralism of Henri de Lubac: Not Everything Is Grace* (New York: Peter Lang, 2011); Stephen Long, "On the Possibility of a Purely Natural End for Man," *The Thomist* 64 (2000): 211-37; Long, "On the Loss, and the Recovery, of Nature as a Theonomic Principle: Reflections on the Nature/Grace Controversy," *Nova et Vetera* 5, no. 1 (2007): 133-84, and Long, *Natura Pura: On the Recovery of Nature in the Doctrine of Grace* (New York: Fordham University Press, 2010); Reinhard Hütter, *Dust Bound for Heaven: Explorations in the Theology of Thomas Aquinas* (Grand Rapids: Eerdmans, 2012), especially chapter 5; Hütter, "Aquinas on the Natural Desire for the Vision of God: A Relecture of *Summa contra Gentiles* III, c. 25 *apres* Henri de Lubac," *The Thomist* 73 (2009): 573-79; and Hütter, "*Desiderium Naturale Visionis Dei — Est Autem Duplex Hominis Beatitudo Sive Felicitas:* Some Observations about Lawrence Feingold's and John Milbank's Recent Interventions in the Debate Over the Natural Desire to See God," *Nova et Vetera* 5 (2007): 81-131; the collection of essays edited by Serge-Thomas Bonino, O.P., in *Surnaturel: A Controversy at the Heart of Twentieth-Century Thomistic Thought,* trans. Robert Williams (Ave Maria, Fla.: Sapientia, 2009); Nicholas Healy, "Henri de Lubac on Nature and Grace: A Note on Some Recent Contributions to the Debate," *Communio* 35 (2008): 535-64; Peter A. Pagan-Aguiar, "St. Thomas Aquinas and Human Finality: Paradox or *Mysterium Fidei?*" *The Thomist* 64 (2000): 375-99; Mansini, "Henri de Lubac"; David Braine, "The Debate between Henri de Lubac and His Critics," *Nova et Vetera* 6, no. 3 (2008): 543-90; Edward T. Oakes, S.J., "The *Surnaturel* Controversy: A Survey and a Response," *Nova et Vetera* 9, no. 3 (2011): 625-56; Christopher J. Malloy, "De Lubac on Natural Desire: Difficulties and Antitheses," *Nova et Vetera* 9, no. 3 (2011): 567-624.

inevitable development of nature and therefore not gratuitous."[13] Or as Lawrence Feingold articulates the problem, de Lubac's position would "divinize the nature of the creature, or make grace inscribed in nature."[14] Even though de Lubac himself consistently defends the gratuity of grace, these scholars are correct in noting that if the supernatural is tethered too closely to the essential and intrinsic qualities of human nature, then the doctrine of grace as a gift given by God's pure generosity may become obscured. Ironically, in de Lubac's form of theological integralism the free gift of grace may come to be seen as equally unnecessary as de Lubac thinks it is for those who uphold the theory of a pure nature since it already appears to be "given" in the natural created order itself.

Those who levy these more recent critiques share de Lubac's pastoral concern to defend the necessity and gratuity of grace for ultimate beatitude, yet they see the solution to lie in stressing the second set of texts from Aquinas noted above — those that uphold the inability of human nature to merit salvation without the aid of grace. Such a perspective requires greater attention to the contours of "the natural" in precision from grace than de Lubac allows. Indeed, the cause of some of the problems recognized in the post–Vatican II church — such as "declining vocations, a confused moral theology, a revitalized secular hostility to the Christian religion"[15] — are ironically considered by some of these scholars to be the unfortunate consequences of the very hypothesis that de Lubac had defended to prevent such outcomes. Within such a contentious atmosphere of seemingly contradictory claims, how is one to make sense of the relationship between nature and grace and its implications for civic virtue?

On the face of it, Aquinas himself seems to affirm quite clearly that human persons do indeed have a natural desire for the vision of God's glory, which lends weight to de Lubac's thesis. The quote from *Summa contra gentiles* III 57 noted above affirms the natural desire of every created intellect for the divine essence. But what Aquinas himself does not make entirely clear is

13. Braine, "The Debate between Henri de Lubac and His Critics," p. 574.

14. Lawrence Feingold, *The Natural Desire to See God According to Saint Thomas and His Interpreters,* 2nd ed. (Washington, D.C.: Catholic University of America Press, 2004), p. 442. Torrell also writes that Aquinas's discussion of "integral nature" (that is, human nature speculatively considered as abstracted from sanctifying grace) helps to safeguard the autonomy of the natural order of creation and demonstrates that "grace does not enter into the definition of nature" ("Nature and Grace in Thomas Aquinas," p. 171).

15. This quote is taken from the publisher's annotation of Bonino's *Surnatural,* and is quoted by Oakes, "The *Surnaturel* Controversy," p. 635.

just how far this natural desire can carry the human intellect in pursuit of the contemplation of God as pure essence. Is it a natural desire for knowledge of God only insofar as God can be known as the First Cause of all that exists, an inchoate conclusion reached on the basis of natural human reasoning?[16] Or is it an implicit desire for the vision of God in God's own essence *(ipsum esse)* — that is, a desire to know the Trinitarian God who is revealed in Scripture and in the person of Jesus Christ? While de Lubac's position is carefully researched and nuanced, on the whole he seems to prefer the latter interpretation.[17]

Three schools of thought emerge among those who want to reconsider de Lubac's thesis. Among recent scholars, Dennis Bradley most strongly defends the natural desire for God's innermost being in Aquinas as *implicitly* contained within the innate, natural human desire for perfect happiness.[18] Among those who uphold the strongest criticisms of de Lubac are Steven Long, Lawrence Feingold, and Reinhold Hütter, each of whom claims that Aquinas speaks of two types of desire, one innate (or natural) and the other that must be elicited by grace and revealed knowledge.[19] For Long, Feingold,

16. Aquinas explores the possibilities and limitations of such natural knowledge of God in *Summa contra gentiles* III 25-51. Elsewhere Aquinas indicates the value of inquiring into the nature of the natural love of God when he states the following: "because it was possible for God to have made man in a state of purely natural endowments *(in puris naturalibus),* it is useful to consider how far natural love *(dilectio naturalis)* could be extended" (*Quodlibet* I, q. 4, a. 3); I am grateful for the reference to this quote from Long, *Natura Pura,* p. 57, note 4. Long, however, translates *in puris naturalibus* as "pure nature," an unfortunate error that imposes the language of later commentaries on Aquinas onto the original text.

17. A more adequate defense of this claim would require a separate monograph, but see de Lubac's appendix to *Surnaturel: Etudes Historiques* (Paris: Desclée de Brouwer, 1991), "Desir Naturel du Surnaturel," pp. 431-38; *The Mystery of the Supernatural,* chapter 11, pp. 207-21; and *Augustinianism and Modern Theology,* trans. Lancelot Sheppard (New York: Crossroad, 2000), chapter 6, pp. 147-83.

18. It should be noted, however, that even Bradley qualifies this as a desire that must proceed from some form of knowledge of God consequent on rational inquiry into the necessary First Cause of existent phenomena. For example, Bradley writes: "The desire to see God, then, is *implicit* in the desire for perfect beatitude" (*Aquinas on the Twofold Human Good: Reason and Human Happiness in Aquinas's Moral Science* [Washington, D.C.: Catholic University of America Press, 1997], p. 459). In other places, however, he qualifies this implicit desire by stating that "humans naturally desire happiness, and therefore *implicitly* desire to know the First Cause of all that is, but that does not mean that they *explicitly* desire to see God in God's essence" (*Aquinas on the Twofold Human Good,* p. 437; see also pp. 446-47).

19. Long, "On the Possibility of a Purely Natural End for Man," p. 221, and Feingold, *The Natural Desire to see God,* pp. 15-16, 44, 397. Reinhard Hütter concurs with Feingold's

and Hütter the desire for God as *ipsum esse* is made "natural" only to the person in the state of sanctifying grace and in possession of faith. In a third group a number of other scholars express reservations about de Lubac's thesis, while defending a more nuanced position on the status of the natural desire for God. These scholars want to provide a corrective to de Lubac's supernaturalizing of the natural without going so far as those who seem to move too far back toward the neo-scholastic preference for Cajetan's language of "pure nature" and the Suarezean language of "elicited desire."[20]

For those in this third group, one may speak of a very qualified natural desire for God, insofar as within the natural dynamism of the intellect there is an innate desire for the true and the good, concepts that are only inchoately and analogically related to transcendent ideals. For Aquinas, this natural desire expresses itself in a dynamic curiosity that is activated by wonder, leads into philosophical inquiry, and proceeds toward metaphysical truths by way of analogical inference and logic (*Summa theologiae* I 12.1; I-II 3.8). This natural desire, however, is not yet an *implicit* desire for the fullness of the beatific vision as it seems to be for de Lubac. Indeed, even in order for this natural desire to become the more particular desire to know God as First Cause of all that is (and here one is still within the realm of natural reason or natural theology), this desire must be further extended by the intellect's innate desire to know the causes of the observable phenomena within creation.

---

reading of Aquinas on elicited desire in *Dust Bound for Heaven,* pp. 225-27. It should be noted that Feingold correctly notes that Aquinas does not use this language of innate and elicited desire, and that it is attributable to Suarez's later commentary on Aquinas (*The Natural Desire to See God,* pp. 15-16, 44). Rather, Feingold believes that the use of the distinction is legitimate insofar as it more adequately expresses Aquinas's original intent (p. 397). This admission, it seems to me (see also Oakes, "The *Surnaturel* Controversy," p. 636), undermines the strength of his argument from the beginning, insofar as he claims to be retrieving an authentic and accurate reading of Aquinas rather than articulating a necessary development of the master's thoughts.

20. In this group I would include Torrell, "Nature and Grace in Thomas Aquinas"; Mansini, "Henri de Lubac"; Braine, "The Debate Between Henri de Lubac and His Critics"; Oakes, "The *Surnaturel* Controversy"; Healy, "Henri de Lubac on Nature and Grace"; and Malloy, "De Lubac on Natural Desire." In addition, although she is arguing against Rahner's fundamental option as opposed to de Lubac's construal of nature and grace, Jean Porter expresses similar reservations when she writes that "Aquinas does not believe that the human person's natural desire for the good involves any *implicit* or *pre-thematic desire* for, or awareness of God (*Summa theologiae* I 12.1, I-II 5.8 *ad* 2)" ("Moral Language and the Language of Grace: The Fundamental Option and the Virtue of Charity," *Philosophy and Theology* 10 [1996]: 169-98, p. 186, italics added).

Even this natural desire, however, may remain in mere potency without anything essential being lost to the underlying nature of the human person. The innate desire for truth proceeds by a process of rational inquiry into the effects of the observable order in creation and seeks to learn of the cause(s) of natural phenomena. All rational creatures are naturally capable of this kind of speculative reasoning, but the intellect can also remain in mere potency through dullness of mind (*Summa contra gentiles* III 38), distraction by the more pressing demands of daily life, or even laziness (*Summa contra gentiles* I 4), not to mention because of mental illness or developmental disability. Thus, the nature of the rational creature is not altered if this capacity for analogical inference remains inactivated or undeveloped for any of the reasons just noted. If this is true of naturally acquired knowledge of the causes of observable phenomena, all the more so is this true of the desire for the beatific vision that transcends the capacities of the unaided intellect.

That which is essential to human nature is the *capacity* for a more fully developed desire for God's revealed essence — the *capax Dei*. For example, in *De veritate*, Aquinas comments on the desire for the beatific vision in relation to Paul's comment that "no eye has seen, nor ear heard, nor the human heart conceived, what God has prepared for those who love him" (1 Cor. 2:9). In this article he describes natural desire as sufficient for pursuing the natural end of the kind of knowledge "of which the philosophers speak." The infusion of faith in the intellect, however, also activates a desire in the will that "is made to exist inchoately [*inchoatio*] within the human being" (*De veritate* 14.2). It is inchoate precisely because the intellect needs to be moved from potency to act by some object external to it through the will's affection. This is true even for acquiring natural knowledge of God as First Cause. It is all the more true when it comes to the activation of intellect and will through the infused knowledge of God made possible by faith through revelation.

At the same time, however, the more particular and explicit desire that is activated by infused faith remains intrinsic to human nature insofar as all created human persons are made in the image of God as endowed with intellect and will. If this were not true, infused faith would remake the person into a new and distinctive nature. Grace would no longer perfect, but would rather supplant nature. As Aquinas states it, the possibility of a more explicit desire for God's inner Triune Being is possible for human persons "because nothing desires a good unless it has some similitude to that good" (*De veritate* 14.2). Therefore, natural desire alone is not directed toward God's essence until it too is elevated by grace and made possible through the revealed knowledge of God in faith.

This suggests that Aquinas's argument for the natural desire to see God is intended to establish the *possibility* that the blessed will truly come to see God's essence. He does not therefore conclude that every person implicitly desires to come to such a particular end in the absence of additional, revealed or infused knowledge. If such supernatural knowledge of God is beyond the capacity of unaided reason, the desire itself cannot exist in the absence of more specified knowledge of God that is made available through revelation and faith. Although the *potential* for natural contemplation of God as First Cause is essential to human nature, its reduction from potency to act is not guaranteed. Thus, all the more so is contemplation of God's Trinitarian nature in need of further specification and aid to be moved from potency to act. All of this presupposes the existence of a natural desire (made explicit in the desire for knowledge of causes leading to the metaphysical postulation of some kind of First Cause) that is the natural *foundation* on which a more explicit desire to know the God revealed as the true cause and end of all that is may be developed through infused, supernatural gifts.

In this analysis the paradoxical status of the human intellect and will is again displayed, but this paradox does not imply a collapsing of the distinction between nature and grace as de Lubac seems to do. Rather, it presupposes just such a distinction. The natural desire for God as a capacity remains inscribed within the contours of human nature, particularly because human persons are made in the image and likeness of God, and as rational creatures possess a potential capacity to see and know God. Thus, when explicit knowledge of God is revealed in Scripture or via infused grace, this is not something imposed over and above human nature (as de Lubac feared), but rather the activation and transcendent extension of a capacity that had resided inchoately in the intellect and will all along.

Two further steps toward clarifying the paradoxical status of the natural desire for God are provided in articles by Jean Pierre Torrell and David Braine. Torrell's comments are more historical in nature while Braine's are more philosophical, but taken together they further help to clarify how to best interpret Aquinas on the paradoxical status of the human person's desire for God. Torrell notes that Aquinas always considers the human person within the actual order of providence that humans experience in this world as it has been revealed in the biblical narrative and the person of Jesus Christ. While some scholastics prior to Aquinas had debated whether the first created human being was endowed with sanctifying grace from the first moment of existence, Aquinas takes the position that human nature from the very moment of creation was endowed with the gift of sanctifying grace.[21] What this signifies, according to Torrell, is that Aquinas is primarily concerned with articulating the natural desire for God as it exists in all human persons who have been irrevocably influenced by the gift of sanctifying grace at the moment of creation and its subsequent loss due to original sin.

If we follow Aquinas on this point, then the natural desire for God functions on an existential level much like the inchoate desire that Paul recognized among the Athenians who "search for God and perhaps grope for him and find him" (Acts 17:27). Prior to the fall, human beings created in a state of grace would have had a qualified "natural" desire to see God's essence, not because of the inherent principles of human nature but because of the gratuity of grace from the first moment of creation. This gift of habitual grace in the moment of creation conferred an explicit desire for God on the first human beings. After the fall this natural desire is in need of further aid and specification through faith (and the other theological virtues) to be elevated and directed toward God's innermost being as it had originally been at the moment of creation. This subtle but important distinction between nature as such and nature from the very moment of creation enables us to appreciate that the desire for God as an original imprint within human nature is felt without it being inscribed within the contours of human nature as such. Thus, de Lubac is correct to note that this desire for a supernatural finality is experienced by those human persons who exist in this order of creation and providence. This does not entail, however, that it is fully inscribed within the natural capacities of human reason itself.

David Braine's observations help to build on this point by identifying a tendency for de Lubac to conflate human *nature* as such with human *persons* existing after the fall. Braine writes that de Lubac "should have said that supernatural finality is something given to *persons* in virtue of a relation,

---

21. Torrell notes the ways in which Aquinas's assertion on this point becomes stronger through the course of his career, against those who held that the human person was created first and given sanctifying grace later. For example, in *Scriptum super Sententiarum* II, d. 29, q. 1, a. 2 he writes that "since man was created in the integrity of his natural faculties *(in naturalibus integris)* and they could not stay inactive, *it is more probable* that, turned toward God in the first instant of his creation, he received grace" (italics added). However, by the time of writing *De malo,* he is much more forceful in his assertion where he writes that "original justice includes sanctifying grace and I do not believe that it is true that the first man was created with purely natural endowments" (*De malo* q. 4, a. 2, *ad* 1, quoted in Torrell).

rather than that it gives them a *distinct nature.*"²² De Lubac's thesis provides an existentially correct description of human *persons* after the fall, but it fails to distinguish between human persons qua actual beings existing in this providential order of God's creation and the intrinsic principles of human nature as such. This oversight leads de Lubac to conclude that the supernatural end must be imprinted on human nature itself, rather than seeing it as something given at creation, subsequently lost after the fall, and now experienced as something missing and therefore desired naturally (in the highly qualified, inchoate sense discussed above). Taken together these insights of Torrell and Braine provide important qualifiers that enable a more nuanced appreciation of de Lubac's contribution to the nature-grace discussion. They facilitate a recognition that human nature as such is defined first and foremost in relation to its connatural end rather than its supernatural end, but that human persons nonetheless experience an inchoate desire for what has been lost.

Human persons for Aquinas are therefore defined as a species with respect to the capacities endowed on them in nature *(in puris naturalibus)*, and to their connatural good, even as they remain paradoxically open to a further transcendent end. Aquinas repeatedly affirms that there is only one ultimate end for the human person — the beatific vision — but this one end is analyzable in terms of a twofold aspect *(duplex est)*. For example, he states the twofold nature of the one end quite plainly when he claims the following:

> Final and perfect happiness can consist in nothing else than the vision of the Divine Essence. (*Summa theologiae* I-II 3.8)
>
> The end toward which created things are directed by God is twofold: one which exceeds all proportion and faculty of created nature, and this end is life eternal that consists in seeing God which is above the nature of the creature. . . . The other end, however, is proportionate to created nature, to which end created being can attain according to the power of its nature. (*Summa theologiae* I 23.1)²³

Thus, even as God created human persons with sanctifying grace in this order of providence with the sole end of happiness with God,²⁴ the nature

---

22. Braine, "The Debate between Henri de Lubac and His Critics," p. 553, italics added.

23. See also *Summa theologiae* I 62.1; I-II 62.1, 5.5; *De veritate* 14.2.

24. Defending this historical claim does not forestall the possibility that God could have created human persons in a different order of creation to desire and attain only a natural, immanent happiness. God's omnipotence is in no way restrained by the claim that God

of the human species remains normatively distinguished by its natural capacities and powers. Indeed, the recognition of a common, natural desire for truth forms the foundation for Christian solidarity with all human persons in pursuit of natural human flourishing and the common good, even as the pilgrim church's essential mission is to witness to the transcendent end of friendship with God.

Reading Aquinas's comments on the desire for God through these historical (Torrell) and philosophical (Braine) corrections to de Lubac's thesis preserves Aquinas's insistence on a distinction between nature and grace. At the same time these insights lend further weight to de Lubac's rejection of the theory of pure nature. Indeed, it helps to explain why Aquinas never speaks of a "pure nature" in the way the sixteenth-century commentators would. The concept of pure nature belies a further level of speculative abstraction that Aquinas himself was not primarily concerned with exploring or defending. His primary concern is to present a philosophically and historically accurate analysis of the conditions of human persons in this order of creation once touched by grace, but longing for its loss. Indeed, Aquinas never used the term *natura pura* in any of his writings.[25] On this point de Lubac was correct to criticize later commentators and the neo-scholastic tradition in their reading of a putative pure nature in Aquinas's discussion of nature and grace. At the same time, however, one must note that Aquinas does consider it a useful theological enterprise to determine what is essential to human nature in precision from grace and in relation to its own natural endowments and powers.

To designate this speculative exercise Aquinas frequently uses the phrase *in puris naturalibus*.[26] He also makes reference to the human person in a state of "integral nature" as a means of speculation on human nature as it may have existed had God not given grace at the moment of creation. Integral nature is therefore always compared with the state of corrupted nature as we experience it in human history. For he writes, "even in the state

---

freely chose to create human persons in the order of salvation history as we know it with the ultimate end of happiness with God in eternity.

25. Torrell notes that the term *natura pura* never occurs in the Index Thomisticus ("Nature and Grace in Thomas Aquinas," p. 168).

26. *Scriptum super Sententiarum* d. 29, q. 1, a. 2; d. 30, q. 1, a. 1; *De malo* q. 4, a. 2, *ad* 1; *Summa theologiae* I-II 109.4, *ad* 3. He also notes that "original justice, in which the first man was created, was an accident pertaining to the nature of the species *(accidens naturae specie)*, not as caused by the first principles of the species, but as a gift conferred by God on the entire human nature" *(Summa theologiae* I 100.1).

of integral nature *(in statu naturae integrae)* the person needs a gratuitous strength superadded to natural strength for one reason, that is, in order to do and to wish the supernatural good" *(Summa theologiae* I-II 109.2). Thus, although Aquinas himself does not make recourse "to a chimerical state of pure nature, which mankind had never known,"[27] he does speculate on the condition of human nature as abstracted from the order of grace, primarily to highlight what is essential to human nature in and of itself. This speculative exercise helps to more accurately describe the relationship between nature and grace, and to consider what is morally possible for human persons living after the fall. Therefore, speculation on human nature in precision from grace is not merely "verbal and irrelevant"[28] for Aquinas as de Lubac claimed. Such speculation provides an important theological foundation for considering the effects of sin and its significance for Aquinas's moral theology. (I pick up this discussion on the effects of sin again in the following section.)

Aquinas circumscribes his theoretical speculations on nature abstracted from grace by always referring back to human *persons* in *this* order of creation. These humans (the only ones we know of) are created for the beatific vision and they have been touched by the original gift of sanctifying grace, even if this is only experienced as an inchoate longing for a paradise lost. Hence, the later commentators and contemporary scholars who argue for a pure nature seem to be imposing an additional layer of speculation and abstraction on what Aquinas himself intended to do. For Aquinas, on the basis of critical human reason and revelation, there never was nor will there ever be such a thing as pure nature.[29]

The linguistic distinction between *in puris naturalibus* and *natura integra* (terms Aquinas does use) and *natura pura* (a term that Aquinas never used, but others have used to articulate his doctrine) is not merely semantic. De Lubac feared that the use of the term "pure nature" would lead to a complete divorce between nature and grace and to theologically hostile forms of secularism and/or atheism. The more nuanced distinction between nature and grace that I defend in this account of civic virtue provides a means for dialoguing with those who may hold philosophical viewpoints distinct from Christianity, whether religious in nature or of a more secular worldview. When it comes to cultivating public dialogue based on a theological con-

27. Torrell, "Nature and Grace in Thomas Aquinas," p. 179.

28. De Lubac, *The Mystery of the Supernatural*, p. 67.

29. Recent scholars who explicitly advert to the term "pure nature" to describe Aquinas's speculations on human nature include Lawrence Feingold, Steven Long, Bernard Mulcahey, and Peter Pagan-Aguiar.

strual of civic virtue, the nature-grace distinction provides a more helpful model than some recent Christian rhetoric of issuing condemnations against others who do not share our basic philosophical or theological presuppositions. Such denouncements are reminiscent of Pope Pius X's failed "paper wars" discussed in Chapter 1. In addition, denunciation fails to provide a positive vision for moving forward in pursuit of the common good. The distinction between nature and grace defended in this account can also help to avoid the theoretical problems that arise from defending either a pure nature or a supernaturalized nature. That is, it enables Christians to avoid baptizing secularism (as a theological account of pure nature seems to invite) and to avoid temptations toward some form of theological-political integralism. This late modern form of theological integralism collapses all political considerations into theological terms and categories that may not be shared by all members of a body politic (as supernaturalizing the natural seems to invite). My Thomistic account of civic virtue seeks a middle way between these two extremes, and the nature-grace distinction defended above provides the theoretical foundation for such an approach (just as a similar distinction provides a theoretical foundation for Aquinas's account of the rational creature's return to God in the *Secunda Pars*).

Thus, de Lubac's instinct to defend Aquinas from being understood to have postulated a pure nature is correct, but the preceding analysis provides one very important qualifier. That is, human nature is defined by and analyzable in relation to its natural capacities and end (not only or primarily by its supernatural end), even as in actual human experience each person remains open to and called to an end that transcends such natural categories. This turns out to be a highly significant qualifier, however, when one considers the implications of the twofold end of human persons for the natural law morality that animates work on behalf of the common good by those within a pilgrim church. The distinction between nature and grace that undergirds natural law reasoning provides a theoretical paradigm for understanding how Christians can avoid the temptations toward theological integralism, epistemic superiority, or paternalistic elitism in public discourse regarding the common good.

Nature, Grace, and Natural Law: Epistemic Superiority or Humility and Solidarity?

I noted in the previous chapter that the retrieval of a Thomistic account of civic virtue for late modern democratic societies requires an emendation of the kind of elitism found in John Courtney Murray's defense of the political prudence of the wise political leader. In the final section of this chapter, I argue that upholding a distinction between nature and grace provides the necessary tools for Christian engagement in public deliberation about the good with the kind of humility and solidarity that such a task requires. I also critique a more recent form of elitism and epistemic superiority that arises within the discourse of Catholic natural law. Although Murray overemphasizes the role of the wise legislator in determining the middle axioms of natural law, his account of natural law has the merit of upholding a distinction between nature and grace that is required for its ongoing viability as a means of public discourse. Despite Murray's proclivity for a certain kind of elitism, natural law for him ultimately provides the philosophical tools necessary to create a "charter of essential humanism."[30] In this section I contrast Murray's form of elitism with the kind of Christian epistemic superiority in Steven Long's recent work. Although Long's defense of pure nature upholds a very strong distinction between nature and grace, he moves dangerously close to what I would call a quasi-Jansenist position by denigrating the natural goodness and capacity for moral reasoning in human persons after the fall. His analysis of pure nature and natural law reasoning suggests that sin has so wholly corrupted nature that right practical reasoning — even with regard to the temporal goods of the political community — is only possible with the aid of grace, revelation, and the magisterial authority of the church. This position results in a form of Christian epistemic superiority and theological integralism that is incongruent with a Thomistic account of civic virtue.

Although Murray's account of the role of the wise political leader is problematic, he does uphold an appropriate distinction between nature and grace. The goal of natural law theory for Murray is simply "to give a philosophical account of the moral experience of humanity and to lay down a charter for essential humanism."[31] For Murray, natural law supplies Christians with a means of articulating a cogent moral philosophy in regard to public life that is accessible to reason, and is best suited to the conditions of pluralism that define late modern political life. It also remains open to the transcendent claims of revelation and faith. Since natural law is ultimately tethered to metaphysical first principles and an anthropology that are congruent with the basic tenets of Christian faith, it provides Christians (Murray was specifically thinking of Catholic Christians) with a coherent philosophy

---

30. Murray, *We Hold These Truths*, p. 297.
31. Murray, *We Hold These Truths*, p. 297.

with which to engage in public dialogue with others that is congruent with the principles of revelation and revealed faith. One upshot of this is that those in a pilgrim church need not live a divided existence between their public, civic lives and their private lives of faith. Natural law provides a philosophical foundation for living an integrated human life without resorting to theological integralism to justify one's political positions.

A very different form of elitism, however, may emerge from overemphasizing the distinction between nature and grace. This form of elitism becomes particularly problematic if it is combined with a more aggressive interpretation of the effects of sin as a radical wounding of the natural capacities of the human person. Among those scholars in the second group who critique de Lubac's thesis noted in the previous section, Steven Long most consistently follows these criticisms to their logical implications for natural law and the church's public witness to moral and political deliberation.[32] He criticizes de Lubac for the loss of what he calls the "ontological density" of nature. In response, Long resurrects the language of pure nature and suggests it as a cogent manner of interpreting Aquinas. He then applies the implications of his critique of de Lubac to the natural law tradition and to contemporary Western culture and politics. For example, Long criticizes scholars such as Jacques Maritain, Jean Porter, and David Schindler for claiming that Christians may find rational agreement with others on practical matters such as the affirmation and defense of human rights. For him the global consensus that emerged in public discourse and international law on the existence of such rights in the latter half of the twentieth century is not a witness to the cogency of natural rights based on natural law. Rather than providing a foundation for upholding human dignity and justice, he believes that such practical agreement — devoid of speculative agreement on the metaphysical principles of natural law — will only fan the flames of "incessant political and social conflict."[33]

In Long's view true social cohesion will only be practically possible when all persons can agree on the speculative foundations of natural law, the teleological ordering of ends, direct and intentional "advertence to revelation," and the privileged location of the Roman Catholic Church as "our tutor in natural law."[34] Whereas Murray and Maritain had claimed that because of

---

32. See in particular chapter 4 of *Natura Pura*, pp. 140-99. Long, along with others in this second group, relies heavily on the work of Feingold's *The Natural Desire to See God*.

33. Long, *Natura Pura*, p. 153.

34. Long, *Natura Pura*, p. 178.

particular historical circumstances and intellectual commitments within the church, natural law had survived in the Catholic intellectual tradition, Long argues that natural law is *only* intelligible within the Catholic tradition.[35] He thus seems to reject natural law as the proper inheritance of all humankind or as a foundation for a universal kind of humanism, as defended by the International Theological Commission's recent statement, "In Search of a Universal Ethic: A New Look at the Natural Law."[36] He also rejects John Courtney Murray's contention that the First Amendment of the U.S. Constitution can be rightly understood as an article of peace divorced from, or at least neutral with respect to, distinctively theological or Christian beliefs or doctrines.[37] In this regard, the kind of Christian integralism and epistemic superiority in Long's analysis far surpasses any of the problems encountered in Murray's work. In the final analysis, it is difficult to see how Long's argument is a natural law argument at all, as the normative dimensions of human nature remain vacuous outside the additional content provided by revelation and magisterial authority.

In *Natura Pura* Long argues against de Lubac and his followers — particularly Hans Urs von Balthasar — in favor of interpreting Aquinas as upholding a concept of pure nature. He claims that such a conception of pure nature is necessary to protect not only the gratuity of grace, but also for an accurate comprehension of natural law. He argues for a conception of nature that has true "ontological density." In referring to human nature's ontological density I take him to mean that human nature remains morally intelligible within its own natural endowments and capacities. In and of itself this claim is perfectly congruent with Aquinas's speculation on humans *in puris naturalibis* or *in statu naturae integrae*. Furthermore, Long rejects the position defended by Balthasar that the "theological concept of nature is

---

35. Maritain writes, for example, that "the idea of natural law is a heritage of Christian and classical thought." It belongs to the heritage that leads back "to Grotius, and before him to Suarez and Francisco de Victoria; and further back to St. Thomas Aquinas; and still further back to St. Augustine and the Church Fathers and St. Paul; and even further back to Cicero, to the Stoics, to the great moralists of antiquity and its great poets" (*Christianity and Democracy and the Rights of Man and Natural Law,* trans. Doris C. Anson [San Francisco: Ignatius, 2011], p. 103).

36. An English translation is available on the Vatican's website at http://www.vatican.va/roman_curia/congregations/cfaith/cti_documents/rc_con_cfaith_doc_20090520_legge-naturale_en.html. Accessed September 25, 2013.

37. Long discusses Murray and David Schindler's use of Murray's work in *Natura Pura,* pp. 184-90, especially p. 190.

primarily a negative one"[38] that provides an empty vacuole for sanctifying grace, along with the position defended by Karl Rahner that nature is simply a "residual" or "remainder concept" abstracted from the graced horizon of the supernatural existential.[39] With regard to these particular criticisms of Balthasar's and Rahner's denigration of the theological integrity of nature, I remain quite sympathetic with Long, as my comments in the previous section indicate. The natural intelligibility of human nature, however, can be defended without recourse to the chimerical state of pure nature and without adverting to a form of Christian epistemic superiority with regard to natural law reasoning.

In the practice of natural law reasoning within the moral and political life of contemporary societies, Long and Reinhard Hütter seem to believe that all forms of natural law reasoning will be intrinsically flawed if they are not subsumed into revelation and the church's magisterial authority. For Hütter, the wounding of human nature is so deep, and the healing effects of grace so profound, that forms of natural law reasoning that do not *explicitly* advert to divine law (revelation), tether human reason to eternal law, or defer to the church's magisterial authority will *always* be incapable of providing any effectively normative order to human morality and civil law. Hütter, for example, writes that "the natural love of God above all that orders a society to the common good is no longer efficaciously operative in the state of wounded human nature."[40] Because of this, "genuine, theologically enlightened liberalism"[41] is only possible when liberal thought submits to the catechesis of the church regarding natural law. Hütter's theologically enlightened liberalism is quite different from the kind of positive laicity or moderate liberalism that I traced in the first chapter, and which laid the foundation for the endorsement of religious freedom as a universal human right and proclaimed the state's incompetence in regard to theological truth in *Dignitatis humanae.* Rather, his position seems to insinuate that the state must recognize the church as its tutor in natural law. It is difficult to see how this does not lead to a new form of theological

---

38. Long quotes from Balthasar's *The Theology of Karl Barth: Exposition and Interpretation,* trans. Edward T. Oakes (San Francisco: Ignatius, 1992), p. 282, quoted in *Natura Pura,* p. 67.

39. Rahner presents this oft-cited claim in his essay, "Concerning the Relationship between Nature and Grace," in *Theological Investigations,* vol. 1, trans. Cornelius Ernst (London: Darton, Longman, & Todd, 1974), pp. 301-3.

40. Hütter, *Dust Bound for Heaven,* p. 108.

41. Hütter, *Dust Bound for Heaven,* p. 108.

integralism in which the state has a duty with regard to the promulgation and defense of religious truth.

Long's and Hütter's analyses of natural law reasoning therefore implicitly reject Murray's claim that "the natural law has no Roman Catholic presuppositions."[42] Rather, for Long "the condition of philosophy in the life of the Christian is superior both because (1) subjectively, there is the aid of the superior illumination of grace, and (2) objectively, revelation both *medicinally* reveals certain truths nonetheless properly natural and available to reason, while it also provides negative and positive norms that help to inspire and guide [moral] inquiry."[43] By denigrating the moral significance of human nature and its teleologically ordered inclinations to virtue after the fall, and by upholding the church as a privileged location of grace-infused reasoning, he ends up granting epistemic superiority to Christian moral discourse. This superiority seems to apply to both public reasoning about the political good and matters relating more directly to dogmatic and moral theology.

What is missing from these accounts of Christian moral reasoning is — in a word — humility. It is worth recalling Augustine's insight that in human history the earthly and heavenly cities are an admixture of saints and sinners — of the tares and the wheat — whose true destiny is only revealed after this human pilgrimage (*Civitate Dei* XX 9). Being a member of the pilgrim church does not guarantee salvation, let alone superior capacities for reasoning, any more than being outside the church guarantees one's damnation or inferior capacity for reasoning. Without an awareness of the uncertainty regarding the ultimate destiny of the people of God on pilgrimage through this life, Long fails to recognize that although grace heals and elevates wounded human nature, Aquinas never makes the further claim that therefore any particular individual Christian or the church as a whole is *necessarily* in a position of superiority when it comes to moral reasoning. History should provide sufficient examples to disabuse one of this kind of moral hubris.

---

42. Murray, *We Hold These Truths,* p. 109. While it may be true that the natural law tradition has developed in a distinctive manner within the Catholic tradition, Long's claims seem to undercut the sense in which natural law is an inheritance of all of humanity, and has been and continues to be expressed in a multitude of forms depending on the cultural context in which human reason develops. Stephen Pope provides an excellent historical and thematic survey of the ways in which the concept of natural law has developed from classical antiquity, into medieval theology, and finally into the modern era (see "Natural Law and Christian Ethics," in *The Cambridge Companion to Christian Ethics,* 2nd ed., ed. Robin Gill [New York: Cambridge University Press, 2012], pp. 67-87).

43. Long, *Natura Pura,* p. 187.

Aquinas provides a foundation for this kind of humility in at least two different places. First, as discussed in relation to the passions in Chapter 3, he recognizes that even in a state of grace the Christian wayfarer still experiences the previously acquired dispositions that work against the theological virtues that function as the principles that order the infused cardinal virtues.[44] The uncertainty regarding one's ultimate destiny is why the Christian wayfarer must work out the drama of salvation "with fear and trembling" (Phil. 2:12).

A second example can be found in Aquinas's discussion of the role of *industria* in relation to prudence. He writes about *industria* as a form of "diligence" or "wise effort" in the pursuit of virtuous goods. He claims that those in a state of grace possess a particular form of *industria* with regard to "things necessary for salvation." But it is entirely possible that a person with habitual grace may possess the infused form of civic virtue without ever having had the opportunity to cultivate these principles into an actively engaged capacity for justice.[45] In discussing what he calls a "fuller diligence" Aquinas writes that

> there is also another, fuller diligence *(industria plenior),* whereby a person is able to make provision both for himself and for others, not only in matters necessary for salvation, but also in all things relating to human life, and such diligence as this is not in all who have grace. (*Summa theologiae* II-II 47.14, *ad* 1)

And elsewhere Aquinas states that "there is no necessity that political virtue be had by infusion of grace" (*De virtutibus in communi* q. 9, *ad* 18).[46] Thus, one need not conclude that Christians, considered qua individuals or collec-

---

44. "One may experience difficulty in performing the actions proper to the habitus of the infused moral virtues because of certain contrary dispositions surviving from previous acts" (*Summa theologiae* I-II 65.3, *ad* 2; see also *De virtutibus* 5.2, *ad* 2; quotations are found in Michael Sherwin, "Infused Virtue and the Effects of Acquired Vice: A Test Case for the Thomistic Theory of Infused Cardinal Virtues," *The Thomist* 73 [2009]: 29-52, p. 44).

45. Michael Sherwin describes this phenomenon in the following manner: "the beginner finds himself in the unique position of having virtues that he does not psychologically feel like he has" ("Infused Virtue and the Effects of Acquired Vice," p. 46). Nor has such a person yet had the opportunity, often through no fault of her own, to employ *industria* to the perfection of certain virtues.

46. It should also be noted that in this context Aquinas seems to be using the term "political" to refer not simply to politics, but more broadly to the naturally acquired virtues in pursuit of the human good (see William Mattison, "Can Christians Possess the Acquired Cardinal Virtues?" *Theological Studies* 72 [2011]: 558-85, p. 572).

tively in the church, necessarily have a greater capacity to reason with regard to pursuit of the goods of this life.

The possession of political prudence (whether in its acquired or infused form), as discussed in Chapters 2 and 3, is manifested by repeated acts of wise decisions with regard to laws and acts that order the community toward the common good. Such virtue may be found in non-Christians who have acquired it naturally by *industria,* or in Christians who have likewise demonstrated infused political prudence — albeit with the aid of grace — through similar effort. Thus, the criterion that qualifies one for political office rests on a publicly demonstrated capacity for political prudence as an essential component of civic virtue. On Aquinas's account it may be the case that there are many holy and wise persons in things pertaining to salvation who have very little or no political prudence with regard to the terrestrial common good. A discerning person might choose a Father Zosima for spiritual direction, but not necessarily to run for political office. In a case where a person has demonstrated *industria* with regard to things necessary for salvation but not for the civic good, it would be better to appoint a virtuous and politically prudent pagan (or Buddhist, or Muslim, etc.) to govern than to insist on Christian epistemic superiority with regard to political prudence.

A better approach to natural law may be discovered in trusting the inherent capacity of human reason to know (moral) truth — in what Aquinas calls the *adaequatio rei et intellectus* (*De veritate* 1.2) — while simultaneously cultivating the requisite humility demanded of one's pilgrim status in this world. David Hollenbach suggests, for example, that inquiry into the nature of human social existence demands both "epistemological humility" and "intellectual solidarity."[47] Hollenbach writes, for example, that epistemological humility

> is a cognitive stance that begins with the acknowledgement that one does not have ready answers to all questions of how people ought to live together. Nor does it presume that a moral orientation that seems reasonable or even necessary to the inquirer is evidently desirable to all other reasonable people. It acknowledges that one can attain genuine

---

47. Hollenbach first discusses epistemological humility in *Claims in Conflict: Retrieving and Renewing the Catholic Human Rights Tradition* (New York: Paulist, 1979), p. 131. He discusses the relationship between epistemological humility and intellectual solidarity in *The Global Face of Public Faith: Politics, Human Rights, and Christian Ethics* (Washington, D.C.: Georgetown University Press, 2003), pp. 46-50.

knowledge only through receptivity to the world beyond the mind of the inquirer.[48]

It seems that Long is rightly concerned to propose natural law as an alternative to modern, scientific rationalism or postmodern skepticism with regard to the human capacity to know and live according to moral truth. However, he replaces these modern or postmodern epistemological stances with a form of intellectual superiority that is inimical to democratic values of equality and autonomy and to the church's tradition of natural law. The natural law tradition as it has survived in the Catholic Church has always upheld natural law as a possession and capacity of the entire human family. Hollenbach's epistemological humility provides a way to uphold the church's high regard for reason by charting a middle way between skepticism and relativism on the one hand, and a moral-intellectual superiority and domination on the other.

When this humility is combined with intellectual solidarity, it becomes possible to reason together with all people of good will toward moral truth in the pursuit of creating the political structures that support the attainment of the common good. For Hollenbach "intellectual solidarity also presupposes a commitment to *mutual* listening and speaking" and a recognition that researchers and theologians "are not demigods but fellow travelers with other human beings through the course of history."[49] It is difficult to find a space for such listening to others in the mutual pursuit of moral truth in Long's account of natural law. And it is difficult to understand how solidarity and dialogue may be fostered when one assumes to have superior knowledge of the truth even prior to entering into dialogue. Moreover, epistemological humility and intellectual solidarity are quite fitting for the members of a pilgrim church who hold out hope for a good that transcends the terrestrial common good, but who are simultaneously committed to the good of others with whom they travel in this life.

I am willing to defend the claim that the tradition of moral inquiry that emerges from the Christian people of God on pilgrimage through history yields distinctive and important insights into the nature of human morality and political life. However, such insights will only emerge and come to be appreciated by the body politic through a dialogue that respects the capacity for natural law reasoning by all participants committed to seeking the com-

48. Hollenbach, *The Global Face of Public Faith*, p. 46.
49. Hollenbach, *The Global Face of Public Faith*, p. 48.

mon good.[50] Moreover, this dialogue is most capable of advancing toward moral truth when the basic rights of free assembly and free speech of all the participants in the conversation are justiciable as guaranteed and protected by law. According to Hollenbach, "nurturing such humility and solidarity requires a social atmosphere where equality and freedom are valued and institutionalized. In this sense they are 'liberal' virtues, and they require the building and strengthening of the institutions of constitutional government, free speech, free exercise of religion, etc."[51] Jean Porter has similarly claimed that natural law inquiry is best fostered within the political conditions of modern democratic societies that defend a free space of public discourse and disagreement without enforcing one, monolithic vision of the good.[52]

When it comes to his more specific comments on the moral normativity of natural inclinations as the foundation for natural law, Long seems to undercut the strength of his own claims regarding the "ontological density" of human nature. For example, Long criticizes Porter's construal of natural law for failing to recognize how what he calls the "close-in" teleologies of natural order and inclination can provide directly normative conclusions. Porter claims that the natural inclinations "underdetermine" the directly normative precepts of natural law because they are in need of further specification. For her the remote precepts of natural law that provide particular direction to the inchoate inclinations only become logically coherent within the cultural context and practices that further specify those inclinations into particular acts of virtue.[53] Long's comments considered above, however, seem to indicate that it is *only* within the church and its tradition of speculative metaphysics that any morally relevant conclusions can be drawn from nature's ontological density. His assertions, however, seem to lend support to rather than undercut the strength of Porter's claim. Long believes that such close-in teleologies can only be fully understood within the traditions of practices

50. Meg Wilkes Karraker provides an excellent example of this kind of mutual reasoning and solidarity. In *Diversity and the Common Good: Civil Society, Religion, and Catholic Sisters in a Small City* (Lanham, Md.: Lexington, 2013) she reveals ways in which the religious sisters of a small Midwestern city were able to leverage their social capital to work with other civic leaders to address instances of racial prejudice and violence in their community.

51. Hollenbach, *The Global Face of Public Faith*, 49.

52. Porter argues that such moral inquiry and dialogue "both presupposes and lends support to the classical liberal virtues of tolerance and openness to pluralism" ("Openness and Constraint: Moral Reflection as Tradition-Guided Inquiry in Alasdair MacIntyre's Recent Works," *Journal of Religion* 73, no. 4 [1993]: 514-36, p. 515).

53. See Jean Porter, *Nature as Reason: A Thomistic Theory of Natural Law* (Grand Rapids: Eerdmans, 2005), pp. 126-27.

that are embodied in the social and institutional structures of the church itself, not by a close-in analysis alone. It is not so much that Long disagrees with Porter on the necessity of social practices and institutions to further specify and order the natural inclinations. Rather, he seems to disagree with her claim that there are multiple, valid natural law moralities expressed in various social and historical contexts.[54] Rather than surviving and being expressed in a particular historical form (as it does for Murray), natural law morality for Long is *only* expressed in the Roman Catholic Church.

Moreover, Long is not entirely consistent in applying his own conclusions to his critique of Porter's analysis. When it comes to issues of sexual morality, Long is entirely willing to assert moral normativity for the "close-in" teleological structure of the human body, or more precisely of human sexuality. The concept of family as naturally rooted in marriage between one man and one woman and of the intrinsic immorality of contraception and abortion are for him accessible to unaided human reason. These moral truths are accessible to all rational persons because they are based on the natural teleological order that can be seen in the biological processes of sex and reproduction.[55] For Long, the rejection of such moral claims in Western culture and law provides examples of how corrupted natural law reasoning — even with regard to such close-in teleologies — has become in a world that has rejected the direct influence of the church's authority in morality and politics.

On the other hand, however, he sees little intrinsic value in the kind of moral asceticism cultivated in popular culture by concern for physical health and the health of the environment. These he believes to be mere secular errors that leave their followers pursuing a false and empty spirituality.[56] It is not clear, however, on premises that Long himself defends regarding the ontological density of nature, why the close-in teleologies of the sexual organs are universally intelligible whereas similar teleological patterns noted in relation to physical health and to ecological sustainability are not. I suggest that a more fruitful approach may be found if Christians recognize the cultural phenomena of practices such as concern for the health of the body and the health of the planet as manifestations of the human capacity to exercise natural reason to discern order within the human body and within

---

54. Porter, *Nature as Reason*, p. 165.

55. Long discusses the universally accessible intelligibility of the family on p. 175 and sexual ethics on p. 208 of *Natura Pura*.

56. Long, *Natura Pura*, p. 107.

creation. These could be taken as particular examples of the exigencies of human reason exercising its capacity to recognize the moral normativity of the created natural order, and as reasonable attempts to live in accord with the natural order discernable in creation.

These more secular forms of natural law reasoning and moral practices will not be the final word for Christians, of course, as they will be understood to function within an extended sense of the ordering of ends that includes God as final end of all things and as sustained by divine providence. What this more dialogical approach does suggest, however, is that natural law is a powerful intellectual tool for engaging in reasonable dialogue with others, not a blunt weapon for proclaiming the epistemological superiority of the church. For those within a pilgrim church, these points of rational congruence between traditions are sought out and affirmed because they may become the touchstones for dialogue and witness. They present opportunities for Christians to affirm natural goodness and to publicly explain and defend how such natural goods may be ordered toward the ultimate good and are rationally congruent with a commitment to faith. Indeed, in certain contexts such congruence of ends may serve as a moment of possible witness and evangelization by first affirming and then extending the natural inclination to good that is inscribed within the human heart (see Rom. 2:15). It is precisely such affirmation and analogical extension of natural goodness toward its ultimate source that the people of God in a pilgrim church can provide to dialogue in a pluralistic, secular culture. The natural law tradition provides a foundation for a theologically informed public rhetoric that can provide answers to ultimate questions of human life that liberalism itself cannot answer on its own principles of neutrality with regard to the good.

One of the challenges of such a public witness to natural law reasoning is that it rests on a defense of certain metaphysical principles such as the teleological ordering of ends and a theory of final causality that are not generally accepted today. Murray and Long are both aware of the challenges involved trying to secure agreement on the metaphysical foundations of natural law reasoning in a pluralistic context. I remain sympathetic with both of these thinkers on this issue. Murray notes, for example, that

> the whole metaphysic involved in the idea of natural law may seem alarmingly complicated; in a sense it is. Natural law supposes a realist epistemology. . . . Secondly, it supposes a metaphysic of nature, especially the idea that nature is a teleological concept. . . . Thirdly, it supposes a natural theology. . . . Finally, it supposes a morality, especially the principle that

for man, a rational being, the order of nature is not an order of necessity, to be fulfilled blindly, but an order of reason and therefore of freedom.[57]

Thus, Murray affirms the necessity of defending these aspects of natural law theory, while using these principles to work toward constructive dialogue. Long, on the other hand, writes that "those whose theology rests exclusively with a broadly theistic, historicized, cultural hermeneutic will tend to lack the metaphysical entry capital to commence interpretation of Aquinas on these points."[58] While both Murray and Long recognize the inherent complexity of these metaphysical components of a natural law ethic, Murray uses this as a basis to begin constructive dialogue whereas Long uses it to exclude those who "lack the metaphysical entry capital" to engage in rational dialogue. Murray's approach belies a greater faith in the universal human capacity for natural law reasoning and in the possibility that such claims could be discussed rationally and persuasively defended in the face of the many arguments against it that are characteristic of modern, liberal thought.[59]

57. Murray, *We Hold These Truths,* pp. 327-28.

58. Long, *Natura Pura,* p. 17. The entire question of the role of history and hermeneutics in natural law reasoning are actually separate questions that are worthy of study in their own right, but on these points Long's interpretation of Aquinas seems much closer to the lack of attention to the historical context of practical reason encountered in nineteenth-century neo-scholasticism. Gerald McCool writes, for example, that the "great weakness" of neo-scholasticism is its "lack of historical sense and blindness to the role of historical development in theology" (*From Unity to Pluralism: The Internal Revolution of Thomism* [New York: Fordham University Press, 1989], p. 24).

59. The discussion of a teleological metaphysic of nature and natures has remained a central point in attempts to retrieve and defend a natural law ethic up to this day. For example, in his earlier work, MacIntyre makes the well-known point that as we recover an ethic of virtue, we must reject the "metaphysical biology" that serves as a foundation for Aristotle's virtue ethics in *After Virtue: A Study in Moral Theory,* 2nd ed. (Notre Dame, Ind.: University of Notre Dame Press, 1984), p. 162. Yet in his later work, he has reversed his opinion and believes that we must retrieve some kind of overarching teleological aim that makes sense out of all the teleological striving of each individual nature, as well as providing some sense of order in a hierarchy of goods that acts as a guide to moral choices in the use of practical reason. He indicates this need in *Whose Justice? Which Rationality?* (Notre Dame, Ind.: University of Notre Dame Press, 1988), where he argues that justice can only fully be comprehended in Aquinas's work if it is placed in light of Aquinas's "metaphysical biology" (p. 198). Other significant contributions to this effort to retrieve, defend, and extend the implications of asserting a metaphysics of the nature of the human person in theological ethics have been undertaken by Jean Porter (see *Nature as Reason,* pp. 82-124), and Stephen J. Pope in *Human Evolution and Christian Ethics* (Cambridge: Cambridge University Press, 2007), especially pp. 129-57, 268-96.

The possibilities for dialogue in natural law discourse also rest on a defense of the abiding, albeit wounded, capacities for virtue that Aquinas describes as the result of original sin, and the correlative humility that it entails. These considerations are essential for considering what can be expected of those in possession of civic virtue as well as for the kind of rhetoric that animates Christian public discourse on the common good in democratic societies. In describing the effects of sin, Aquinas delineates three modalities of the good of human nature:

> First, there are the principles of which nature is constituted, and the properties that flow from them, such as the powers of the soul, and so forth. Secondly, since the human person has from nature an inclination to virtue, as stated above, this inclination to virtue is a good of nature. Third, the gift of original justice, conferred on the whole human nature in the person of the first man, may be called a good of nature. (*Summa theologiae* I-II 85.1)

For Aquinas the first good constituting the principles and powers of human nature is neither destroyed nor diminished by sin. The third good, original justice, was entirely destroyed. But the second good, the natural inclination to virtue, is not destroyed but rather "diminished by sin" (*Summa theologiae* I-II 85.1). Thus, the wound inflicted by sin results in the loss of the ultimate end for which humans were made, and a wounding of the natural inclination to virtue, even as the underlying principles that characterize that nature and its capacity for virtue remain intact. Hence, grace as it is experienced by human persons performs both a healing and an elevating function, healing insofar as it begins to restore the capacity for virtue and elevating insofar as it makes possible acts directed toward the ultimate end that transcends the natural end of human persons.

In the treatise on grace, Aquinas again considers what good the human person can accomplish in this world. There he reminds his readers that there are two ways of looking at human nature — as it is now (that is, post-fall) and as it could be considered in the state of integral nature. In the theoretical state of integral nature, the human person could have achieved her connatural end. In both states, however, grace is necessary to do the good proportionate to the supernatural end. Thus, even in the state of integral nature where the natural inclination to virtue was not yet wounded and the human person could have achieved her connatural end, she would still need "a gratuitous strength superadded to natural strength for one reason, which is in order to do and wish the supernatural good" (*Summa theologiae* I-II 109.2). In the state of corrupted nature, however,

> the human person falls short of what he could do by his nature, so that he is unable to fulfill it by his own natural powers. Yet because human nature is not altogether corrupted by sin . . . it can, by virtue of its natural endowments, work some particular good, as to *build homes, plant vineyards, and the like;* yet it cannot do all the good natural to it. (*Summa theologiae* I-II 109.2, italics added)

Thus, original sin not only leads to the removal of the supernatural gift of sanctifying grace, it further corrupts even the integrity of human nature vis-à-vis its natural capacities for virtue. And yet at the same time, that nature is not so wholly corrupted that human persons can perform no naturally good acts. Persons are still capable of performing the necessary acts to sustain natural life and to pursue an imperfect state of wellbeing insofar as it is possible in this life.

Aquinas quotes here from a well-known text among scholastics erroneously attributed to Augustine.[60] It is worth considering it in full for it provides insight into the intention Aquinas may have had in including it here:

> For the good, free choice makes him to want those goods that come from nature, such as farming, eating, friendship, marriage, drinking, having friends, wearing clothes, building a house, taking a wife, raising cattle, learning the art of various useful things, in short, to want all the good that belongs to the present life; all things that not only cannot subsist without the government of divine Providence, but still more, come from him, are through him and were begun by him.[61]

The longer quote from Pseudo-Augustine helps to mitigate any sense that for Aquinas corrupted human nature is completely incapable of pursuing its

---

60. For more on Aquinas's and the scholastics' familiarity with Augustine's corpus, and the possibility that they sometimes quoted his works from memory or from *florilegia,* see Bonnie Kent, "Reinventing Augustine's Ethics: The Afterlife of the *City of God,*" in *Augustine's City of God: A Critical Guide,* ed. James Wetzel (New York: Cambridge University Press, 2012), pp. 227-31.

61. Pseudo-Augustine, *Hypognosticon* III, IV 5; quoted in Torrell, "Nature and Grace," pp. 180-81.

connatural good, even as it does so with its natural capacities wounded and in need of divine healing and aid.

The quote from Pseudo-Augustine also helps to highlight the significance of God's "double-gratuity" for the moral life.[62] As the quote itself demonstrates, everything in existence, including human nature and its inclinations toward and capacities to pursue the natural good that persons possess, are already due to a first gift of creation from God. This is the first gratuity, or what Russell Hittinger calls the "first grace," which is the foundation of natural law.[63] The second gratuity — the infusion of grace that heals and elevates wounded human nature — further enables human persons both to more effectively act toward their connatural good (insofar as the nature is healed) and to perform actions meritorious of eternal life (insofar as the nature is elevated and endowed with the theological principles necessary for meritorious acts).

Aquinas's distinction between human nature *in statu naturae integrae* and its wounded modality after the fall helps us to appreciate the falsity of two extreme ways of understanding and applying natural law moral reasoning in the present order of human history. First, one must reject any kind of quasi-Jansenism that would entirely denigrate the capacities of human reason after the fall. The doctrine of Jansenism derives from Cornelius Jansenus (1585-1638), bishop of Ypres, who taught that after the fall the only acts of which human beings are capable are sinful.[64] His teachings completely eliminate any capacity for seeking the connatural good without the aid of divine grace after the fall. Second, one must also reject any kind of semi-Pelagian, utopian hope in the capacities for reason alone to solve the problems of political life. Pelagius was a fifth-century presbyter who rejected the doctrine of original sin and taught that grace enables the human will to avoid sin through the examples of Christ, writings of the Scriptures, and moral exhortation.

62. Mansini refers to this as a double gratuity ("Henri de Lubac," p. 108), as does Hütter (*Dust Bound for Heaven*, p. 159), and de Lubac himself hints toward this double gratuity in *Augustinianism and Modern Theology*, where he writes that "all, rightly speaking, is grace (although a distinction is to be made between one grace and another)" (p. 2).

63. Hittinger draws this phrase from a fifth-century presbyter by the name of Lucidus, who refers to natural law as the "first grace of God" (*The First Grace: Rediscovering the Natural Law in a Post-Christian World* [Wilmington, Del.: ISI, 2003], p. xi). The original citation may be found in Heinrich Denzinger and Peter Hünermann, *Symboles et définitions de la foi catholique* (Paris: Editions du Cerf, 1997), §336.

64. Jacques Forget, "Jansenius and Jansenism," in *The Catholic Encyclopedia*, vol. 8 (New York: Appleton, 1910), http://www.newadvent.org/cathen/08285a.htm. Accessed April 21, 2014.

For Pelagius the will required neither interior healing nor elevation to overcome sin and perform actions meritorious of eternal life.[65] Overcoming sin was for him a matter of human effort and the external aid of Scripture and moral exemplars. Avoiding these two extremes is important because the manner in which one construes the natural capacities of human reason in human history bears directly on how one understands the capacities of human will and reason for natural law and its contribution to political discourse in pursuit of the common good. A critically realistic approach to natural law in public life must navigate between an overly pessimistic quasi-Jansenism and a utopian semi-Pelagianism. Long, it seems to me, moves dangerously close to a kind of quasi-Jansenism in his denigration of moral reasoning outside the visible contours of the church.

On the one hand a Thomistic account of sin, natural law, and human history helps us to appreciate why a realistic consideration of the capacities of human reason in relation to its capacities to achieve its connatural end does not necessarily lead to secularism and atheism as de Lubac had feared. Consideration of the person *in puris naturalibus* is not the same thing as Cajetan's "pure nature." Indeed, Steven Long, Russell Hittinger, and Jean Porter, albeit each in their own distinctive ways, are correct to note that the moral normativity of human nature within the Catholic natural law tradition presupposes a theological and teleological construal of creation and divine providence.[66] A natural law ethic based on a distinction between nature and grace is therefore not a capitulation to a purely natural or secular ethic. Indeed, Aquinas's definition of natural law as the "rational creature's participation in Eternal law" (*Summa theologiae* I-II 90.2) disabuses the notion that natural law is the autonomous, self-governing reason of later Enlightenment and modern moral philosophy. On the other hand, Aquinas's discussion also mitigates against the sense that original sin has completely destroyed any capacity for natural law reasoning, natural virtue, or acting to achieve the

---

65. Joseph Pohle, "Pelagius and Pelagianism," in *The Catholic Encyclopedia*, vol. 11 (New York: Appleton, 1911), http://www.newadvent.org/cathen/11604a.htm. Accessed April 21, 2014.

66. Long argues for a return to an appreciation of the *"theonomic character of natural order and natural law"* (*Natura Pura,* p. 43). Hittinger articulates these claims in *The First Grace,* pp. 24-32. Porter also defends the necessity of reading natural law as a theological concept within the order of providence in *Nature as Reason,* p. 48. Indeed, such a theological foundation for natural law is necessary for amending de Lubac's thesis in favor of a distinction between nature and grace in a way that does not leave natural law devoid of theological content and open to the criticism that it is synonymous with autonomous, secular reason.

temporal good. A Thomistic critical realism provides a space for recognizing, honoring, and cultivating the natural inclinations to virtue that remain after the fall. Politics is one — though by no means the only — important arena in which these natural inclinations may be fostered toward virtue and where persons may be dissuaded from the pursuit of vices that harm the public good, in part through the effective use of the coercive power of law.[67] These natural inclinations to virtue and truth remain intact — albeit in a wounded form — after the fall. They therefore remain universally accessible as a foundation for dialogue in pursuit of the common good for all people of good will. A careful consideration of the distinction between nature and grace and of the effects of sin on the capacities of natural law reasoning suggests that one need not collapse the distinction between nature and grace in the way that de Lubac tends to do. On the other hand, one need not resort to a defense of the state of pure nature as a legitimate interpretation of Aquinas or to a denigration of the natural capacities for moral reason in the manner that Long tends to do. As Murray states it, natural law provides a charter for essential humanism and is best used to foster a reasonable solidarity in pursuit of the common good.

What the doctrines of original sin and the wounding of the capacity for virtue after the fall provide to political discourse is not a denigration of all forms of reasoning outside the church, but rather a sense of the solidarity of all human persons in attempting to achieve imperfect and tenuous justice in the earthly city. One can uphold a Thomistic form of critical realism with regard to moral knowledge and natural law reasoning without a correlative sense of Christian superiority over and against other moral traditions. Rather, natural law provides a more realistic sense of hope that human persons may work together in pursuit of the common good, while the doctrine of original sin moderates that hope from progressing into utopianism.

These considerations also enable a certain kind of freedom for Christians to commit to the common good and the good of all persons that is afforded by recognizing that the highest good of the human person is not found in the terrestrial city. Thus, the paradox of the human person as in possession of the dignity worthy of those called to supernatural grace opens up a space of freedom beyond the claims of the state and the duties of political life. The

67. Here I follow Cathleen Kaveny's claims in *Law's Virtues: Fostering Autonomy and Solidarity in American Society* (Washington, D.C.: Georgetown University Press, 2012) that despite the distinction between morality per se and the coercive instruments of law in liberal politics, legislation and judicial enforcement necessarily inculcate certain virtues and a vision of the human good into human societies.

paradox of the human wayfarer as called to a transcendent end beyond this earthly life enables Christians to recognize a positive role for duly appointed political authority without seeing political life or the state as the arbiter of ultimate authority in human life. Francesca Murphy claims, for example, that this "paradoxical conception of the relation of nature to grace may be [de Lubac's] main contribution to political theology."[68] I believe that the validity of Murphy's claim stands, even as I have amended de Lubac's position in favor of a stronger distinction between nature and grace. De Lubac was correct to note that as long as the pilgrim church witnesses publicly to this paradox of human existence the state cannot demand the total allegiance of human souls. But recognizing an appropriate distinction between nature and grace also carves out a space within which Christians can work with others in pursuit of the common good without needing to impose a kind of theological integralism on others, particularly when it is engaged under the conditions of pluralism. Cultivating such a perspective as an aspect of civic virtue within a pilgrim church frees Christians to experience solidarity with the suffering of others and to commit to creating just social institutions and to defending the common good in political life, rather than denouncing those who do not share their metaphysical or theological presuppositions.

In fact, I argue that the temptation toward Christian privilege and epistemological hubris vis-à-vis those outside the church or in civil society is both spiritually problematic for Christians and practically counterproductive in any effort to seek the common good, to evangelize culture, or to witness to the truth of the gospel. A more fruitful approach is found in the practice of affirming natural goods as gifts of God in creation that all persons can appreciate through the exigencies of natural law morality (the first gratuity). Then Christians may engage in a dialogue that highlights those goods while extending and tethering them to the higher order of goods to be found in the supernatural realm (God's second gratuity). Karraker describes the social capital cultivated by the religious sisters that she studied in Bluffton as "embedded in a civil society that has developed and institutionalized traditions and norms around inclusiveness."[69] These inclusive norms, instantiated in part through the theological convictions of the sisters, have helped the city to successfully address the racial tensions that resulted from recent waves of immigration.

68. Francesca A. Murphy, "De Lubac, Grace, Politics and Paradox," *Studies in Christian Ethics* 23 (2010): 415-30, p. 418.

69. Karraker, *Diversity and the Common Good*, p. 109.

Karraker recounts how the sisters began with direct service to the most poor and vulnerable in Bluffton, but eventually saw the need to more effectively concentrate their resources by creating inter-congregational associations (one of which is called SET: Sisters Engaging Together). Members of SET then began to partner with other religious groups (Protestant, Jewish, etc.), civic bodies (nonprofits, philanthropic organizations, advocacy groups, etc.), businesses, and finally local, state, and even national elected and appointed political leaders. These sisters present powerful examples of how witnessing to moral truth by cultivating relationships of mutual trust can be leveraged toward building up the kind of social capital that leads to measurable, positive social outcomes in economics, public health, altruism, mortality risk, spread of disease, and voting behaviors.[70] What is perhaps surprising is that although not all those civic and business leaders who worked with the sisters on issues such as immigration share the sisters' theological convictions, when interviewed by Karraker almost all of these leaders noted that the strength of these sisters arose from their faith. They commented that the "Sisters see the face of Christ in everyone" and that the "Sisters take on social concerns around the Gospel teachings for the 'least of these' when no one else will do so."[71] This is the kind of natural law moral witness that supports the temporal common good and witnesses to the truth of the gospel in ways that public denunciation simply cannot achieve. It is also a fitting example of the ways in which the middle norms of natural law may be articulated and applied in civil society by engaging distinctively theological convictions and placing them in dialogue with other voices and actors within the body politic.

In this chapter I have attempted to make a modest contribution to the current debate in Catholic moral theology regarding the influence of Henri de Lubac regarding the relationship between nature and grace and its significance for Catholic social and political thought. I have claimed that a Thomistic construal of natural law requires maintaining a stronger distinction between nature and grace than de Lubac's collapsing of this distinction tends to allow. Doing so provides a theoretical foundation for appreciating the necessity of creating and maintaining public spaces within which Christians

---

70. For Karraker's citations of studies on the social impacts of these kind of social capital networks, see *Diversity and the Common Good*, p. 105.

71. Karraker, *Diversity and the Common Good*, p. 100. Karraker also notes that these sisters were persistently willing to witness in less popular ways, as many civic leaders reported being annoyed by the sisters' stance against abortion, even while they respected the sisters for their advocacy work on immigrant rights, environmental issues, and world peace (p. 101).

can engage in dialogue with others while still drawing on our fundamental theological principles and beliefs in witnessing to the pursuit of moral truth in human history. This approach to natural law demands that we find a middle ground between any form of semi-Jansenism that would denigrate the natural inclinations and capacities of human reason outside the church, and any kind of semi-Pelagianism that would expect ultimate solutions to the intransigent issues that confront the human community in the pursuit of justice in political life. I take up the details of this kind of public rhetoric and humanistic solidarity again in Chapter 6. In the following chapter I turn to consider this Thomistic account of civic virtue in relation to some key strands of late modern liberal political philosophy.

CHAPTER 5

Civic Virtue and Contemporary Political Philosophy

*Democratic societies progress by democratic means — that is, when
citizens participate fully and fairly in public life, working for the common good.*

Paul Rogat Loeb

Introduction

At the end of the previous chapter I claimed that natural law provides a
theoretical and practical foundation for Christians to engage in constructive
dialogue with others in pluralistic democracies in pursuit of securing the
temporal goods to be obtained by political means. In this chapter I demonstrate how this natural law methodology might function by engaging some
key thinkers within two predominant strands of political philosophy operative in modern democratic societies — liberalism and classical republicanism
— in relation to a Thomistic account of civic virtue. Each of these traditions
has a distinctive manner of construing the relationship between individual
autonomy and the common good that frames the cultural context within
which I continue to develop a theological account of civic virtue. As such
they provide important touchstones for appreciating how this Thomistic
account of civic virtue functions in dialogue with other traditions of political
thought, even as the Christian tradition offers its own distinctive insights
into the nature of politics and the practices of civic virtue.

Of course, liberalism and philosophies that could be defined as liberal
fill quite a large tent. When I use the term "liberalism" here I am referring
to any political philosophies that are built around the value of individual

freedom as the preeminent political virtue or goal of political life. Joseph Raz, for example, defines liberalism as "a doctrine about political morality which revolves round the importance of personal liberty."[1] This definition of liberalism upholds the primacy of individual liberty as foundational for justice and is also roughly congruent with what Judith Shklar has labeled "fear liberalism." Fear liberalism holds that "cruelty is an absolute evil, an offense against God or humanity. It is out of that tradition that the political liberalism of fear arose and continues amid the terror of our time to have relevance."[2] In Shklar's words, "liberalism has only one overriding aim: to secure the political conditions that are necessary for the exercise of personal freedom."[3] Liberalism, then, applies to any political philosophy that seeks to uphold freedom, human rights, and the value of individual autonomy as a means of curbing the human tendency to utilize political institutions and their powers to dominate others or exclude certain groups from the shared benefits of a common political life.

In this chapter I focus on the work of two key theorists in contemporary liberal thought — John Rawls and William Galston. Since the publication of *A Theory of Justice* in 1971, Rawls's work in political philosophy has had a tremendous influence on the debates about justice in the Anglo-Saxon world. According to the Christian ethicist Robin Lovin, Rawls "changed the terms of the discussion" on justice, and his work continues to have an influence on the discourse of Western political thought.[4] Rawls draws on broadly Kantian and contractarian principles to defend a conception of right from which the foundational principles of justice can be derived. Ideally, for Rawls, all members of society could be reasonably expected to agree with such principles.

Rawls focuses first on describing a set of conditions from which such universal principles can be rationally derived, and then on the institutions and procedures that will sustain these principles. He begins *A Theory of Justice* with the claim that "justice is the first virtue of social institutions."[5] And yet, even as Rawls focuses on the objective elements of justice (standards

---

1. Joseph Raz, *The Morality of Freedom* (Oxford: Clarendon, 1986), p. 17.

2. Judith Shklar, "The Liberalism of Fear," in *Liberalism and the Moral Life,* ed. Nancy L. Rosenblum (Cambridge, Mass.: Harvard University Press, 1989), pp. 21-38, p. 21.

3. Shklar, "The Liberalism of Fear," p. 23.

4. Robin W. Lovin, *Christian Realism and the New Realities* (Cambridge: Cambridge University Press, 2008), p. 118.

5. John Rawls, *A Theory of Justice* (Cambridge, Mass.: Belknap Press of Harvard University Press, 1971), p. 3.

of fairness, institutions, laws, etc.) he also devotes a significant portion of the latter part of this same work to developing a theory of what he calls "a sense of justice." This sense of justice describes the kinds of sentiments, dispositions, attitudes, and habits the citizens of a well-ordered society must cultivate if such a society is to be capable of sustaining itself. I look at how Rawls's analysis of the necessity of "a sense of justice" contributes to considerations of the kind of civic virtue that modern, constitutional democracies demand of their citizens. In doing so, I claim that liberal political theories are more dependent on a sense of justice, or civic virtue, than is typically recognized even by Rawls himself and other liberal theorists. If this is true, it also entails a correlative claim that some vision of the good ultimately must undergird even liberal notions of right in ways that thinkers such as Rawls are reluctant to allow.

Rawls's ongoing dialogue with communitarian philosophers such as Michael Sandel led him to continue to refine his understanding of the nature of justice. For example, in *A Theory of Justice* Rawls distinguishes between thick and thin theories of the good, and claims that his approach is a thin theory capable of rational agreement by all members of a particular political community in the absence of broad agreement on thicker notions of the good — what might be called first principles in natural law tradition. A thin theory of the good lays out the minimum agreements of procedural justice on which the members of a political community must agree to sustain the political institutions that protect our basic commitments to liberty. In his later work, however, particularly with the publication of *Political Liberalism* (1993), Rawls came to recognize his theory of justice as a thick, comprehensive theory of the good, embedded in a particular history and social context of Western, constitutional democratic thought and practice, especially in America. To demonstrate how individuals in a pluralistic society who hold a wide array of thick, comprehensive theories of the good might find agreement on the basic principles of justice, he develops the notion of an "overlapping consensus." An overlapping consensus emerges when individuals and groups within a society find common agreement on principles of justice despite holding distinct, and often incompatible, thick doctrines of the good. Despite some of my disagreements with Rawls's priority of the right over the good, his notion of an overlapping consensus is precisely the kind of common ground that may provide the starting point for Christians in a pilgrim church to engage in public dialogue about the nature of the good to be pursued in pluralistic, democratic politics. Toward the end of this section I conclude by challenging Rawls's defense of the priority of the right over the good. I claim both that the priority of the good over the right is more philosophically coherent, and that Rawls's later work itself seems to suggest that principles of right or justice are better understood as deriving from a conception of the good.

After considering the influence of Rawls on contemporary discussions of justice and civic virtue, I turn to the work of William Galston. Galston has made significant contributions to the effort to make the goods and purposes of liberal democracies explicitly known and articulated so that they can be most efficiently pursued in late modern political life. A more stable and descriptively accurate conception of justice than the Rawlsian-contractarian view can be derived from placing these goods, and the means of achieving them, at the center of democratic deliberation. These underlying sets of culturally embedded assumptions about what constitutes the good are frequently implicit in liberal political thought, but are not as commonly recognized in an explicit manner. One of the benefits of Galston's work is that he clearly recognizes and names these goods. His work helps to provide a language for speaking about the goods within liberal societies that engages the deeply and passionately held convictions about the nature of the public goods that animate civic virtue. Galston's theory of the goods to be pursued by the liberal state and his emphasis on "value pluralism" lend further weight to the claim that principles of justice or right are best derived from a coherent conception of the good.[6]

I conclude by noting that liberal thought on the whole evinces a consistent aversion to speaking about the common good. For example, neither Rawls nor Galston employs the language of the common good in developing their accounts of the goods of liberal politics. However, a thick notion of the common good is central to a Thomistic account of civic virtue. It is precisely the articulation and rational defense of this conception of the common good, combined with a lived commitment to it, that a pilgrim church can offer to the discussion of politics among all persons with whom Christians journey in solidarity through this earthly existence. A theological account of civic virtue can make use of Rawls's overlapping consensus and Galston's articulation of the goods of liberalism, while continuing to insist that a cognitive conception of the common good and the will to defend it are essential for

---

6. William Galston, *Liberal Pluralism: The Implications of Value Pluralism for Political Theory and Practice* (Cambridge: Cambridge University Press, 2002). He explains the basic foundations of the concept of value pluralism, which he draws from the political philosopher Isaiah Berlin (pp. 3-11), and then defends the concept throughout the entire book.

cultivating the kind of civic virtue that will best support the goods pursued within liberal, democratic societies.

In the second section of this chapter I place my account of civic virtue in dialogue with classical republican thought. Classical republicanism has also informed the development of liberal, democratic thought in ways that are not always appreciated in popular and scholarly debates regarding the tension between communal flourishing and individual autonomy. As the title of his recent book *(Our Divided Political Heart)* suggests, the Catholic journalist and political commentator E. J. Dionne notes that American civic identity has been informed by two competing traditions that need to be kept in balance. These two traditions emphasize on the one hand "freedom and a healthy brand of individualism," and "a strong sense of community" on the other.[7] Liberalism tends to stress freedom and individualism, while civic republicanism tends to uphold a stronger sense of commitment to the common good. Both have deep roots in Western political thought. Additionally, Emile Perreau-Sassine notes a logical congruence between Catholic political thought and classical republicanism. He writes that one of the marks of the modern Catholic dialogue with political philosophy is "the reconciliation of classical republicanism with Catholicism in the name of civic and moral virtue."[8] This should come as no surprise since classical republicanism draws on some of the same political thinkers of Roman classical antiquity as Aquinas did, especially Cicero. Highlighting the ways in which republican thought remains (implicitly) operative in the political ideals of liberal democratic societies will therefore further underscore some of the ways in which a Thomistic account of civic virtue can build on these already existing affinities between classical and late modern political ideals.

While various political philosophers have done much to advance historical research on classical republicanism, Philip Pettit has promoted republicanism as a living tradition by incorporating its insights into a constructive account for the late modern period. He highlights the way in which classical defenses of freedom were based on a theory of "freedom as non-domination" as the most solid foundation for the legitimacy of political authority.[9] In de-

---

7. E. J. Dionne Jr., *Our Divided Political Heart: The Battle for the American Idea in an Age of Discontent* (New York: Bloomsbury, 2012), p. 17.

8. Emile Perreau-Saussine, *Catholicism and Democracy: An Essay in the History of Political Thought,* trans. Richard Rex (Princeton, N.J.: Princeton University Press, 2012), p. 141.

9. The main lines of Pettit's constructive account of freedom as non-domination are taken up in *Republicanism: A Theory of Freedom and Government* (Oxford: Clarendon, 1997), which I consider in more detail below.

fending this notion of freedom, he pushes liberal societies to move beyond an overly narrow emphasis on negative rights (considered as spheres of freedom from the influence of others) and to articulate more clearly how freedom from coercion and domination requires more positive commitments to the common good from all members of civil society. This insight requires him to defend a more robust account of the place of the common good and civic virtue than most liberal theories. His work fosters a greater appreciation for how liberal ideals of freedom and autonomy are supported by these more ancient or classical traditions' manner of construing the relationship between the civic virtue of the members of the body politic and the common good. Engaging his work lends greater weight to my claim that late modern democratic societies depend on the cultivation of a robust notion of civic virtue among its citizens, and further underscores the claim that Christians need not partition their lives between public and private virtue in the way that many of the standard accounts of liberalism tend to foster.

Rawls and Galston on the Goods of Liberalism

In *A Theory of Justice* Rawls sets out to derive two fundamental principles of justice that function as a heuristic device to guide the institutions, laws, and practices of a just liberal society. The challenge for Rawls — and for all liberal theory — is to derive these principles in a manner that is rationally defensible to all persons in the absence of shared conceptions of human nature or the good. To accomplish this task he draws on a broadly Kantian epistemology and contractarian thought to create a non-metaphysical foundation for his two principles of justice. He avoids the question of metaphysics by postulating a hypothetical thought experiment from which these principles could be derived. In this hypothetical situation mutually disinterested individuals are placed in what he calls the "original position," who are located behind a "veil of ignorance." In this non-historical, purely hypothetical context, each individual has no information about what his social location will be, but must come to an agreement with other potential members of this society in regard to how the basic principles of justice or fairness should be organized. Thus does Rawls skirt the question of the metaphysical and anthropological foundations of the nature of justice.

Since these actors behind the veil of ignorance do not know what their position will be in society it is assumed that, if they are rational, they would choose a situation in which equality of opportunity would be available to all. In this context, "they must protect their liberties, widen opportunities, and enlarge their means for promoting their aims *whatever these are.*"[10] Notice that no clear ends are supplied to these agents but they are free to pursue "whatever these are." These individuals are to freely choose their ends and then arrive at what Rawls calls a "reflective equilibrium," in which they agree on the basic principles of justice, prior to having any knowledge about what their aims or goals might be once they are placed in an actual, historical context.[11]

Since individuals behind the veil of ignorance do not know what goods they are to pursue, and they are to be free to pursue whatever goods they may choose, Rawls defends his theory as upholding the priority of the right over the good.[12] That is, the principles of justice cannot be derived from a theory of the good life for human persons since there is not only an endless plurality of definitions of the ultimate human good to choose from, but also the choice of such a good for Rawls is to be left to individual choice. Instead, the principles of justice must be grounded in what is right or fair for all members of society, regardless of the goods or ends that they choose to pursue. The epistemology of Rawls's approach remains Kantian insofar as practical reason functions in precision from any metaphysical commitments or considerations of human nature or anthropology. Likewise, his account remains a contract theory insofar as its legitimacy rests on the hypothetical agreement that these principles represent the fairest arrangement for any and all potential members of a political community who consent to live under these procedural norms.

In the hypothetical context of the original position, Rawls proposes two basic principles of justice that would be chosen by rational agents working together toward a reflective equilibrium behind the veil of ignorance. These are as follows:

First: each person is to have an equal right to the most extensive basic liberties compatible with a similar liberty for others.

Second: social and economic inequalities are to be arranged so that they are both (a) reasonably expected to be to everyone's advantage, and (b) attached to positions and offices open to all.[13]

10. Rawls, *A Theory of Justice,* p. 143, italics added.
11. Rawls does not suggest that this kind of deliberation has ever actually taken place, but rather that it provides a heuristic and epistemological function by providing a non-metaphysical, theoretical foundation for the validity and reasonableness of the principles of justice that follow. In *Political Liberalism* (New York: Columbia University Press, 1993), he refers to the original position as "a device of representation" (p. 24).
12. Rawls, *A Theory of Justice,* p. 31.
13. Rawls, *A Theory of Justice,* p. 60.

The first principle ensures the basic protection of individual rights such as political liberty, liberty of conscience, personal freedom, private property, freedom from arbitrary arrest and seizure under terms defined by law, and the like.[14] The second principle helps to ensure the democratic principle of fairness and equality of opportunity. The first part of the second principle (2a) is what Rawls also calls the "difference principle," which states that "the higher expectations of those better situated are just if and only if they work as part of a scheme which improves the expectations of the least advantaged members of society."[15] The difference principle indicates that despite the inequalities in wealth, privilege, and power that tend to accrue over time, his theory of justice is designed to create the conditions under which these inequalities would be to the benefit not only of the privileged but also of the least advantaged members of society. The two principles of justice, and especially the difference principle, offer a heuristic principle for judging the justice of certain institutional arrangements in the absence of shared metaphysical or transcendent notions of the good. At the same time it provides a set of parameters within which the procedural elements of justice must function.

Thus, *A Theory of Justice* is sometimes interpreted as if it focuses exclusively on the procedural elements of justice, and support for this claim may be found in the fact that the actors in the original position are described as acting out of mutual disinterest and in accord with strict conceptions of what is considered reasonable and fair. Rawls's theory of justice would provide the grounds for fairness in a modern democracy if "there is an independent standard for deciding which [distributive] outcome is just and a procedure guaranteed to lead to it."[16] This does not indicate, however, that Rawls adheres to a strictly procedural or social constructed conception of justice such as one might find in legal positivism. As a philosophy of law, legal positivism claims that law is not tethered to any independent principles of the good or justice, but rather that law is purely posited as the social construction of a particular society. In contrast to legal positivism Rawls claims only that the two principles of justice are a heuristic device that provides some of the motivating force behind the structures, laws, and institutions that uphold fairness and equality of opportunity in the modern state.

Rawls has been criticized by communitarians for holding a more for-

14. Rawls, *A Theory of Justice*, p. 61.
15. Rawls, *A Theory of Justice*, p. 75.
16. Rawls, *A Theory of Justice*, p. 85.

mal or abstract form of justice that does not take seriously the embodied, historical existence within which actual persons must make choices.[17] Even as the original position functions as a "device of representation,"[18] it does tend to assume that practical reason can function (even if only in theory) in precision from the histories and sociopolitical contexts in which political philosophies emerge and are refined through trial and error over time and through ongoing practices. Although many of these criticisms are accurate, Rawls is not entirely unaware, however, of the need to account for the ways in which moral agents live and act within just societies in concrete, historical circumstances. He addresses these concerns in at least two different places in his work. The first is in part III of *A Theory of Justice,* where he outlines his account of the good that emerges from his two principles of justice, and of the sense of justice required of citizens in a well-ordered society. The second is in *Political Liberalism,* where he pays closer attention to the manner in which individuals tend to draw on what he calls "comprehensive philosophical and moral doctrines"[19] of the good in their own political deliberations. These examples demonstrate Rawls's insights into the nature of the kind of moral agents that are necessary to sustain a well-ordered society.

While the original position provides a theoretical foundation for deriving the two principles of justice, Rawls also notes that to provide a complete theory of justice as fairness he must take account of the kind of sentiments and dispositions that are required of citizens to maintain a well-ordered society over time.[20] In providing such an account, he proposes three phases of moral development that a person would normally move through in coming to provide intellectual assent to the principles of justice. The first is what he calls the morality of authority, in which children come to reciprocate the love they receive from their family by obeying their commands. The second phase is called the morality of association, in which the person accepts "the moral standards appropriate to the individual's role in the various associations to which he belongs," and in which the basic "cooperative virtues"

17. Much of Michael Sandel's critique of Rawls's theory of justice focuses on these concerns in *Liberalism and the Limits of Justice* (Cambridge: Cambridge University Press, 1982).

18. Rawls, *Political Liberalism,* p. 24.

19. Rawls, *Political Liberalism,* p. xv.

20. While he does sometimes use the language of the virtues (see *A Theory of Justice,* p. 437), he prefers to use the more Humean language of sentiments, which he defines as "permanent ordered families of governing dispositions, such as the sense of justice and love of mankind (§30), and for lasting attachments to particular individuals or associations that have a central place in a person's life" (p. 479).

are inculcated.[21] In the third and final phase, the individual comes to accept and to act out of the basic principles of justice as if they were the guiding principles of their own individual, moral conduct. He describes this process, culminating in a mature sense of justice, in the following manner:

> once the attitudes of love and trust, and of friendly feelings and mutual confidence, have been generated in accordance with the two preceding psychological laws, then the recognition that we and those for whom we care are the beneficiaries of an established and enduring just institution tends to engender in us the corresponding sense of justice.[22]

It seems, then, that on closer inspection, even though justice for Rawls is the first virtue of social *institutions* he also has a significant account of the sense of justice that must necessarily be inculcated into *persons* to sustain a just, well-ordered society.[23]

One difficulty that emerges from Rawls's theory is found in the tension between his manner of construing the relationship between the more personal sense of justice in part III of *A Theory of Justice* and the more abstract principles of justice in part I. For example, on Rawls's account the agents in the original position are said to be acting from a thin account of the good as mutually disinterested agents. As Susan Moller Okin points out, however, Rawls's sense of justice "recognizes the importance of feelings," and is more dependent on a realization of mutuality, reciprocity, and concern for the perspective of others than is typically accounted for in the more formal elements of part I. Part I of *A Theory of Justice* tends to emphasize the way in which individuals can be expected to make decisions about justice based on disinterested practical reasoning. However, if the sense of justice developed in part III requires agents in the original position to recognize their mutual interdependence, this perspective is in tension with the earlier language of rational choice that undergirds the process of deriving the two principles of justice.[24] Thus, there seems to be a tension between part I and part III of Rawls's *A Theory of Justice*. This tension arises out of Rawls's insistence on

---

21. Rawls, *A Theory of Justice,* p. 472.

22. Rawls, *A Theory of Justice,* pp. 473-74.

23. Indeed, he writes that "a correct theory of politics in a just institutional regime presupposes a theory of justice which explains how moral sentiments influence the conduct of public affairs" (*A Theory of Justice,* p. 493).

24. Susan Moller Okin, *Justice, Gender, and the Family* (New York: Basic, 1989), pp. 98-101.

the priority of the right over the good. Ultimately, this tension between the recognition of mutual affection and the procedural elements of justice may be more adequately addressed if the shared conceptions of the good are recognized as foundational and the principles of justice are derived from it. More specifically, such a conception of the good is best articulated through an appreciation of the common good as the purpose toward which the principles of justice are directed. This requires rethinking Rawls's repeated assertion of the priority of the right over the good.

To be fair, Rawls does not contend that his theory of justice as fairness is the only or the best theory that could conceivably be identified, but he does insist that it provides a better account of the striving for justice than that provided by his primary interlocutor — that is, by utilitarian theory. Thus, Rawls repeatedly appeals to the superiority of contract theory, which upholds the priority of the right, in comparison with utilitarian theory, which derives its sense of justice from a theory of the good that is grounded in seeking pleasure and avoiding pain.[25] Rawls therefore identifies the superiority of his Kantian contract theory over against the relative weaknesses of the utilitarian theory. On this point I agree with Rawls. The problem, however, is that Rawls never seriously entertains the possibility of other "teleological" approaches that derive a theory of justice from a conception of the good such as that provided by pre-modern classical or medieval thinkers. In pre-modern theories of the good and of virtue (which to my knowledge Rawls never directly engages), it is not necessary to assume that those who reasonably arrive at principles of justice for a well-ordered society must begin from such an ahistorical position of mutual self-interest.

Before moving on from Rawls, however, it will be important to consider the rather different manner in which he construes the role of the good in relation to right in his later work, especially in *Political Liberalism*. The most

---

25. This contrast is made throughout *A Theory of Justice*, but a very clear comparison is made between these two approaches to justice when he writes that "the contrast between a teleological theory and the contract doctrine may be expressed in the following intuitive way: the former defines the good locally, for example, as a more or less homogeneous quality or attribute of experience, and regards it as an extensive magnitude which is to be maximized over some totality; whereas the latter moves in the opposite fashion by identifying a sequence of increasingly specific structural forms of right conduct each set within the preceding one, and in this manner working from a general framework for the whole to a sharper and sharper determination of its parts. Hedonistic utilitarianism is the classical instance of the first procedure and illustrates it with compelling simplicity. Justice as fairness exemplifies the second possibility" (p. 566).

important development between *A Theory of Justice* and *Political Liberalism* is the distinction Rawls makes between "comprehensive philosophical and moral doctrines and conceptions limited to the domain of the political."[26] In *A Theory of Justice,* Rawls had articulated a distinction between what he calls "thick" and "thin" conceptions of the good. Rawls came to believe that the theory of justice put forth in *A Theory of Justice* was a comprehensive philosophical doctrine of the right that, although it propounded to be a thin theory of the good, actually upheld a thick theory of the good. One of the problems with *A Theory of Justice* is that as a thick, comprehensive philosophical doctrine, it excluded other views of the good from the conversation, and thus did not leave space for individuals to choose their own comprehensive theory of the good. In the realm of Christian political engagement, the predominant strands of liberalism tended to foster a more aggressive form of political rhetoric as Christians drawing on thick notions of the good felt more and more excluded from the formal-procedural liberalism of Rawls and other liberal theorists.

In rethinking his theory, however, Rawls made several important modifications to his account of justice as fairness. These changes help to further clarify the difficulties encountered in his construal of the relationship between parts I and III of *A Theory of Justice* that were noted above. In *Political Liberalism* Rawls develops the "political conception of the human person,"[27] which recognizes that for individuals to act according to a rational plan of life, they need to adhere to full, thick conceptions of the good in their daily choices and actions. Thus, he could account for the undeniable reality that every individual leads her life based on some comprehensive view of the good. There are no actual human persons who live or make choices behind a veil of ignorance. He proposes that his political conception of the human person, on the other hand, could be developed to account for the ways in which individuals place outlying limits on their conception of the good to engage in political deliberation in a context of pluralism. Within the parameters of right set by his theory of justice as fairness, individuals could conceivably agree on these basic parameters while still being free to pursue their own conception of the good within the bounds set by the principles of justice.

For the purposes of *Political Liberalism* Rawls defines the political conception of the human person primarily in terms of her role as a citizen and

26. Rawls, *Political Liberalism,* p. xv.
27. Rawls, *Political Liberalism,* p. xvii.

as possessing two basic powers: moral powers and the powers of reason. The moral powers include "a capacity for a sense of justice and for a conception of the good," and the powers of reason include "judgment, thought, and inference."[28] Rawls also assumes, however, that every person in society will adhere to a certain comprehensive moral, philosophical, or religious doctrine, which defines the good that she chooses to pursue and which is drawn on to make political and moral decisions.[29] It is precisely these comprehensive commitments that lead individuals to adopt a "rational plan of life" that they use to order and rank the various values and goods that guide moral decision-making.

On the face of it, this seems like a reasonable solution. However, Rawls's position in *Political Liberalism* seems to imply a distinction between the private individual who acts consistently out of a comprehensive theory of the good and the public individual, the "political" person, who limits her conception of the good based on the requirements of the principles of justice. Thus, he allows that individuals can, and almost always do, formulate their political viewpoints and commitments by drawing on their own comprehensive theory of the good. He agrees that they can draw from such doctrines to raise issues of justice for consideration within the public discourse. This is legitimate as long as they are *eventually* willing to defend these ideas using the principles of "public reason"[30] that are *in theory* accessible to all. This is what he describes as *"the proviso."*[31]

Rawls's solution to the problem of the need for persons to draw on comprehensive notions of the good to engage in a rational plan of life therefore tends to bifurcate the human person between the private individual and her engagement in public life. One is free to draw on thick notions of the good in personal life, but drawing on such a notion in public or political life demands a certain additional degree of justification limited by the constraints of public reason. The natural law account of moral reasoning and civic virtue developed in the previous chapter, however, does not depend

28. Rawls, *Political Liberalism*, p. 19.

29. He writes that citizens are "regarded as having at any given time a determinate conception of the good, that is, a conception specified by certain definite final ends, attachments, and loyalties to particular persons and institutions, and interpreted in the light of some comprehensive religious, philosophical, or moral doctrine" (*Political Liberalism*, p. 74).

30. Rawls, *Political Liberalism*, Lecture VI, pp. 212-54.

31. Rawls, "The Idea of Public Reason Revisited," in *The Law of Peoples: With "The Idea of Public Reason Revisited"* (Cambridge, Mass.: Harvard University Press, 1999), p. 152.

on such a bifurcation between the public and private lives of persons. The middle norms or axioms of natural law that are proposed in a context of public deliberation are already drawn from coherent moral principles that are potentially understood by all members of the body politic. This does not mean that these norms are not in need of additional defense, articulation, elaboration, or deliberation, but rather that this kind of public rhetoric does not demand that one lop off the fundamental metaphysical or theological commitments that undergird one's claims. Just political solutions to issues of justice that concern a community may be more easily integrated into public deliberation, and more capable of rational defense, if they remain tethered to the conception of the good from which they derive. This implies that the ultimate validity of public claims about what is right or just must ultimately be grounded in the conception of the good that provides the foundation for political and social solidarity among the members of the body politic. But this is precisely the kind of deliberation that needs to occur to achieve a lasting overlapping consensus as the foundation for a stable political community, and that cannot occur in theories that do not allow conceptions of the good to enter into public deliberation.

It is worth noting in particular that Rawls affirms the Catholic conception of the common good as falling within the parameters of what he considers an acceptable concept for public deliberation in a pluralistic context. He writes that

> political liberalism, then, does not try to fix public reason once and for all in the form of one favored political conception of justice . . . [it] also admits Habermas's discourse conception of legitimacy (sometimes said to be radically democratic rather than liberal), as well as Catholic views of the common good and solidarity *when they are expressed in terms of political values.*[32]

Rawls's understanding of public reason, then, is explicitly intended to be open to comprehensive philosophical or theological doctrines of the good. The difficulty that has emerged on a practical level is that despite his claim that his theory "does not try to fix public reason once and for all in the form of one favored political conception of justice," many Christians (and others) have come to feel that their viewpoints are less and less acceptable as points of public dialogue precisely because the proviso tends to limit the

---

32. Rawls, "The Idea of Public Reason Revisited," p. 142, italics added.

very foundations from which their comprehensive claims must be articulated and defended.

The key question for Rawls's theory is whether or not all voices do indeed have an equal say within the parameters of his description of public reason. For example, Bryan Garsten indicates that the attempt to make individuals argue for their political beliefs on the grounds of a public, universally acceptable mode of discourse such as in Rawls's public reason can lead to what he calls "liberal alienation." In describing this alienation he writes that

> as a number of commentators have noticed, frustration, disaffection and a move toward fanaticism are common responses to liberal efforts to disengage from substantive conflicts over seemingly intractable matters, especially those involving moral or religious issues.[33]

On this point, Garsten's observations help to demonstrate that the attempt to limit the public discussion on the issue of basic goods to the narrow conception of the good that can in theory be agreed on by all reasonable members of society has actually led some persons who hold other viewpoints to feel pushed out of the discourse of public reason. These persons or groups feel excluded precisely because under the conditions of the proviso they perceive that their own viewpoints of the good are ruled out by the constraints of public reason.

In the first chapter I highlighted a distinction between modern liberal institutions that serve to defend human freedom and dignity (what Perreau-Saussine calls "positive laicity") and a more doctrinaire liberalism that imposes a more rigidly secular moral philosophy from notions of individual autonomy on the body politic. Rawls's work demonstrates how this tension remains within the liberal tradition itself, as notions such as public reason can become a means of excluding religious arguments from public debate. Postconciliar Catholic political thought tries to maintain a consistent critique of doctrinaire liberalism while at the same time promoting positive liberalism. The pilgrim church does this precisely because of a fundamental belief that procedures and institutions (that is, principles of right) must be constructed on a solid anthropology that takes seriously the goods to be pursued in public life. Murray echoes this strand of thought when he writes that "no society in history has ever achieved and maintained an identity

---

33. Bryan Garsten, *Saving Persuasion: A Defense of Rhetoric and Judgment* (Cambridge, Mass.: Harvard University Press, 2006), p. 184.

and a vigor in action unless it has had some substance, unless it has been sustained and directed by some body of substantive beliefs."[34] This is what he recognized as the "public consensus," and what Rawls seeks to articulate from the principles of right as an "overlapping consensus." This dialectic of affirmation of positive laicity and critique of doctrinaire liberalism is one of Catholic social thought's core strengths as a comprehensive political philoso- · phy, and it also contributes to many of the ways that Catholic social thought has been misunderstood. A Thomistic account of civic virtue insists that a viable, flexible, and enduring public or overlapping consensus will only emerge from substantive debate and rational agreement on the fundamental goods to be pursued in public life. I turn now to consider the ways in which William Galston helps to name the substantive goods that a just liberal political community requires.

William Galston's work proves to be especially helpful on the issue of the possibility of upholding the priority of the good over the right while still operating in a broadly liberal paradigm and recognizing the need for certain virtues and dispositions to sustain a just society. For example, Galston notes that in his experience of working during the Clinton administration to find consensus among special-interest groups on matters of domestic policy, these groups did not set aside their desired goods to uphold procedural priorities of right or fairness. Rather, each group argued for what it saw as the good(s) that it wanted to promote. Despite the existence of plural conceptions of the good, Galston contends that this did not lead to "deliberative anarchy,"[35] but rather to the conclusion that "there can be right answers, widely recognized as such, even in the absence of general rules for ordering or aggregating diverse goods."[36] Even though he does not use the phrase, Galston seems to be hinting that something like a conception of a common good can emerge even without shared agreement on a comprehensive doctrine of the good among those who deliberate in democratic societies.

To show how this is so, Galston provides an account of the goods, values, and purposes of liberal theory that is in fact a comprehensive doctrine, but one that is still capable of being applied amid the contemporary reality of pluralism. In doing so, he begins to outline what I would call a critical con-

---

34. John Courtney Murray, *We Hold These Truths: Catholic Reflections on the American Proposition* (New York: Sheed & Ward, 1960), p. 84.

35. This is precisely the fear expressed by Alasdair MacIntyre in *After Virtue*, that a lack of consensus about the good or about justice in society will lead politics into being "war carried on by other means" (p. 253).

36. Galston, *Liberal Pluralism*, p. 7.

ception of the common good. In Stephen Macedo's words, Galston's theory of the goods of liberalism is properly "limited but *pervasive.*"[37] It is limited to the political realm, but it is also pervasive enough to be a coherent philosophical doctrine. Galston's approach to value pluralism combined with his insistence that we start from the standpoint of analyzing our shared conceptions of the good makes it considerably easier to engage in public dialogue about the kinds of values and goods that we want to promote within liberal communities dedicated to human freedom and autonomy.

Another advantage of Galston's account of liberal goods is that it allows for a thicker description of the kinds of virtues that are necessary to sustain modern democracies in a manner that is not in tension with the basic principles of justice. Rather, he shows how the kinds of people who make up a political community derive the procedural elements of justice and shape their civic institutions in accord with their image of the good life. Thus, his work highlights the kinds of moral subjects that are fostered within liberal political communities, and evades the tension that arises between parts I and III of Rawl's *A Theory of Justice.* His emphasis on the development of the human person as a necessary correlate to the liberal commitment to equality of opportunity means that there is significantly more room for "self-discipline and sacrifice" than is typically recognized by liberal political thinkers.[38]

Galston insists that these liberal virtues will not entail the same level of perfectionism or sacrifice required of civic republicanism or of Christianity. Nevertheless, they do place demands on citizens, such that some visions of the good will be ruled out and the pursuit of certain goods will be legitimately curtailed through the coercive power of the state or through more subtle social pressures. The securing of justice in society means that certain instantiations of the good will need to be curtailed through the force of law or other forms of social pressure, even while allowing for the widest range of expression and freedom possible. This further underscores my contention that a Thomistic conception of civic virtue can account for the need to develop a certain basic level of virtue in citizens, while also leaving room for the development of more perfectionistic doctrines of virtue such as are found in the Christian tradition or others. It can also help to account for the manner in which upholding the primacy of the good over the right will not necessarily lead to seeing the state as the privileged locus of virtue and identity.

37. Stephen Macedo, "Charting Liberal Virtues," in *Virtue,* ed. John W. Chapman and William A. Galston (New York: New York University Press, 1992), pp. 204-32, p. 212.
38. Macedo, "Charting Liberal Virtues," p. 220.

To introduce the language of the virtues, which in contemporary philosophy is most often cast in Aristotelian language, is to court a certain amount of criticism from liberal thinkers. There is a general tendency to read Aristotle as advocating civil life as *the* privileged locus for the exercise of the excellence (that is, virtue) of the good person, and thus to value a certain kind of perfecting of the human person as the responsibility of the state. The liberal fear, exemplified in Shklar's fear liberalism, is that this desire to foster perfection will lead to totalitarianism, tyranny, paternalism, and arbitrary use of state power and social institutions to enforce a monolithic vision of the good on the body politic. For example, Rawls indicates that political liberalism has no problem with a form of classical republicanism that insists that citizens "must also have to a sufficient degree the 'political virtues' (as I have called them) and be willing to take part in public life."[39] But he takes issue with the tradition that he believes to be rooted in the virtue ethics of Aristotle and that he calls "civic humanism," which insists that "taking part in democratic politics is the privileged locus of the good life."[40]

A similar concern can be found in Charles Larmore's criticism of Aristotle's understanding of justice. He claims that since Aristotle "embraced the much stronger claim that political life is the domain in which the moral virtues are best exercised," then the state's role is to at best foster, and at worst enforce, the good life for its citizens as it sees fit.[41] His reasons for this claim rest on his interpretation of the *Politics* where Aristotle asks "whether the excellence of a good person and a good citizen is the same or not" (III 4 1276b16-17). Larmore interprets Aristotle as if he claimed that the virtue of the good person and the virtue of the citizen are interchangeable. In Chapter 3 I concluded that for both Aristotle and Aquinas there is room for a distinction between the fullness of virtue required of the good person and the virtue required of the citizen. Aristotle himself writes that "it is evident that the good citizen need not of necessity possess the excellence which makes a good person" (*Politics* III 4 1276b34-35). Galston arrives at a similar conclusion and argues that the good person and the good citizen "are nearly always different."[42]

While this could be dismissed as simply an exegetical dispute, the implications for the way in which virtue language can or cannot function within

39. Rawls, *Political Liberalism,* p. 205.
40. Rawls, *Political Liberalism,* p. 206.
41. Charles Larmore, "The Limits of Aristotelian Ethics," in Chapman and Galston, eds., *Virtue,* p. 190.
42. Galston, *Liberal Pluralism,* p. 218.

liberal political thought are quite significant. For this point opens up the possibility that there may be certain political virtues that are required of all citizens, but that these virtues do not represent the pinnacle of human excellence such as would be pursued or demanded in a more extensive religious or philosophical doctrine than liberalism purports to be. In other words, there is room for talk of liberal virtues that represent a sort of minimum requirement for those living in civil society in such a way that there also remains a conceptual space for a fuller vision of virtue and human perfection to function alongside the minimum virtue required of members of a community or society. Thus, even as a Thomistic account of civic virtue recognizes the necessity of the existence of a functioning civil authority or state, it does not demand that political authority is solely responsible for enforcing the totality of the virtues on the citizens. The state and its legal mechanisms will certainly be one facet of a complex set of social institutions that instantiate civic virtue, but it need not — in fact, it cannot — demand the total and uncritical assent of citizens when it comes to instantiating the virtues. The paradox of the human person on pilgrimage defined by one, twofold end, protects against such totalizing demands of allegiance. Civic virtue recognizes that the human power and creativity of civic engagement resides not in the state apparatus, but in the persons and the *ethos* that form part of the conception of the common good that sustains and motivates civil society as a whole and individual acts of civic virtue. In Maritain's words, the state exists to serve the body politic and the good of its members, not the other way around.

Liberalism then, for Galston, represents a vision of political life in common with other free and equal citizens who are called to take responsibility for their own lives in a way that is not necessarily as inherently individualistic as many communitarian critics charge it with being.[43] Once again,

43. Raz has also made a concerted effort to show that liberal values are not individualistic in the sense that they are often criticized for being. This is a theme running throughout *The Morality of Freedom*, where he writes that "if there is one general thread to the argument of this book it is its critique of individualism and its endeavour to argue for a liberal morality on non-individualistic grounds" (p. 18). Some of the specific details of this argument become most clear when he expresses the manner in which personal autonomy and rights require a deeper appreciation of the values, virtues, and goals that are only expressed as "collective goods" (p. 199) that transcend the individualism that is often thought to be the bedrock of liberal political thought. Moreover, as we noted above, Rawls's account of the sense of justice indicates that there is more room for talk of mutual interest and concern for the other in his own liberal theory than he is often credited with recognizing.

Galston's theory seems to hint at something like the common good, even though he never draws on the term. For Galston, the tension between positive and negative notions of liberty or between "virtue and self-interest is a tension within liberalism, not between liberalism and other traditions."[44] Negative notions of liberty simply uphold a realm of non-interference from the state and others, but say nothing about the choices regarding the good that individuals make. Positive liberty, on the other hand, claims that negative freedom is a necessary but insufficient condition for the exercise of true moral freedom. True moral freedom can only be achieved when one commits to a vision of the good as the animating force of one's moral life. Indeed, there is good reason to critique an account of civic virtue founded on self-interest or negative liberty alone from within Catholic tradition. The liberal virtues articulated by Galston or the sense of justice articulated by Rawls function analogously within liberal thought to restrain the tendency toward *pleonexia* — that is, the vice of desiring more than one is due, which Aristotle takes to be the vice most opposed to justice (*Nicomachean Ethics* V 1 1129b). The challenge for those Christians in a pilgrim church who seek to instantiate civic virtue and are formed in liberal societies, then, is to find ways of recognizing the goods that are secured by liberal institutions without capitulating entirely to an ethic that upholds the atomized individual over and against the common good.

By engaging two prominent liberal political theorists, John Rawls and William Galston, liberal thought is seen as dependent on an anthropology that recognizes persons as socially embedded in communities with particular histories that have come to define their shared, thick conceptions of the good. This means that for liberalism to survive as a viable political philosophy in general, and for Christians in particular to continue to support it, it must recognize its own debt to these kinds of concrete commitments on which the modern structures and laws that have promoted freedom exist. Rawls's sense of justice is a necessary element of his theory of justice as fairness that is often overlooked, and it demonstrates the need for citizens to develop certain virtues, attitudes, dispositions, or sentiments to sustain a well-ordered society. Moreover, Galston's account of liberal goods and virtues, and Raz's construal of collective goods, demonstrates that there are other ways of construing the relationship between the good and the right in liberal thought than the one provided by Rawls's contractarian theory. Despite the collective aversion among liberal theorists to discuss the common

44. Galston, *Liberal Pluralism*, p. 217.

good, it seems that liberalism itself struggles to articulate what exactly the role of shared conceptions of the good is in modern democratic political institutions, and that it demands a more coherent articulation of what these goods are. By engaging in the dialogue within the sphere created by what Rawls calls an overlapping consensus and what Murray refers to as a public consensus, the Thomistic account of civic virtue articulated here provides some of the intellectual tools necessary to help clarify what those common goods are, even amid significant disagreement and pluralism. A strong ally in this dialogical task can be found among those who continue to defend a constructive account of classical republican thought.

Virtue, Freedom, and the Good in Classical Republicanism

As noted above, Philip Pettit has developed the historical insights of classical republicanism to create a modern, constructive account of republican political thought. He notes that many of the essential commitments of this tradition have functioned to create and sustain the institutions and practices that have been forged to uphold modern, liberal politics. Liberal political thinkers have often overlooked these republican influences. Thus, Pettit is interested in furthering the aims and goals of liberal freedom, and therefore sees himself working as a classical republican thinker in congruence with the modern liberal tradition's emphasis on freedom. But he wants to do so by drawing attention to the implications of some of the neglected elements in liberalism that were formed by traditions of political thought with more ancient roots and more substantive notions of community and virtue than liberal thinkers typically recognize. Pettit is particularly critical of those liberal ideologies that follow Isaiah Berlin's influential thesis by placing a sole emphasis on negative rights — that is, rights merely as spheres of freedom from external influence.[45] For him, such rights are formal abstractions in the absence of a civic community in which they can be justiciable. Because of this awareness, his account has a much more robust appreciation of the

---

45. Berlin develops these notions of liberty and strongly endorses negative liberty as the only legitimate foundation for liberalism in *Two Concepts of Liberty* (Oxford: Clarendon, 1958), pp. 7-15. Pettit's thinking on this topic seems to have developed, as he, following Quentin Skinner, initially endorsed republican freedom as a form of negative freedom (see Eric MacGilvray, *The Invention of Market Freedom* [New York: Cambridge University Press, 2011], pp. 187-88). In *Republicanism* Pettit now considers republican freedom to be "a third concept of liberty" in distinction from mere positive or negative conceptions of liberty (p. 18).

common good and the manner in which a certain conception of virtue is necessary to sustain liberal commitments to the value of freedom.

Pettit's republicanism shares with liberalism an overriding concern with the centrality of individual freedom as the defining characteristic of modern political institutions in the West. However, he adds an important clause to the political notion of freedom by basing his theory of government on the conception of "freedom as non-domination."[46] Domination is defined as "having your choices blocked or inhibited by others"[47] in an arbitrary manner, and it is significant for Pettit that one can be considered to possess freedom in a negative sense, while still not being free of arbitrary forms of coercion from other persons, groups, and/or social forces such as the market. That is, one could be formally free in the sense of not being coerced directly by the force of law into a particular set of choices, but still be constrained by those with other forms of cultural power. For example, a person may be free under the law to apply for a permit to build a home for his family, but if he is forced to pander to the whims of a locally elected city official — say through a bribe or by needing to please him by returning a favor — then although he is formally free, he is not free of arbitrary interference by political officials. Pettit stresses that even if the terms of a relationship are consensual or contractual (these are the basic requirements of fairness for those who defend market freedom), arbitrary forms of coercive power can still be present. The recent debates over predatory lending in the mortgage and credit card industry are particularly poignant examples of such forms of arbitrary power despite the presence of a consensual, contractual agreement between borrower and lender. To determine the justice or fairness — and ultimately the legality — of such exchanges, more sophisticated conceptions of virtue and the common good are a necessary counterbalance to moral judgments based on the impersonal forces of a free market exchange.

To make his case for the superiority of a republican theory of freedom as non-domination versus a formal, negative freedom, Pettit claims that what is needed is another way of conceptualizing freedom that predates the two options laid out by Isaiah Berlin in his widely influential essay "Two Concepts of Liberty" (1958). Berlin's two concepts are what he calls negative and positive freedom. The negative conception is, in a basic sense, "the area within which a man can do what he wants,"[48] whereas positive liberty derives

46. Pettit, *Republicanism*, p. 4.
47. Pettit, *Republicanism*, p. 83.
48. Berlin, *Two Concepts of Liberty*, p. 7.

from the capacity to be the master of one's actions and destiny.[49] Ultimately, Berlin claims that basing a political philosophy of government on a positive notion of freedom is likely to lead to tyranny, as particular notions of perfectionistic self-development become enforced by the external apparatus of the state and of the legal system. This fear of an enforced vision of the good by the state is an abiding concern of all liberal theorists. In his analysis of rights, Wesley Hohfeld calls this negative sphere of freedom either a "privilege" or an "immunity," as opposed to the kinds of "claim rights" that would place more responsibility on others to fulfill an obligation toward one with such a right.[50] Thus, Berlin and most liberal political theorists argue that the best way to prevent abuses of power by the state is to focus exclusively on securing a space for the negative freedom of individuals.

Eric MacGilvray claims that the initial defenders of market freedom from the seventeenth to the twentieth centuries — such as Francois Quesnay, Adam Smith, David Hume, Ludwig von Mises, Friedrich Hayek, and Milton Friedman — blended classical republican notions of freedom with liberal (that is, negative) conceptions of freedom to create a "qualitatively different conception of freedom that took economic rather than political life as its model."[51] Although I have neither the competence nor the intention of dealing directly with economics in this work, it is worth noting that economic and liberal conceptions of freedom have significantly shifted the social and political purposes and meanings of freedom and civic virtue. Classical republican thought claims that citizens may only be free when there is a creative tension between the civic virtue of the members of the body politic and the social institutions that defend their freedom. In particular, republicanism demands that the members of the body politic exercise their civic virtue in such a way that they exert enough collective control over the mechanisms of

49. Berlin, *Two Concepts of Liberty*, pp. 16-19.

50. Wesley Hohfeld, *Fundamental Legal Concepts as Applied in Judicial Reasoning: And Other Legal Essays*, ed. Walter Wheeler Cook (New Haven, Conn.: Yale University Press, 1923), pp. 36-38, 60-63. As Hohfeld notes, the term "immunity" "is far more likely to be used in the sense of physical or personal freedom (i.e. absence of physical restraint), as distinguished from a legal relation" as indicated by the technical sense of a claim right (p. 49). Elsewhere he states the relationship between positive, claim rights and negative immunities and privileges in the following manner: "A right is one's affirmative claim against another, and a privilege is one's right or freedom from the claim of another. Similarly, a power is one's affirmative control over a given legal relation as against another; whereas an immunity is one's freedom from the legal power or 'control' of another as regards some legal relation" (p. 60).

51. MacGilvray, *The Invention of Market Freedom*, p. 119.

politics and the state so that the needs of the entire commonwealth, rather than the narrow interests of particular persons or groups, are being served. Such are the conditions for freedom in classical republican thought, and Pettit's notion of freedom as non-domination is congruent with this notion. The cultural shift toward liberalism's emphasis on negative rights combined with neoclassical economic preferences for allowing the forces of the market (rather than the state) to determine social outcomes significantly shifts how we talk about freedom. But also, and more important, it shifts how we understand the social function of civic virtue.

In the liberal-neoclassical-economic synthesis that defines much public rhetoric in late modern democratic discourse the state and its laws exist primarily to ensure the free functioning of the autonomous, decentralized, and anonymous forces of the market. In fact, the state becomes the single largest threat to freedom. On the other hand, the function of civic virtue is to pursue (economic) self-interest without any direct intention of maximizing the social benefits of one's actions in pursuit of the common good. The free market ensures a just outcome and absolves the citizen of moral or political responsibility for any unjust social outcomes. At the end of the day these outcomes are nobody's fault and are "natural" consequences of the laws of free market behavior. MacGilvray writes that despite the many claims that free markets are the last bastions of human freedom in the face of tyrannical political regimes, "the contrast between republican and market freedom presents us, in other words, with a choice between *responsibility* and *irresponsibility* as models of human freedom."[52] Friedrich Hayek claims, for example, that we should — indeed, we must — prefer the neoclassical economic conception of freedom, not because it is any less arbitrary or unpredictable than tyrannical political regimes, but simply because we "feel" freer in a market society.[53] The alternative vision of freedom presented within a Thomistic account of civic virtue must articulate a notion of freedom that is not bound by impersonal, mechanistic, and deterministic forces such as the market and/ or the absolute authority of political regimes — whether despotic or just. A theological conception of civic virtue frees us from seeing the exercise of free and authentic human action as bound by any form of mechanistic laws, whether these are scientific or economic laws. As the free, rational, created, social creatures that God created us to be we have more choices about how

---

52. MacGilvray, *The Invention of Market Freedom*, p. 197.

53. Friedrich Hayek, *The Road to Serfdom* (Chicago: University of Chicago Press, 1944), p. 224. Cited in MacGilvray, *The Invention of Market Freedom*, p. 173.

to organize our political lives together than the defenders of the laws of free markets would have us believe. A Christian anthropology that understands human persons as free in a sense that transcends the deterministic, material world provides essential correctives to the deterministic models that dominate secular political discourse.

If the anonymous forces of the market are truly as arbitrary, mechanistic, and deterministic as even the most radical defenders of market freedom claim them to be, then it seems that the one thing the defenders of market freedom have in common with their much-maligned Marxist and socialist counterparts is the belief that history is driven by impersonal, materialistic market forces and that human freedom is radically limited by these historical forces. If MacGilvray's analysis of the ways in which free market systems provide the illusion, but not the fact, of greater freedom is correct, then the current cultural pervasiveness of market language of freedom is potentially even more corrosive to freedom and civic virtue than the communist or socialist threats of the twentieth century. It is also much more difficult to notice, to name, and to provide a viable alternative that respects humanity's deeper spiritual freedom. To the extent that the state and its laws (perhaps inadvertently) give preference to market notions of negative freedom and virtue, it tends toward the kinds of negative laicity or doctrinaire liberalism that is rejected in Catholic political philosophy. Given Catholic social thought's explicit and repeated condemnations of Marxism, in large part because its historical dialectical materialism is both implicitly and explicitly atheistic, it is hard to imagine how neoclassical economics, even when defended by theological notions such as those neoconservative thinkers I identified in Chapter 1, is any less materialist or atheistic. A Thomistic and theological construal of civic virtue has much in common with classical republicanism's understanding of the value and purpose of human freedom.

There are two consequences of adopting this negative market sense of freedom that are in tension with an account of civic virtue, either in the Thomistic sense or as articulated in republicanism. One consequence is that it tends to understand the use of classical language in regard to virtue as a threat to individual freedom. The second consequence is that it tends to overlook the space of civil society as a locus of civic virtue by pitting individuals and their self-interest against the state. In other words, it reinforces the image of the person as an asocial monad in possession of negative rights whose civic role is reduced on the one hand to commercial activity and to a relationship between one's self and the state on the other. The latter, moreover, is always experienced as a threat to one's negative freedom. The first concern partially explains why there is such an allergic reaction on the part of many liberal thinkers to virtue language that is too strongly perfectionistic or elitist.

Pettit is also concerned with the "tyranny of the democratic elite."[54] The advantage of his approach is that he presents a way of defending more classical notions of freedom and virtue that do not reduce rights to negative spheres of freedom or individuals to lone consumers and/or agents in relation to the state. His approach recognizes the inherent goodness of rights and autonomy in contemporary political life, while placing the individual in a proper social context in which freedom can be recognized and defended. In other words, his theory upholds the importance of civic virtue in such a way that it is applicable in the conditions of democratic forms of government. He upholds a strong role for a republican form of civic virtue without enforcing a monolithic view of the good on society. His theory of freedom as non-domination is compatible with the liberal notion that the state cannot and should not enforce a fully comprehensive view of the good on its citizenry, but it is also dependent on robust conceptions of civic engagement and virtue that take place in a social context of which the state itself is only the topmost authority charged with coordinating the actions of all members and groups of the body politic in the direction of the common good through the mechanisms of law and its enforcement.[55]

In moving from the principle of freedom as non-domination into a theory of government, Pettit must provide some middle axioms for demonstrating how this notion of freedom can be used to support the actual functioning of modern governments. In its most basic elements, Pettit's recommendations resemble that which is standard in most liberal constitutional democracies: he promotes "an empire of laws, rather than men"; dispersal of legal powers in a bicameral congress, executive, and judicial branch; and the idea that the law should be relatively resistant to rapid change through

54. Pettit, *A Theory of Freedom: From the Psychology to the Politics of Agency* (Oxford: Oxford University Press, 2001), p. 162. Pettit is also concerned to demonstrate that his theory can draw on classical sources in such a way that it does not rely on the narrow conceptions of citizenship as the property-owning, male-only class of individuals that it was in ancient Greece or Rome. He also recognizes that this makes modern statecraft much more complex and demanding, but that this is a price we must be willing to pay to uphold the freedoms that we cherish (*Republicanism*, pp. 95-96).

55. Recall here that this is the way in which Jacques Maritain describes the legitimate function of state authority in *Man and the State* (Chicago: University of Chicago Press, 1951), pp. 12-19.

majority will, such as through a constitution or common law arrangement.[56] The philosophical differences between Pettit and those liberals considered above does not lie directly in the constitutional or legal arrangement of the modern state (the basic principles of right or justice), but rather in the way in which a republican notion of freedom as non-domination functions as a heuristic principle to guide acts of civic virtue and public policy, and how this principle supports a greater appreciation for virtue and the common good. Moreover, freedom as non-domination does not presuppose that the principles of justice alone will suffice to bring about just government action and policy. Rather, it looks to the active involvement of the members of body politic to create, sustain, and hold accountable the institutions and the offices of those who are responsible for directing the actions of the state. In other words, it calls on citizens to partake in active forms of civic engagement such as are required of civic virtue, and to engage their most deeply held passions and commitments when doing so.

This means that government power will have a considerably wider scope for classical republicans than for those who adhere more strictly to negative-rights and neoclassical economic-based theory. It also suggests that the instantiation of virtue that this requires is not something that comes top-down from the state, but rather that it is the ground-up cultivation of virtue within members in a civil society that forms, sustains, and holds government accountable. While this republican ideal of freedom is more demanding on the state, it is so precisely because it is more demanding on the members of the body politic. Although this is not its primary function in the earthly city, the pilgrim church is one essential component of civil society that instills such practices of civic virtue and appreciation for the necessity of defending the common good in its members. The need for such institutions increases in direct proportion to the size of the state because as it increases in size and scope the more likely it is to begin to exercise arbitrary power in a way that would contradict the very foundational principles of non-domination that are central to republicanism and civic virtue.

Pettit is fond of repeating the truism that "the price of liberty is eternal vigilance,"[57] as well as the belief that political power by its very nature has a corrupting tendency on those who possess it. He seeks to provide a middle way between "the sparse and heartless sort of government with which rightest liberals pretend to be satisfied," and the "interventionism,

---

56. Pettit, *Republicanism,* p. 173.
57. Pettit, *Republicanism,* p. 6.

majoritarian rule — the potentially tyrannical sort — which populists have to countenance."[58] He is seeking a middle way between a negative-rights only approach that leaves the government too little power to protect the most vulnerable, while trying to avoid the pitfalls of an overly centralized state. The middle axioms of such an approach are instantiated in the civic engagement of the members of the body politic — that is, in their active commitment to civic virtue.

The way to "keep the bastards honest"[59] for Pettit is to claim that the state may only intervene in ways that track the common interests of the members of civil society. Here one can see elements of Cicero's and Augustine's conceptions of the common good as an ongoing communal way of life in pursuit of certain shared values or goods. Thus, freedom as non-domination must be accepted by the majority of the body politic to be a part of the manner in which persons conceive of and act on the common good. Freedom is, of course, primarily an individual good in the sense that subjection to arbitrary coercion by any one person is an affront to modern notions of liberty. This conception is shared by all liberal thinkers. But what other contemporary liberals, especially those whose work is grounded in a theory of negative freedom or liberty rights, have a difficult time articulating is why freedom as non-domination should be seen as a an essential aspect of the *common* good.[60]

Pettit provides at least two reasons that a republican conception of freedom is best understood as an essential component of the common good. The first has to do with the ways in which it will be seen as "a common good from the point of view of each vulnerability class."[61] That is, if freedom as non-domination is a central good and aim of liberal societies, then it will be an affront to the good of all if even one group or individual is subjected to arbitrary coercion. In fact, these groups, or vulnerability classes, will often be the best situated agents to point out the forms of arbitrary power that are being perpetuated against them. Recall how in the previous chapter Bryan Massingale's commitment to justice emerged out of his participation in the black community's exclusion from many of the basic goods of American

---

58. Pettit, *Republicanism,* p. 12.

59. Pettit, *Republicanism,* p. 6.

60. To be even more precise we should note that freedom is always an individual good, but that Pettit helps us to see how sustaining this good as a good for all requires communally shared values and ideals that are embodied in a society's way of life, in its structures, institutions, and laws.

61. Pettit, *Republicanism,* p. 124.

society. Similar to the kind of elitism in Murray that can provide a veneer of reasonableness over unjust conditions, a procedural or formal account of justice may in practice become relatively blind to those who may be excluded from the benefits of the common good. Thus, Pettit's heuristic with regard to the exclusion from the common good of particular vulnerability classes functions analogously to Catholic social thought's and liberation theology's emphasis on the preferential option for the poor and vulnerable.

The second reason that freedom as non-domination is a necessary component of the common good is that one can argue that if the principle is violated for any one group, it makes it that much more likely that an unchecked power of the government or the market could subject other groups, including one's own, to such power. This second consideration implies that a sense of solidarity and mutual interest in defending the common good is a precondition for the principles and institutions that support the full flourishing and autonomy of each person and group in society. This consideration is analogous to Okin's comments regarding the kind of socially embedded agents that Rawls's theory demands. But notice that this directly challenges the neoclassical construal of civic virtue as tethered directly to the pursuit of one's self-interest. Thus, all have a common interest in upholding freedom as non-domination as a part of the shared values that constitute the common good in liberal societies. Even those who are not directly affected by such arbitrary coercion, whose negative rights have in no way been violated, have a stake in upholding freedom as non-domination as a common good for everyone in society. Leaving such concerns to the arbitrary forces of the market is an abdication of the responsibility to civic virtue that is demanded of both justice and charity, as discussed in Chapter 2. One of the goals of a constitutional democracy, then, must be to work toward the conditions in which freedom as non-domination is accepted as a common element of the language in which members of civil society talk about and conceptualize justice. And to accomplish this, it will also be necessary to have a language for recognizing and discussing the common good. As MacGilvray states, an alternative notion of freedom and civic virtue "must show that this republican conception of freedom provides a viable alternative not only to the negative and positive liberty traditions, but to market freedom itself."[62] The Catholic conception of the common good, and its analogues in other traditions such as classical republicanism, is an absolutely central and essential component of such an alternative language. It is the only language I know of

---

62. MacGilvray, *The Invention of Market Freedom*, p. 183.

that is capable of providing a conceptual vision of the flourishing of human persons that is directly tethered to and dependent on social and structural considerations that transcend individual self-interest. Thus, Pettit's classical republican notion of freedom and virtue helps us to see that a critical conception of the common good is an essential element of developing the kind of virtue required of citizens to uphold a just society.

The preceding considerations lead to the heart of why classical republicanism and Catholic political thought overlap in their understanding of the civic virtue demanded of the members of the body politic in democratic states. To maintain a robust sense of justice grounded in a concern for freedom as non-domination, Pettit revives classical notions of virtue and a critical conception of the common good. He is, however, able to revive notions of virtue in ways that maintain the concerns with individual freedom as a necessary but insufficient condition for the exercise of authentic moral and spiritual freedom. He also is able to account for the reality of pluralism, especially in giving special attention to vulnerability groups, and therefore he is able to avoid some of the problems typically associated with the use of virtue language in the liberal tradition. A theological account of civic virtue adds the further distinction between the transcendent common good that is the ultimate good of creation, and the temporal, penultimate common good that serves as the goal of just social institutions and practices. To the extent that Christians can witness to this twofold good in civic engagement and public dialogue possibilities will emerge to find and then work out of that overlapping consensus on which the enduring liberal institutions that uphold the legitimate rights and freedoms of human persons depend.

Thus, Pettit claims that "republican laws must be supported by habits of civic virtue or good citizenship — by habits, as we may say, of civility."[63] When this habit of civility, required of all members of the body politic, is combined with the heuristic device of seeking out and identifying those cases of marginalization in which individuals or groups are subject to arbitrary domination and coercion, we have a much more robust conception of civic virtue and the common good than is usually presented within liberal political thought. My claim, based on the work of Pettit and others who study the tradition of classical republicanism, is that these notions are not alien to liberal political institutions, but have formed our core values in ways that we are not always directly cognizant of. By emphasizing the classical and medieval conceptions of freedom and the common good operative in

---

63. Pettit, *Republicanism*, p. 245.

liberal thought, civic virtue may gain a significant amount of critical power beyond the usual liberal virtues of civility, tolerance, equality, and respect for rights, necessary as these are. Civic virtue demands that citizens go one step further and take a stand for those who are most vulnerable and subjected to arbitrary power precisely because this is a way of protecting the common good and creating sustainable, just political institutions. By drawing on the classical language of goods and virtues that constitutes a significant portion of the Western heritage of political thought, Pettit further helps to illustrate my claim that the right is more securely defended when it is derived from a "limited but *pervasive*"[64] sense of the good shared by the entire body politic.

One of the continuing weaknesses of much liberal political theory that has emerged from the preceding analysis is a difficulty in identifying or recognizing the common good, or any conception of the good that is not reducible to a sum of individual goods or a good identified solely on the basis of individual preference or self-interest. Since civic virtue is identified by its object, which is the common good, it entails a capacity to critically conceptualize the common good in the intellect and to orient one's intentions and desires toward it. Pettit helps to demonstrate that liberal, democratic societies continue to benefit from engaging in more ancient or medieval forms of thinking about political theory that provide robust philosophical accounts of the common good and civic virtue. His distinctive manner of drawing on some of these sources while upholding freedom as non-domination as an element of the common good, and the theory of civic virtue that can be developed out of it, form part of that public consensus within which Christian pilgrims may articulate, defend, and pursue the common good in late modern liberal societies.

By placing a Thomistic, theological account of civic virtue in dialogue with some of the central strands of contemporary liberal political philosophy we are one step closer to understanding how Christian civic virtue practiced by the members of a pilgrim church may engage in authentic witness to the moral good in democratic societies. Despite my criticisms of Rawls's insistence on upholding the priority of the right over the good, it is possible to appreciate his sense of justice and his notion of an overlapping consensus for creating a public space for the practice of civic virtue by all members of the body politic. Galston's articulation of the goods of liberal societies makes even more explicit what seems to be implied in Rawls's theory of justice, which is that even liberal, pluralistic societies require a certain limited but

64. Macedo, "Charting Liberal Virtues," p. 212.

pervasive sense of the good and virtue that are required of the body politic. Finally, Pettit's defense and development of classical republican thought demonstrates how classical notions of virtue and freedom have formed and continue to inform the liberal tradition itself, even when they are not always directly acknowledged. In the following chapter I consider how a Thomistic form of civic virtue may be practiced by the members of a pilgrim church by engaging in public rhetoric as a means of witnessing to the common good within pluralistic, liberal societies.

CHAPTER 6

Toward a Constructive Account of
Civic Virtue and Public Rhetoric

In condemning spiritual tepidity, Jesus was not condemning political moderation.

Emile Perreau-Saussine

Introduction

In 1996 the Barna Group, an evangelical Christian research firm dedicated to studying the intersection between faith and culture, found that among "outsiders," which they defined as "atheists or agnostics, those of a faith other than Christianity, or unchurched individuals with no firm religious convictions," 85 percent held a favorable view of the influence of Christianity on society.[1] About a decade later, public opinion seems to have shifted. By 2007, 38 percent of outsiders held a "bad impression of present-day Christianity,"[2] representing a 22 percent shift toward a negative public perception of Christians by those outside the church. When the Barna Group investigated the reasons that outsiders held a negative view of Christianity, they found that "the three most common perceptions of present-day Christianity are antihomosexual (an image held by 91 percent of young outsiders), judgmental (87 percent), and hypocritical (85 percent)."[3] The changing public perception of Christianity seems to have been exacerbated by the efforts of

1. David Kinnaman and Gabe Lyons, *UnChristian: What a New Generation Really Thinks about Christianity . . . and Why It Matters* (Grand Rapids: Baker, 2007), p. 24.
2. Kinnaman and Lyons, *UnChristian,* p. 24.
3. Kinnaman and Lyons, *UnChristian,* p. 27.

Christians (usually, but not exclusively, associated with the political right) to impose their views on the public through political and legal means. Indeed, their research indicates that these concerns are expressed not only by outsiders, but also by many Christians who are concerned that Christianity has become too politicized.[4]

While Christians are indeed called to be a sign of contradiction to the values of the world (see Luke 2:34 and Acts 28:22), these statistics are alarming. They suggest that it is not the authentic quality of Christian public witness to Christ's uncompromising love that is driving the perceptions of others, but rather Christian engagement with the most vulgar forms of political power and its rhetorical expressions in popular media. If the members of a pilgrim church are going to fulfill their role of witnessing to the beauty of the gospel and the virtues of justice and charity, and if Christian discourse about the common good is to have any significant impact on the culture and institutions of late modern democratic societies, Christians are going to need to find new and creative means of living and dialoguing together with those who do not share their fundamental moral convictions. Christians are also going to need to find more authentic and charitable ways of talking to each other within the church because the lines of the present cultural and political divide cut right down the middle of traditional ecclesial identities. A Thomistic account of civic virtue offers a way for the members of a pilgrim church to witness to the social, moral, and political significance of their theological convictions through natural law reasoning with humility and charity, while also respecting the legitimate plurality of late modern cultures and the relative autonomy and penultimate value of the civil sphere vis-à-vis the ultimate aims of the pilgrim church.

Following the aggressive politicization of the church in the 1980s, the sociologist James Davison Hunter has developed an incisive account of how Western culture has arrived at the current political gridlock that he refers to as the "culture wars." As a committed Christian he has also developed his own suggestions for how Christians might move beyond the culture wars. He draws on his work as a sociologist to claim that the predominant forms of Christian engagement in American politics in the late twentieth and early twenty-first centuries are not only ineffective and

4. The Barna Group studied two groups, which they defined as Mosaics (born between 1984 and 2002) and Busters (born between 1965 and 1983) (Kinnaman and Lyons, *UnChristian*, p. 17). Kinnaman and Lyons write that nearly "two-thirds of Mosaic and Buster outsiders and *nearly half of young born-again Christians* said they perceive 'the political efforts of conservative Christians' to be a problem facing America" (*UnChristian*, p. 155, italics added).

necessarily doomed to failure, but also incongruent with the primary task of the church to witness to the gospel. In virtue language, the most common methods of political engagement used by Christians are both imprudent and uncharitable. This suggests that a rethinking and reimagining of Christian civic virtue, drawing on the Thomistic insights cultivated in the previous chapters, is in order.

For Hunter, culture is more foundational to a community's vision of the good than politics. Politics is only one aspect of a society's shared vision of the good that is embodied in political institutions, written into positive laws, and enforced through legal processes. Culture, on the other hand, is more fundamental. Political institutions and ideals emerge out of a shared symbolic meaning of the culture itself, what Murray calls a public consensus. This suggests that Christians would be well-advised "to decouple the 'public' from the 'political.' Politics is always a crude simplification of public life and the common good is always more than its political expression."[5] If it is true that politics emerges out of some form of a shared conception of the good, then Christian civic virtue best contributes to the common good not by forcing Christian values onto others through legislation, but by witnessing and contributing to a rational public dialogue about the good that informs the culture. Indeed, as I have been claiming throughout this book, the natural law tradition provides rich resources for addressing precisely this need, especially if it is interpreted in ways that that provide room for the members of the body politic to reason together toward the middle axioms of natural law, while eschewing any tendencies toward elitism, paternalism, or epistemic superiority.

Ultimately, culture is about the power to define "a normative order by which we comprehend others, the larger world, and ourselves and through which we individually and collectively order our experience."[6] As the Thomist philosopher Josef Pieper states it, the root of our word for culture is

---

5. James Davison Hunter, *To Change the World: The Irony, Tragedy, and Possibility of Christianity in the Late Modern World* (New York: Oxford University Press, 2010), p. 185. This insight is also captured in Maritain's distinction between the state (the political realm) and the body politic (the public realm of the people), and by Bernard Lonergan's distinction between culture and society. For Longergan culture is a symbolic system of meaning and values, whereas society is constituted by the material ways in which these meanings and values are expressed in institutions and a people's way of life. In Lonergan's words, "culture stands to social order as soul to body" (*A Second Collection,* ed. William F. J. Ryan and Bernard J. Terrell [Philadelphia: Westminster, 1974], p. 102).

6. Hunter, *To Change the World*, p. 32.

cult, and the heart of a *cult* in the classic sense is the offering of sacrifice or worship.[7] In other words, culture is the embodiment of those highest, transcendent ideals for which one is willing to sacrifice — whether it be time, money, effort, or even one's life. This helps to explain why, even amid our secular age, there remains "a touch of the sacred at the heart of civic life."[8] Ultimately, then, the struggle to control these mechanisms of symbolic meaning and cultural capital is about domination and power. While we tend to focus on politics as the primary locus of power, the culture wars are about nothing less than "a struggle over the right to define the way things are and the way things should be."[9] In short, it is a struggle to define the vision of the good out of which political life and social institutions are *culti*vated.

For Hunter the predominant model of engaging and transforming culture utilized by the Christian churches is based on a faulty understanding of the mechanisms of cultural power. More specifically, it misconstrues the role that politics plays in the creation and maintenance of cultural visions of the good. Understanding these dynamics is an essential component of cultivating realistic expectations about the possibilities of practicing Christian civic virtue and practicing natural law reasoning. A greater appreciation for the complexities of the dynamics of cultural power will lead to a more chastened, but more realistic and humble, set of expectations to guide Christian civic virtue. My goal in this chapter is to provide a vision of Christian civic virtue and public rhetoric to ground such engagement.

The standard narrative of cultural transformation that has come to define Christian political engagement is described by Hunter in the following manner:

> The substance of this view can be summarized something like this: The essence of culture is found in the *hearts and minds of individuals* — in what are typically called "values." Values are, simply, moral preferences; inclinations toward or conscious attachment to what is good and right and true. Culture is manifested in the ways these values guide actual decisions we individuals make about how to live. . . . By this view, a culture is made

7. Josef Pieper, *Leisure: The Basis of Culture,* trans. Alexander Dru (San Francisco: Ignatius, 2009), pp. 68 and 73.

8. Emile Perreau-Saussine, *Catholicism and Democracy: An Essay in the History of Political Thought,* trans. Richard Rex (Princeton, N.J.: Princeton University Press, 2012), p. 104.

9. James Davison Hunter, *Culture Wars: The Struggle to Define America* (New York: Basic, 1991), p. 158.

up of the accumulation of values held by the majority of people and the choices made on the basis of those values.[10]

With this model in view, the vast majority of Christians, on both the political right and the left, have attempted to shape the hearts and minds of individuals to form them into Christian "values." It is believed that these individuals will then translate those values into public policy through the mediation of electoral politics and legislation. In this way, Christian values can directly and indirectly shape the public and political culture through engagement in democratic politics. By supporting those candidates who embody such values in filling positions of political authority, elected officials can instill Christian values in the culture. The hope is that once these values are inscribed in law then there will be a virtuous circle in which the values held by the people will be backed by the coercive power of the state, and the moral core of society will be preserved. Implicit in this view is the belief that cultures change when legislators and politicians shape the public sphere through legal enforcement, and that values can be shaped through legislation.

The problem with this account is that politics does not directly form culture in such a straightforward manner. Hunter writes in regard to politics that "it contributes most effectively to the process of cultural change not when it imposes a cultural agenda but when it creates space for a new way of thinking and living to develop and flourish."[11] There are two implications of this claim for civic virtue. First, it presents further warrant for the church's ongoing endorsement of moderate political liberalism or positive laicity, precisely insofar as the liberal state not only defends rights of individuals and vulnerability classes, but also as it is committed to a kind of freedom that, at its best, has the potential to create the optimal conditions for such cultural and humanistic creativity to grow and flourish. Second, it suggests why the attempt to shape culture only or primarily through political means is doomed to failure. The attempt to shape culture through electoral politics ignores the wider networks of power in which cultures are formed and develop in a long and slow historical process. This process is neither predicable nor controllable through any direct means.

Since the putative goal of democratic politics is to fashion a government that reflects the will (or the "values") of the people, it is understandable why the standard account has broad appeal and a certain logical coherence.

10. Hunter, *To Change the World,* p. 6.
11. Hunter, *To Change the World,* p. 78.

What Hunter claims, however, is that this model is "based on both specious social science and problematic theology."[12] Despite the enduring image of the populist model of cultural change from the ground up outlined above, he notes that cultural change almost always occurs from the top down, when new cultural goods are developed and proposed by elites operating in new centers of power.[13] Cultural power and symbolic capital are formed and develop in the complex interactions between elites who control the means of public media and discourse and the institutions within which they function. According to Hunter, the more densely interwoven these networks are, the more are they able to effectively shape and define culture. Electoral politics, legislatures, and law are only one component of this cultural matrix. More important, in terms of defining cultural power they are not necessarily the most important or influential. The power dynamics of culture and politics overlap in some significant ways, but cultures are defined by a much broader array of factors and power dynamics than politics alone.

This in part explains why, despite immense efforts by Christians on the political right and left to influence the culture through directly political means, American law and politics remain fundamentally shaped by secular values that seem to function in relative autonomy from the more directly religious values of some citizens. Born of the frustration of an obvious lack of effectiveness, Christians and others turn to the more vulgar forms of social communication to discredit the opposition, primarily through vilification and denunciation of whomever is construed as one's political or moral opponents.[14] "Enemies" may be identified either as outsiders to the Christian tradition (secular, atheistic liberals, radical Islamicists, etc.) or as apostate insiders (those who draw on Christian theology or values to support the "heretical" views of the political opposition). Thus is born the culture wars, and along with it the futile pursuit of political power fueled primarily by anger and resentment, backed up by tremendous amounts of time, energy, and money that could be better spent in other ways to witness to the truth of the gospel.

A second and equally important point to recognize is that the standard approach is based on a poor understanding of the kind of power that

---

12. Hunter, *To Change the World,* p. 5.

13. Hunter develops eleven propositions regarding the formation of cultural power; number eight states, "CULTURES CHANGE FROM THE TOP DOWN, RARELY IF EVER FROM THE BOTTOM UP" (*To Change the World,* p. 41). He defends this view with sociological research in the following pages.

14. Hunter, *Culture Wars,* p. 136.

Christians are called to exercise. The power of distinctively Christian virtues in general, and civic virtue in particular, is derived ultimately from the grace and charity freely given by God to the wayfarers who make up the pilgrim church on earth. These virtues are exemplified particularly in humility, charity, and meekness (see Matt. 5:5). However, these virtues do not necessarily call for the total denunciation of power as inherently evil, but rather its transformation in the light of God's grace. Christian humility and meekness are not the same thing as acquiescence or cowardice in the face of injustice, and they often call for tremendous courage and risk in the public sphere. But these virtues do suggest that the means of addressing injustice will be rooted in a vision of power distinct from the forms of domination and exclusion fostered by the culture wars. This is why natural virtue must be "subalternated" (Maritain) or "subverted" (Porter) in light of the transcendent goal of the pilgrim church. Attempts to "win" the culture wars using the standard model's construal of power must ultimately be met with Jesus' question: "For what will it profit them to gain the whole world and forfeit their life?" (Mark 8:36).

I suggest at least three consequences for a Thomistic account of civic virtue of the rhetoric of the culture wars that has become embedded in American public discourse. First, the public language of discrediting, vilification, and denunciation of one's (perceived) opponents contributes to a culture of public shame and exclusion. Anyone who does not fit into narrowly defined "orthodox" positions as defined by the cultural elites who frame public discourse — whether political or religious — is not to be trusted, should be treated as morally suspect, and should be discredited and shamefully driven from public dialogue. Public rhetoric in this context is not about engaging with and debating others' ideas, but rather about dismissing other *persons* — not just their arguments — as inherently irrational. The more fundamental, and more necessary, dialogue about the best vision of the good to be pursued in society cannot even get off the ground in such a cultural context. The tendency toward vilification and exclusion also erodes public trust and civic friendship and fosters what the nineteenth-century philosopher Friedrich Nietzsche describes as *ressentiment,* or resentment. Because of the close association between Christians and these predominant forms of public and political discourse, Christians themselves become what Hunter describes as "functional Nietzscheans, participating in the very cultural breakdown they so ardently strive to resist."[15]

---

15. Hunter, *To Change the World,* p. 175.

A second consequence is that Christian engagement in these forms of political witness further contributes to the breakdown in meaning of the broader culture. Hunter refers to this as "dissolution," which he describes in the following manner:

> The modern world, by its very nature, questions if not negates the trust that connects human discourse and the "reality" of the world. In its mildest expressions, it questions the adequacy of language to make the world intelligible. In its more aggressive expressions, however, it fosters a doubt that what is said has anything to do with what exists "out there."[16]

This problem is grounded in deeper philosophical questions of the congruence between words and the reality that they symbolize. Certain forms of dissolution have been fostered within elite academic institutions where Kantian epistemological skepticism with regard to the capacity of the intellect to understand the nature of the "thing-in-itself" *(Ding an sich)*, Cartesian doubt and mind-body dualism, and postmodern critiques of language and power combine to create a general loss of faith in the capacity for words to effectively convey, and hence to accurately shape, reality. As the sociologist Christian Smith states it, "somehow all of this high theory thus became democratized and vulgarized in U.S. culture."[17] Public discourse focused solely on winning by discrediting the opposition further underwrites this cultural cynicism about our capacity to know reality and to shape ourselves into the kind of moral creatures who desire to live in harmony with the created order and with others in a just social order. The congruence between words and the reality they signify is lost and replaced by language as a form of brute power, put to use as a tool of domination and exclusion. Natural law reasoning as I have described it in previous chapters becomes unintelligible in such a cultural matrix. In the words of John Courtney Murray and Alasdair MacIntyre, two of the most vocal and articulate recent defenders of natural law and moral realism, the barbarians have already stormed the gates of contemporary culture.[18] By inadvertently perpetuating the dissolution of

16. Hunter, *To Change the World,* p. 205.

17. Christian Smith et al., *Lost in Transition: The Dark Side of Emerging Adulthood* (New York: Oxford University Press, 2011), p. 15.

18. Murray writes that "the work of the barbarian [is] to undermine rational standards of judgment, to corrupt the inherited intuitive wisdom by which the people have always lived, and to do this not by spreading new beliefs but creating a climate of doubt and bewilderment in which clarity about the larger aims of life is dimmed and the self-confidence of a

meaning and the moral realism on which natural law depends, Christians contribute not only to Nietzschean resentment but also to cultural nihilism. Christians can no longer simply denounce the specter of meaninglessness and cultural relativism without reflecting on the ways in which we have contributed to the very cultural conditions that serve to sustain it, not least of which by the means we have chosen to engage in politics as an attempt to form and guide culture.

A third consequence, and the most significant for the prospects of practicing civic virtue, is that in the context of the culture wars rhetoric it becomes impossible to speak about the common good as a real and existent good shared by all members of a society. The predominant forms of public and political rhetoric demand that to compete for social prestige, one must do so on the grounds of excluding others from the common good itself. This kind of cultural dialogue erodes any sense of the human goods that unite members of the body politic together in a shared pursuit of justice, moral truth, and genuinely human goods (Aquinas's *bonum honestum*). Instead, the particular vision of the good pursued by each partisan group must be defined by a narrow orthodoxy "without an appeal to the common weal," and must be supported by rational justifications that become "not much more than a veneer over a will to power."[19] To the extent that the church's message and the good news of the gospel become embedded in the negative aspects of these cultural forms of expression, it is no wonder that cynicism and a lack of trust in church leaders come to define the typical cultural response to Christian leaders and the Christian message. A Thomistic account of civic virtue grounded in natural law's moral realism with regard to the common good, however, provides a means for speaking about the common good as a truly existent, cognizable good shared by all members of a community. Trust in the exigencies of natural law suggests that a critical and morally realistic grasp of the basic contours of the common good is possible even amid the conditions of pluralism.

If the standard view is irredeemably flawed, how, then, is cultural power actually generated? And related, how can a more accurate understanding of cultural power help us to reimagine the practices of civic virtue? Hunter

---

people is destroyed" (*We Hold These Truths: Catholic Reflections on the American Proposition* [New York: Sheed & Ward, 1960], p. 12).

MacIntyre famously quips at the end of *After Virtue: A Study in Moral Theory,* 2nd ed. (Notre Dame, Ind.: University of Notre Dame Press, 1984) that "the new dark ages . . . are already upon us. . . . This time however the barbarians are not waiting beyond the frontiers; they have already been governing us for quite some time" (p. 263).

19. Hunter, *To Change the World,* p. 106.

understands culture as emerging from what he calls a "trialectic" between three components: (1) values, beliefs, and ideas, (2) individuals, and (3) institutions (including the material artifacts that they create) that come to shape a culture's vision of the good.[20] He distinguishes his view from both cultural materialism and cultural idealism. The former understands culture as expressed and shaped by the physical artifacts — the "stuff" — that are created within it, while the latter approach understands culture as expressed primarily in abstract ideas. Rather, cultures emerge from the intersection between ideas and ideals, persons, and the social institutions and networks that form a community's way of life. In this way Hunter's critical realism and cultural trialectic is congruent with both the Ciceronian-Augustinian definition of the common good previously defended and the practical example of the Bluffton religious sisters' role in initiating cultural change discussed in Chapter 4. Hunter's trialectic model insists that human persons and cultures are formed by the interaction between ideas or values, relationships, and institutions. The central role of relationships in this model suggests additionally that cultural change will be most effective when the social capital of trust is present. In fact, effective dialogue and disagreement yield to moral truth only when the social glue of trust — both between words and reality, and between fellow members of the body politic — is present to facilitate the pursuit of the common good. I explore the relationship between trust and public rhetoric in the following section.

In this perspective cultural power is defined as "the ability to *successfully* propose a new cultural good."[21] The capacity to instill value in certain cultural goods — and thus to define the ideals, moral values, and institutional practices that shape a culture — emerges from the centers of the networks of elite individuals and the institutions they lead. Instead of the more popular or democratic notions of cultural change that have defined Christian civic and political engagement, Hunter suggests that cultures change when new elite networks of power develop outside the previously existing cultural nerve centers and are able to successfully propose new cultural goods. When done effectively, this shift in symbolic power becomes embodied in new structures and networks. In the beginning new networks initiate and then later come to symbolize a shift in public consciousness about the nature of the goods that define a culture.

---

20. I am grateful to Professor Hunter for clarifying his understanding of this trialectic of culture through a personal email correspondence (March 3, 2014).

21. Hunter, *To Change the World*, p. 29.

While sociologists can analyze how these kinds of cultural changes typically occur, they can neither predict nor demonstrate a means to control how change will unfold in the future. Cultural change is dialectical and complex. That is, it emerges out of a public discourse about the nature of the good that takes place between the elite networks of power that shape the culture, and all of the other actors, agents, individuals, groups, and institutions that make up the civil society. Thus, this model of cultural change is not antidemocratic so much as it complicates our understanding of how democratic power operates. It does not suggest that people and popular movements have no place in the cultural dialogue.[22] But it does suggest that the most effective and most democratic movements of change emerge when the will of the people broadly construed is supported by and embedded in the power networks that also shape cultural perceptions of the good human life that is the goal of society. This process is easier to analyze and describe than it is to control or direct. One must always recall, however, that even with the best of intentions among all those participating in the pursuit of the good, the outcome of the process of forming and reshaping cultures is uncertain and open to the contingencies of history. The rhetoric of the culture wars that places the blame for cultural disintegration on particular persons or groups obscures this essential aspect of contingency in the way that cultures are formed and develop over time. It may provide a temporary outlet for anger at injustice, but, as I explore below, it does not provide an effective channel for directing it toward greater justice or support for the common good.

The bad news, according to Hunter, is that compared to the most powerful networks of cultural creativity in the late modern world, Christianity is a relatively weak culture. This is due in part to the fact that Christians have been pouring large amounts of resources into directly political means of influencing culture, rather than creating the kinds of networks that could successfully propose an alternative set of cultural goods. He writes that

> in the Catholic and Evangelical foundations [that he analyzes], no fellowship program exists at all for supporting the most talented intellectuals, artists, or social innovators. This review is hardly systematic or comprehensive, but the preliminary indications suggest that very few

22. Christian Smith's description of the "sociological imagination" that makes up the core of a culture's and a people's identity is particularly helpful in understanding this dialectical process. He writes that the "sociological imagination seeks to understand the *personal experiences of individual people,* on the one hand, and *larger social and cultural trends, forces, and powers,* on the other, by *explaining each in terms of the other*" (*Lost in Transition,* p. 4).

resources within the Christian community, in all of its diversity, go to supporting leadership in developing cultural capital in the centers of cultural production.[23]

This is sobering news, but not all is lost. It simply suggests that the hope of Christians to engage in the secular, liberal cultures of the twenty-first century is more moderate and humble than the grand claims to win the culture wars by instilling Christian values in society through directly political means.[24]

The good news is that a more realistic understanding of how cultural power is generated and how cultures change, combined with a more humble appreciation of the roles of the pilgrim church and its members in this process, provides some helpful suggestions for reimagining Christian civic virtue in twenty-first-century liberal societies. I have already noted that the theological distinction between nature and grace, and a correlative distinction between the penultimate aims of civic life and the ultimate goals of the church, underscores the relative autonomy of politics vis-à-vis the church. This alone already provides grounds for questioning whether the goal of Christian civic virtue should be to instill distinctively Christian values directly in culture through political means. It also lends further support to the kinds of moderate liberalism and positive laicity that was most fully embraced and articulated at Vatican II in *Dignitatis humanae* and *Gaudium et spes*. Hunter writes that "while politics can only do so much, it is also true that bad politics can do truly horrific things."[25] That is why a Thomistic account of civic virtue remains committed to many of the goods and aims of the modern liberal nation-state. It is also why, despite my respect for much of their theology, I cannot follow the tendency of the second group of interpreters of Catholic social thought to distance Christians from the state as their stance falls short of the full expression of civic virtue.

Coming to terms with the contemporary cultural reality also provides

---

23. Hunter, *To Change the World*, p. 84.

24. Peter Kreeft argues in *How to Win the Culture Wars: A Christian Battle Plan for a Society in Crisis* (Downers Grove, Ill.: InterVarsity, 2002) that the way to "win" the culture wars is simply to create more Christian saints and to try harder. He writes that "if you will look into your own heart in utter honesty, you must admit that there is one and only one reason why you are not, even now, as saintly as the primitive Christians: *you do not wholly want to be*" (p. 103, italics added). This seems to make "winning" the culture wars simply a matter of the purity of Christian desire, and misses the mark in terms of addressing the actual sources of cultural power and change as outlined by Hunter and others.

25. Hunter, *To Change the World*, p. 171.

an opportunity to rethink the predominant forms of public witness and discourse in which Christians engage in culture and politics. One response to Hunter's analysis might be to withdraw into forms of political quietism or religious pietism and let the world go its own way. The previous discussions on the relationship between justice and charity and a theological commitment to the common good of all humankind indicate that those who practice civic virtue necessarily reject such a solution. However, if we step back and reassess our approach to practicing civic virtue, the first place to begin is to look inside the Christian tradition itself and to consider what theological resources are best suited to engaging in late modern culture and politics. In doing so, Hunter suggests that "in the Christian faith, one has the possibility of relatively autonomous institutions and practices that could — in both judgment and affirmation — be a source of ideals and values capable of elevating politics to more than a quest for power."[26] Although Hunter analyzes the Christian churches in the United States as a whole, this is one point where it is possible to bring a distinctively Thomistic account of civic virtue as it has survived and continued to develop in the Roman Catholic tradition into dialogue with the narrative of contemporary culture that he describes.

I suggest that there are two aspects that are central to this account of civic virtue that are particularly salient for reimagining Christian civic engagement in late modern democratic culture and politics. The first is directly related to the ecclesiology of the pilgrim church that undergirds this account. The second has to do with the kind of public rhetoric that is supported by the natural law tradition of moral reasoning. To begin with the ecclesiological dimension, the Catholic Church is a global institution that is constituted by a cultural dialectic between the elite networks of power in the center of its leadership and the more local forms of expression and practice at national, diocesan, parish, and individual levels. The forms of rhetoric and symbolic power that emerge from within the institutional church itself will come to have a tremendous influence on the way that the entire congregation of the faithful, or people of God, will understand their role in shaping the political lives of their native communities.

Indeed, one of the primary tensions in contemporary Catholic ecclesiology revolves around how to best balance the centralized authority of the pope upheld in the ultramontanist position of Vatican I in relation to the collegiality of all the bishops with the renewed emphasis on the laity and the local church highlighted at Vatican II. For example, the kind of internal

26. Hunter, *To Change the World*, p. 172.

self-reflection of the church's inner structure between Vatican I and Vatican II represents how this dialectical process of cultural development can lead to greater insight into the true nature of both the institutional church and the political lives of modern societies. As noted previously, even when the Catholic Church was most actively reasserting its right to preeminence in the spiritual realm and organizing itself institutionally around the papacy in the late nineteenth century, there was already an implicit endorsement of a certain kind of autonomy of the political sphere of human activity (reminiscent of the older Gallican tradition). It was only through the on-going dialectical process, which occurred both *ad intra* between liberals and integralists in the church and *ad extra* in dialogue and conflict with modern nation-states, that the Catholic Church came to a more explicit endorsement of moderate forms of political liberalism or positive laicity. All of this occurred in a complex dialectical process of "affirmation and antithesis"[27] between the timeless truths of the gospel and the contingent, historical expressions of modern politics. But the important point to note here is that although no one could predict or control the outcome of this process, it led to greater insight into the truth that religious freedom and moderate liberalism more adequately uphold and defend the dignity of the human person than either the direct union of altar and throne or political Gallicanism had previously done. I outlined this historical process in greater detail in Chapter 2 but it demonstrates how an ongoing, dialectical process of dialogue can be sustained within the institutional structures of the church that leads to greater insight into the nature of moral truth. It also highlights how such insight has a profound influence on the modalities through which the members of the pilgrim church practice civic virtue.

This example also demonstrates how essential the critical realism of natural law reasoning is to the Catholic tradition and to a Thomistic account of civic virtue. Thus, a second aspect of civic virtue that is particularly salient for addressing late modern culture is the way it remains committed to the epistemological claim that there is and can be broad coherence between the world in which humans live, the language we use to describe it, and a moral response to it. In short, civic virtue demands a critical moral realism as an alternative to the kind of nihilism fostered by the public rhetoric of the culture wars. It will not be the same kind of realism upheld by the neo-Thomists of the late nineteenth and early twentieth centuries. But it will likely be a more hermeneutical realism. A hermeneutical realism takes seriously the

27. Hunter, *To Change the World*, p. 231.

congruence between words, reality, and action, while honoring the limits of human knowledge about contingent social and political issues through the epistemological humility that I described in Chapter 4. While there are complex philosophical issues to be worked out in defense of this claim, my goal in the rest of this chapter is to outline a way in which the tools of rhetoric may be engaged by Christians to strengthen the credibility of critical realism as a practical alternative to cultural nihilism.

If Hunter's analysis of American culture is correct, then one of the most important implications of the practice of Christian civic virtue is found in its model of engaging in and providing support for a public space for dialogue and debate about the nature of the good that is relatively autonomous from the predominant forms of cultural discourse. It is from such a vision of the good that symbolic cultural power may emerge in a way that may truly foster the common good of all. Although Christians cannot predetermine the outcome of this dialectical process, our biblical and theological tradition does provide the resources that enable trust in divine providence that undergirds our understanding of natural law. Faith enables pilgrim Christians to believe that truth and goodness are innate capacities of the human intellect that cannot be destroyed even amid the worst forms of cultural nihilism, dissolution, and resentment. Civic virtue seeks to witness to and reestablish this kind of trust.

Critical Realism, the Common Good, and Public Rhetoric

Defending a critically realist notion of the common good as the object of civic virtue is therefore a central task of the practices of civic virtue. In what follows I want to consider what form of public rhetoric is most congruent with the pursuit of the common good. The common good provides a language grounded in the moral realism of natural law for identifying, cognizing, and making actionable the highest ideals shared by the members of a political community and expressed through the cultural trialectic of ideals, persons, and institutions. At this point it is helpful to review the following features of the common good that have emerged from the previous analysis as the object of acts of civic virtue. The common good is:

- formally distinct from the individual good or the sum total of individual goods in society;
- the object and goal toward which all positive (human) law aims;

- the highest natural or temporal good of both individuals and communities; this point implies that each individual's good is inextricably tethered to the common good;
- a real, appetible good — a substantive good that is capable of being cognized in the intellect and of attracting the will through the affections and also (indirectly) through the passions. And therefore
- the common good is identifiable in what Cicero defines as a set of ideals or values that are embodied in a particular way of life and that provide a meaningful context in which members of a community are enabled to engage in common endeavors,[28] or what Augustine calls "common objects of love."[29]

In all of these ways, then, the common good refers to a state of affairs, a way of living together within a particular society or culture, that somehow reflects that which the members of the body politic uphold together as the most important values and goods that will sustain and foster their flourishing

28. It seems that there is a similar notion at work at work in the way that Oliver O'Donovan describes the aim of justice as providing members access to the social means of communication and engagement that support their flourishing. For example, he maintains that "we can be deprived of the structures of communication within which we have learned to act, and so we can find ourselves hurled into a vacuum in which we do not know how to realize ourselves effectively" (*The Ways of Judgment: The Bampton Lectures, 2003* [Grand Rapids: Eerdmans, 2005], p. 68). We should note, however, that O'Donovan's manner of construing the common good and political judgment differs from our account in at least one important way; that is, he considers political judgment to be an act that follows on an act of injustice to defend the common good or rectify the harm done. For example, he writes that "political judgment, then, is a response to wrong as injury to the public good" (p. 59). The account of judgment that I continue to develop below is much more constructive than reactive.

29. See Jean Porter, *Ministers of the Law: A Natural Law Theory of Legal Authority* (Grand Rapids: Eerdmans, 2010), p. 161, where she references Cicero's *De republica* I 25.42 and Augustine's *De civitate Dei* XIV 28 (note 15). See also Oliver O'Donovan's reflections on similar themes in *Common Objects of Love: Moral Reflection and the Shaping of Community* (Grand Rapids: Eerdmans, 2002). Eric Gregory also provides insights into Augustinian notions of the good. Understanding these dynamics as an *esse* of love is a foundational notion for civic engagement, as when he writes, for example, that "we do well also to consider Augustine's insight that how a political society thinks about the directions of its desires and loves has important consequences for the sort of life such a society might lead" (*Politics and the Order of Love: An Augustinian Ethic of Democratic Citizenship* [Chicago: University of Chicago Press, 2008], p. 372). Although Gregory's work has much to commend it in regard to reflecting on the continued significance of Augustine's notion of love for civic engagement, I believe his account could be further strengthened by a more sustained reflection on the common good in Augustine's thought and in relation to modern liberal thought.

both individually and collectively as well as the social institutions that make such flourishing possible. On this account, the common good can refer to specific instances of tangible goods (such as those goods produced through exercising a right to engage in economic activities, own property, have access to health care, etc.), and it can also refer to more abstract goods such as freedom, autonomy, or solidarity (among others). In this respect, "the common good" is not only conceived as one, distinct object, but rather captures a community's shared sense of identity based on the values and goods that it upholds as essential to each member of the community, ranging from the most tangible to the most abstract forms of goods.

Taking this approach to the common good has much to recommend it. For example, it allows the common good to maintain its normative, critical purchase on any given society, without attempting to spell out a universal common good that could be applicable in each particular context.[30] As William Barbieri describes it, "what we have instead is a complex, open-ended picture in which different [cultural] goods exist, in different social contexts, both for individuals and for members of a broad range of types of community."[31] On the one hand, this feature of the common good is natural and to be expected, and is even in accord with what Aquinas maintains. For he writes that "the common good comprises many things . . . [and it] is procured by many actions" (*Summa theologiae* I-II 96.1). Therefore, a genuine plurality of natural expressions of the common good that sustains human flourishing is in line with the manner in which the basic inclinations toward the good as the foundation of natural law reasoning are legitimately expressed in a variety of contexts.[32]

On the other hand, if this open-ended nature of the common good is taken too far, then the common good becomes too diffuse and starts to lose its normative purchase. Even though the common good is not instrumental or reducible to individual goods, it must also somehow allow a community to sustain and foster a genuine form of human flourishing for each member qua

30. This seems to be one of the more prominent ways of conceiving of the common good in the encyclical tradition and much of Catholic social thought in general. See, for example, Lisa Cahill's "Toward Global Ethics," *Theological Studies* 63, no. 2 (2002): 324-44.

31. William A. Barbieri Jr., "Beyond the Nations: The Expansion of the Common Good in Catholic Social Thought," *Review of Politics* 63, no. 4 (Fall 2001): 723-54, p. 744.

32. Porter also notes some of the ways in which viable conceptions of the common good that sustain human flourishing in non-Western contexts have been considered and developed by recent scholars, such as Lawrence Rosreen has done in Muslim societies and Benezet Bujo has undertaken in African contexts (*Ministers of the Law,* p. 166, note 17).

individual. In other words, the critical test for the efficacy of the common good within any given community remains the extent to which it allows all individuals and in particular those members of vulnerability classes within the body politic access to some set of goods, ideals, values, and practices that enable them to seek flourishing as rational, self-directed creatures, and to participate in the goods of a community's civic life.

This feature of the common good also suggests why attempts to build public consensus to support the institutions of modern political life cannot be derived from principles of right or procedural justice alone in the manner that Rawls insists. Hunter, for example, disagrees with the claim "that in a liberal democracy, the state is or should be neutral when it comes to questions of the good. This is wrong mainly because it is impossible. Law infers a moral judgment; policy implies a worldview."[33] Although Rawls develops his political notion of the person and his idea of an overlapping consensus to address this need, he still maintains that liberal political institutions are based on the priority of the right over the good. As I argued in the previous chapter, his notion of an overlapping consensus can be used to develop a shared conception of the good that may be broadly accepted by members of a community and that provides for the stability of just social institutions without accepting his insistence on the priority of the right over the good.

For example, in the context of liberal, constitutional democracies autonomy, freedom, tolerance, and equality are essential components of the way in which the common good is symbolically represented and understood. These are goods that are capable of sustaining and fostering a distinctively human manner of flourishing only if they are available to each and every person within the community, even as such common goods, considered as an ongoing way of life informed by intelligible ideals, are in and of themselves goods that transcend the individual good. Thus, Michael Sherwin accurately describes the common good in the following manner:

> The whole of all of these goods which make up the cultural heritage of a people, and which promote the full human life . . . this totality is the temporal common good. . . . The common good is thus the good of the whole shared by each of its parts.[34]

---

33. Hunter, *To Change the World*, p. 103.

34. Michael Sherwin, O.P., "St. Thomas and the Common Good: The Theological Perspective: An Invitation to Dialogue," *Angelicum* 70 (1993): 307-28, pp. 320, 322.

The common good is thus formally distinct from, yet intrinsically tethered to, the good of each individual, in such a way that each person's individual good is dependent on the manner in which the common good is made accessible to all within a particular community. One of the greatest needs in late modern culture is the cultivation of a capacity to extend our emotional sensitivities and cognitive grasp to include aspects of reality that take into account goods that are not reducible to individual goods.

This manner of construing the common good upholds the Aristotelian notion, which is also defended by Aquinas, that the common good is the highest, most noble, and most divine good of natural human life and communities.[35] It remains flexible enough to be applicable in a wide variety of human cultures and contexts, and is thus applicable in the context of late modern pluralism, and it simultaneously retains its normative purchase because of the way that the common good is tethered to, indeed constitutive of, the good of each and every individual within a community. Moreover, as I continue to claim in what follows, it functions as a way of defining and providing a language for the way in which a particular community upholds its distinctive manner of life in such a way that it defines that community's moral core — its *ethos*. As such, it provides a starting point for practical deliberation about the good and the best means of achieving it, while also remaining open-ended and flexible enough to leave room for deliberative judgment within the body politic in an ongoing process of critical reflection on the best means of achieving a healthy, flourishing, and just society. With this conception of the common good more firmly in place, it is now possible to move into a closer analysis of how Christians may witness publicly to the common good in ways that enable others who may not share our foundational theological or philosophical commitments to critically conceive of the common good such that it can function as the aim of acts of civic virtue.

I want to turn now and propose that the deeper implications of the analysis of the role of the passions in practical reasoning begun in Chapter 3 can be extended into the public discourse of late modern democratic cultures by looking backward (as it were) to Aristotle's *Rhetoric* and to some contemporary commentators on Aristotle's moral and political thought. I suggest that doing so will provide much needed practical means of cultivating a rhetoric that more adequately reflects Christian commitments to the common good and to the exercise of forms of power that are more in line with the values of the gospel. Additionally, despite what may seem at first to

---

35. *Nicomachean Ethics* I.2 1094b; *Sententia libri ethicorum* 1.2, no. 12.

be a paradoxical claim, such an impassioned approach to rhetoric can serve to increase civic friendship and the capacities for rational deliberation about the practical truths to be pursued in the civic life of democratic societies. Aristotle's discussion of the passions in the *Rhetoric* is his most sustained and in-depth account of the role of the passions in practical reasoning, and thinkers such as Martha Nussbaum and Eugene Garver bring Aristotle's discussion forward in a very helpful manner by placing it in the discourse of contemporary ethical and political thought. Moreover, as Aristotle famously notes in the *Nicomachean Ethics,* the practice of virtue requires not *only* the rational discernment of binding moral norms, but he adds the important insight that right practical reason entails having certain dispositions or "feelings at the right times on the right occasions toward the right people for the right motive and in the right way" (II.6 1106b11). There is much to get "right" here, and one of the things we must get right is our emotional responses to particular situations in relation to our perceptions and judgments insofar as they lead to particular actions. The culture wars make this difficult, but civic virtue provides resources for more wisely and effectively dealing with our dispositions and appetites in pursuit of justice.

Although Aquinas does not engage Aristotle's *Rhetoric* with the same level of detail as he does other works of the philosopher,[36] I suggest that it is entirely appropriate to extend a Thomistic analysis of civic virtue by revisiting Aristotle's analysis of public rhetoric. First, it is possible to draw on the *Rhetoric* in a manner that does not contradict Aquinas's own thought on the role of the passions in practical reason, but rather helps us to extend an analysis of the passions for a contemporary application of civic virtue. Second, Aristotle himself does not see the *Rhetoric* as completely separate from his aims in the *Nicomachean Ethics* and the *Politics,* even as he does not make these connections as explicitly as one may wish. The quotation noted above from the *Ethics* shows that feeling the right way with regard to one's

36. While there is evidence that Aquinas was familiar with Aristotle's *Rhetoric* (for example, he quotes from it in his discussion of anger; see *Summa theologiae* I-II 23; II-II 158), it is also clear that he did not engage in a more in-depth analysis of *Rhetoric*. Aquinas does not quote *Rhetoric* as extensively as he does *Nicomachean Ethics* or *De anima,* nor has he provided a commentary on *Rhetoric*. Moreover, Aquinas was not necessarily concerned with developing a full-fledged political theory, but was only concerned to develop his political thought insofar as it was necessitated by the theological aims of analyzing human action that defined the *Secunda Pars* of *Summa theologiae* (see Jean-Pierre Torrell, *Saint Thomas Aquinas,* vol. 2, *Spiritual Master,* trans. Robert Royal [Washington, D.C.: Catholic University of America Press, 2003], p. 302).

passions and reasoning the right way with regard to potential objects of one's actions is an essential element of the practice of the virtues in general, and of prudence in particular. The congruence of reason and emotion is a necessary component of following the rule of reason and the mean, a notion foundational to Aquinas's construal of natural law reasoning. Indeed, the capacity to effectively channel anger through courageous and prudential acts of civic virtue in ways that do not foster greater resentment is an essential component of Christian civic virtue. Likewise, the discussion of the virtues in the *Ethics* leads naturally into Aristotle's reflections in the *Politics,* as the life of virtue and practical reason that Aristotle upholds as the ideal model is one that is rooted in a particular kind of *polis,* city, or state (*Nicomachean Ethics* I 2, X.9; *Politics* I 1-2). The aims of ethics and of politics converge insofar as rhetoric is put to use in the pursuit of building the kind of community that seeks to live well together in the pursuit of authentic human flourishing. Thus, it is fitting to think of the *Ethics* and the *Politics* as having an intrinsic, natural connection. What is less common, however, is to consider the impact of the discussion of collective deliberation and persuasion found in the *Rhetoric* in relation to Aristotle's ethical and political thought.[37] Indeed, Aristotle's comments regarding the unreasonable use of rhetoric on the part of the Sophists (at the end of the *Ethics* and the first book of the *Rhetoric*) might be taken to indicate that his discussion of persuasion has nothing to do with the rational demands intrinsic to his ethical or political thought.

On closer inspection, however, it becomes clear that in the *Rhetoric* Aristotle is attempting to rescue the art of rhetoric from the Sophists precisely by tethering it more closely with the kind of rational deliberation that is the hallmark of virtue in the *Ethics* and the *Politics.* Moreover, this kind of communal and public deliberation that draws on the rational goods and passions internal to the art of persuasion in regard to the common good is central to a Thomistic account of civic virtue. Under the conditions of the culture wars, it is clear that moving beyond moral nihilism and collective resentment requires a rethinking of the means used to find and cultivate a public consensus on the shared human goods of political life. As noted by the sociologist Christian Smith, late modern liberal cultures do not seem to instill in young adults the linguistic or moral reasoning skills to identify,

---

37. For example, Alasdair MacIntyre writes that "no issue is more central to contemporary concerns than the relation of ethics to rhetoric. No book has more to teach us than Aristotle's *Rhetoric.* But we have been unable to learn from Aristotle for lack of adequate commentary and exposition" (quoted from the back cover of Eugene Garver's *Aristotle's Rhetoric: An Art of Character* [Chicago: University of Chicago Press, 1994]).

much less act in pursuit of, the common good. They lack the skills and the language to pursue any moral considerations beyond references to the needs of the individual, subjective self.[38] The *Rhetoric* can provide some much-needed building blocks for constructing a contemporary account of what it means to engage in a realistic form of moral reasoning as part of the practice of civic virtue.

My decision to draw on the *Rhetoric* in the context of Thomistic civic virtue that is tethered to a natural law understanding of critical moral realism means that the art of persuasion itself is intimately associated with reason as the rule of human behavior. Effectively persuasive speech can only be wrested from the control of the Sophists (in Aristotle's time), or from the public culture wars that seek to persuade by fear and irrational argument (in our time), if it is subject to rational scrutiny, while simultaneously maintaining a legitimate space for emotion and passionate commitment in public persuasion. Public rhetoric about the common good must be made capable of being undertaken with rational and emotional integrity. In other words, rhetoric cannot be the mere manipulation of passions and logic to convince one's audience to go along with the orator's goals, but rather must serve the rational aim of striving for the common good, civic virtue, and practical moral truth *together* as a community. As Eugene Garver states it, reason itself must be a good internal to the practice of rhetoric for Aristotle's analysis to remain both internally coherent and connected to his aims in his ethical and political thought.[39]

Thus, the kinds of passions that Aristotle discusses in the *Rhetoric* are *civic* passions in that they are related to (a) ethical deliberation and (b) our life together as community members. If persuasive speech is not subject to the ends and constraints of reason itself, then rhetoric is doomed to the ir-

---

38. Smith writes that "it is hard for emerging adults *to see an objective reality beyond the individual self.* . . . In philosophical terms, most emerging adults are functionally (meaning how they actually think and act, regardless of theories they hold) 'soft ontological anti-realists,' 'epistemological skeptics,' and 'perspectivalists' — although few are aware of these terms" (*Lost in Transition*, p. 221), and "almost none have any vision of a common good" (p. 223). I also want to follow Smith in concluding that this is not the fault of emerging adults themselves, but rather reflects the manner in which late modern liberal cultures have failed to provide young adults with any viable vision of the common good or internally coherent social morality.

39. Eugene Garver, *Confronting Aristotle's Ethics* (Chicago: University of Chicago Press, 2006), pp. 28, 31, 35. The notion of a "good internal to a practice" is drawn from Alasdair MacIntyre's analysis of the importance of this concept for understanding the virtues in *After Virtue* (p. 187).

rational manipulation of fears and desires, especially ones that are reducible to economic and material analyses and manipulation.[40] It is not surprising, therefore, that in popular language a speaker's argument is frequently dismissed as being merely "rhetorical" (in a pejorative sense, indicating that the speaker's conclusions are not true or are motivated by ulterior motives such as self-interest, power, or domination) when she is suspected of not following reason. "Rhetorical" in this case suggests that the speaker is manipulating the audience by playing on their fears or immoderate desires to convince them to pursue ends that are ultimately in the speaker's narrow field of self-interest. This popular manner of dismissing a speaker's argument also indicates that we continue to expect those who speak and act publicly in regard to our civic life together to be held to a certain ethical standard *precisely as public speakers who influence the body politic,* even if this expectation is not always consciously articulated. Public rhetoric thus becomes another arena in which the implications of the kind of political prudence expected of those who hold roles of political authority becomes more evident. In this sense rhetoric is intimately connected to the *ethos* and the character of both the speaker and the audience — that is, of the entire body politic and its sense of the common good. Rhetoric, therefore, only serves its true end as an art when it helps the members of a community to deliberate together about the best goods to be pursued and the best means of achieving such genuinely human ends.

Aristotle's *Rhetoric* provides important clues for how persuasive speech can lead to a more adequate rational grasp of the true political ends that humans pursue together in a political community. First, Aristotle insists that the end of rhetoric is "not so much to persuade, but to find out in each case the existing means of persuasion" (*Rhetoric* I.1 1355b14). This is why rhetoric is an art rather than a science in Aristotelian terms. Ethics and politics are the technical sciences that investigate, discover, and articulate the best ends or goods to be pursued in political life, but rhetoric provides an atechnical but nonetheless essential means for pursuing those ends in ways that are congruent with the moral aims discovered via the technical sciences of ethics

40. Smith's observations are particularly enlightening on this connection between consumerism and awareness of responsibility toward the common good. He writes that "what disappears with the cultural takeover of mass consumerism are shared social identities, organic communities of solidarity, the civic virtues of duty and responsibility, and the learned processes of public deliberation, consensus building, and conflict resolution," and that "the more emerging adults are into consumerism, the less they are into politics and civic engagement" (*Lost in Transition,* pp. 217-18).

and politics.[41] Without this tethering to moral truth and the pursuit of the genuinely human good — that is, without tethering the aims of the *Ethics* and the *Politics* to the means described in the *Rhetoric* — rhetoric devolves into manipulation, power, and domination. In the contemporary context of the culture wars, where rhetoric has been divorced from these rational goods, it is the particular responsibility of Christians and others who practice civic virtue to witness to this intrinsic connection between the means and the ends of politics and morality. This witness is in fact an act both of friendship (in the Aristotelian sense) and of charity (in the Thomistic sense). The first task will thus be to relearn the art of public persuasion and then to put it into practice in the institutional contexts that are most likely to support it.

Second, Aristotle suggests that listeners will be persuaded when they are convinced that the speaker has provided what he calls in Greek *pisteis,* and is often translated as "rhetorical proofs" (I.I 1355a11).[42] The kinds of proofs provided by rhetoric are not the same as the kinds of technical, dialectical proofs that are found in the sciences or logic, but are based on the kind of atechnical, syllogistic reasoning that he calls an "enthymeme" (*Rhetoric* I.I 1355a11). Enthymatic syllogisms occur when the major premise from which the conclusion is derived cannot be proven using strictly logical, dialectical reasoning. Aristotle notes that enthymemes frequently begin from something that is assumed (but not strictly proven) to be common knowledge, or from popular maxims that state an apparent or assumed truth. For example, I did not provide a technical proof of the fact that we expect a speaker to exhibit a certain level of ethical virtue in the example provided above. However, we were able to draw the conclusion that we do in fact expect such truthful conduct from public speakers from the maxim that a fallacious argument is often referred to as "merely rhetorical." In such an instance, shared common sense provides the grounds for a rhetorical proof.

Garver therefore suggests that *pisteis* could be rendered as "credibles,"[43] or what might be translated as "statements worthy of belief," in capturing the intended meaning of the original Greek. Thus, my readers could go along

---

41. I am grateful to Eugene Garver for pointing out the distinction here between technical and atechnical means of moral inquiry and deliberation (personal email correspondence, March 6, 2014).

42. Garver notes that although *pisteis* is usually translated as "proof," it is also translated into English as "argument, reasoning, persuasion, belief, trust, faith, conviction, obligation, and confidence" (*For the Sake of Argument* [Chicago: University of Chicago Press, 2004], p. 3).

43. Garver, *Confronting Aristotle's Ethics*, p. 17.

with my conclusion as a credible and reasonable outcome of my argument, even though I did not use dialectic to prove that *ethos* and character matter for the truthfulness and effectiveness of persuasive speech. Moreover, such proofs only function when there is a level of *trust* in the fact that my statements can be counted on as reflecting a truth about the world in which we live. In other words, *ethos* (the possession of certain virtues of honesty as a speaker) is intimately connected with *logos*, or the logic of persuasive speech. Correlatively, it means that the *ethos* and *logos* exemplified by the speaker have a formative role in the creation of the *ethos* and what counts for rational argument *(logos)* by the members of the body politic.

These claims lead to two very important further conclusions. First, they provide even further substantiation for the claim that there is a certain level of political virtue and political prudence that we demand of those who hold public offices and perform public roles. Second, they suggest that participating in a dialogue in which truthful public speech is upheld is one way that individuals within a culture (re)learn to trust in a correlation between language, reality, and morality. In other words, it fosters the kind of critical moral realism that is essential for natural law and for a limited, but pervasively shared conception of the common good. The atechnical, hermeneutical process of rhetorical practical deliberation is itself constitutive of these goods internal to natural law reasoning.

The preceding raises the following question: Precisely what is the nature of the truth that we are pursuing when we engage in public dialogue about the common good in the civil sphere? Garver writes that the comprehensive nature of religious arguments with regard to moral truth represents both an advantage and a disadvantage for those who defend distinctively religious arguments in pluralistic, democratic societies.[44] On the one hand, liberal political institutions are built on the notion that political consensus must be cultivated under conditions that assume the absence of universal agreement on comprehensive moral truths. On the other hand, the religious person

---

44. In describing the comprehensive nature of religious rhetoric as both a challenge and an opportunity, he writes that "in each case comprehensiveness is not a logical property but an ethical one: it makes community harder to establish, and so the more comprehensive an appeal, the more an audience will mistrust and resist it. For the same reasons, though, the more comprehensive an appeal, the deeper the community that is established when the appeal is successful" ("How Can a Liberal Listen to a Religious Argument? Religious Rhetoric as a Rhetorical Problem," in *How Should We Talk about Religion? Perspectives, Contexts, Particularities,* ed. James Boyd White [Notre Dame, Ind.: University of Notre Dame Press, 2006], pp. 164-93, p. 173).

feels simultaneously compelled to respect the pluralism of the body politic while witnessing to the universal normativity of the moral truth that she cherishes as part of her religious heritage and identity. Rhetorical proofs provide a middle way beyond the usual stalemates between liberals and religious thinkers in much contemporary political thought.

Rhetorical truth is distinctive from the kind of absolute truths expressed in matters of "faith and morals" that are essential for defining the beliefs and boundaries of the Catholic, Christian faith. This task is the legitimate function of the magisterium of the church. Rhetorical proof is a deliberative, practical truth. But it remains truth nonetheless. Public rhetorical deliberation is not meant for, nor is it well suited for, the kind of technical, rational inquiry that seeks to establish absolute and certain principles of speculative or practical reason. Rather, rhetoric is an atechnical art perfectly suited to the civil and political context in which, even amid generally shared agreement on first principles or a rough public consensus, the practical outcome is not immediately deducible from the principles and shared values that constitute the people's sense of the common good. In other words, the move from a religious person's public witness of her own comprehensive moral truth to political solutions that result in legislation or public policy is a move from an atechnical public witness toward technical judgments of laws, either in their creation via legislation or in their interpretation via the judicial system. Garver writes that the "citizen may speak religiously, but the state cannot act on religious grounds. Between the speaking citizen and the acting state lies the civic audience, midway between the speaker's voluble freedom and the state's deafness."[45] Thus, technical pronouncements from a discipline such as moral theology, even when canonically binding within the church, must be presented in liberal societies as a form of atechnical witness in which they may be submitted to rational, communal deliberation by the members of the body politic. This kind of deliberation is in fact best secured under the conditions of positive laicity or moderate liberalism. In this process of rhetorical deliberation, shared public values and principles may emerge from public discourse that then become part of the public consensus that defines the people's sense of the common good. It is the distinctive role of legislators and interpreters of the law to draw on these atechnical rhetorical proofs and to formulate them into laws or interpret them through legal pronouncements. This kind of democratic, atechnical witnessing that moves into communal deliberation, and from there into technical policy and the interpretation

45. Garver, "How Can a Liberal Listen to a Religious Argument?" p. 168.

and application of law is an essentially hermeneutical enterprise. It also describes, in a general way, the manner in which the middle norms or axioms of natural law are developed and made actionable within civil society and the state. Although negative laicity or doctrinaire liberalism tends to stifle this rhetorical process of deliberation, positive laicity or moderate liberalism sustains the conditions under which this kind of public, moral, and legal truth may be pursued and established.[46] Moderate liberalism enables the rhetorical pursuit of practical moral truth in civil society, and secures the possibility that religious arguments may legitimately contribute to this process of deliberation through witness, argumentation, and dialogue.

A second feature of the nature of rhetorical truth is that it is closely tethered to the character and *ethos* of those who speak and those who listen in the process of deliberation. The inquiry into practical truth sought in public rhetoric takes place in what Garver describes as a "real hermeneutical circle" between *ethos* (character) and *logos* (reason). In Garver's words, "the more credible someone's arguments, the more I trust the speaker; the more I trust the speaker, the more I find his or her arguments credible."[47] In other words, credibility is fostered not by the strength of argument alone, or by appeals to authority alone, but also by the amount of trust that exists between the speaker and the audience. And trust is possible only when there is a certain kind of civic friendship. The speaker bears the responsibility for placing trust in her audience. Correlatively, this act of trust and goodwill actually serves to enhance the amount of trust that the audience perceives to be warranted by the character of the speaker. Rights to free speech ensure the negative freedom for religious persons or groups to present their arguments, but they do nothing to ensure that anyone else will want or have to listen.

---

46. Despite my indebtedness to Garver's analysis, the one point at which I part company with his conclusions is his discussion of the priority of the right over the good in liberalism. He writes, for example, that the "supposed priority of the right to the good is a metaphysical thesis about the nature of value. I recommend instead its rhetorical equivalent, the priority of agreement to truth. That essential strategy of liberalism, bracketing truth and aiming at agreement, seems unavailable for many religious thinkers" ("How Can a Liberal Listen to a Religious Argument?" p. 177). The priority of agreement to truth seems to prioritize procedural justice over and against Aristotle's understanding the process of communal deliberation as ultimately leading to practical truth. It does not seem to me that Aristotle brackets truth in favor of procedural justice in the way that a liberal priority of the right over the good tends to do. Rather, rhetorical deliberation becomes the appropriate means of discovering and implementing practical truth in the political realm.

47. Eugene Garver, "Why Should Anybody Listen? The Rhetoric of Religious Argument in Democracy," *Wake Forest Law Review* 36 (2001): 353-99, p. 380.

Therefore, the onus is partly on the speaker to create the conditions of trust under which his words may be taken as credible. As Aristotle and Aquinas both acknowledge, the only way to discern one's character is to analyze the nature of the ends that a person seeks in both word and deed. Attempts to circumvent this process by claims to direct authority will automatically undercut the audience members' trust in the character of the speaker. They will undercut the perceived rationality of the ends and means proposed by the speaker, even when the audience may be predisposed to agreement.[48] The public rhetoric of the culture wars has sought to exploit the negative side of this claim by discrediting the opposition, and Christian engagement in these forms of rhetoric only exacerbates the problem. Civic virtue practiced by the members of a pilgrim church can seek to put the positive side of this claim to good use in the pursuit of the common good by engaging in witness and rhetoric that builds rather than destroys civic trust and friendship.

Aristotle demonstrates that there are three, interconnected forms of proof *(pistis)* to be cultivated within the art of rhetoric:

> the proofs furnished by the speech are of three kinds. The first depends upon the moral character of the speaker [*ethos*], the second upon putting the hearer into a certain frame of mind [*logos*], the third upon the speech itself, insofar as it proves or seems to prove . . . [since] the orator persuades by means of his hearers, when they are roused to emotion by his speech [*pathos*]. (*Rhetoric* I.II 1356a3, 5)

I have discussed both *ethos* and *logos,* but *pathos* is the third component that must be creatively engaged for restoring public trust in rational deliberation. The best persuasive speech is capable of attaining all three, and thus it is worth looking closely at the manner in which passions contribute to rhetorical truth. Aristotle's *Rhetoric* helps us to understand that when trust is fostered in public dialogue, emotions can help to extend and support the capacity of reason to deliberate well about the most fitting political goals to be pursued in civic life.

I noted in Chapter 2 that Aristotle does not have a power of the human soul called the will, but he does write frequently about the faculty of

---

48. Garver writes that in situations where religious leaders claim absolute authority the "audience perceives this lack of character and consequently mistrusts the speaker, sometimes even when [or in spite of the fact that] it accepts his conclusion" ("Why Should Anybody Listen?" p. 392).

human desire (in Greek, *boulesis*) that is the result of proper rational deliberation about an end or good to be chosen. In the *Ethics* Aristotle refers to this as the "deliberative desire" that is the motivating force behind human acts (*Nicomachean Ethics* III.3 1113a). Thus, it is not surprising that when Aristotle deals with desire as the basis for the cause of the passions in the *Rhetoric,* he distinguishes between desires that are rational and those that are irrational:

> Now, of desires some are rational, and some are irrational: I call irrational those that are not the result of any assumption *(hypolambanein).* Such are those which are called natural; for instance those which come into existence through the body — such as the desire for food, thirst, hunger. . . . I call those desires rational *(meta logou)* which are due to our being convinced; for there are many things which we desire to see or acquire when we have heard them spoken of and are convinced that they are pleasant. (*Rhetoric* I.XI 1370a5)

The goal of truthful persuasion is thus to induce those who deliberate together to bring their desires into harmony with their sense of what is most noble, excellent, or rational. When this congruence occurs the members of a community are able to align their actions to contribute to pursuing both their individual good and the common good together. Both civic virtue and civic friendship are cultivated under these ideal conditions of communal deliberation. Aristotle writes that "the better and nobler the object, the better and nobler the desire" (*Rhetoric* I.VII 1364b19). For Bryan Massingale, a hopeful vision of this noble good tethered to passionate desire is essential to justice because desire and emotion possess "the power to transform even recalcitrant realities."[49] Or as Smith states it, "Good human societies have always been built on the very human belief that there's got to be something better than this."[50] A Thomistic theory of civic virtue maintains that the common good is the highest and most noble terrestrial good that is naturally desired by all persons, and that each person's individual flourishing and that of the community as a whole is dependent on a healthy perception of the common good. Thus, a primary goal of Christian public rhetoric is to draw the attention of the body politic to the common good itself and to the various

49. Bryan Massingale, *Racial Justice and the Catholic Church* (Maryknoll, N.Y.: Orbis, 2010), p. 143.
50. Smith et al., *Lost in Transition,* p. 237.

ways that it is best pursued and defended by engaging persons' passionate commitments and ideals.

Aristotle thus recognizes a distinctive role for the passions *(ta pathē)* in public rhetoric. For him "all those affections which cause persons to change their opinion in regard to their judgments, and are accompanied by pleasure or pain" (*Rhetoric* II.I.8 1378a8) may be put to effective and rational use in public deliberation. Since the goal toward which deliberation aims is a judgment in regard to a matter of contingent action to be taken (*Rhetoric* II.XVIII 1391b1), the passions contribute to the art of persuasion insofar as they can be analyzed as states of mind, the objects toward which they are directed, and the occasions that cause their arousal (*Rhetoric* II.I 1378a8-9). One of the goals of public rhetoric, then, is to create the conditions that facilitate the process by which the passions become properly oriented or well-ordered toward authentic human goods. They can then be put to effective, rational use by the speaker and the audience in an effort to contribute to a community's capacity to deliberate well together in regard to the best means for pursuing the common good.

It is worth pausing here to note that both Aristotle and Aquinas believe that the end or good toward which humans are naturally inclined is fixed and given by nature. This is one reason that Rawls and some other liberals want to avoid what they see as perfectionistic moral theories that uphold one vision of the good as one, fixed aspect of human nature. But for Aristotle and Aquinas (among others), deliberation occurs only when one or more persons form a judgment about a contingent situation in which the *means* to achieving a particular good or end are open to the choices of the agents. For example, Aristotle writes in the *Ethics* that "we do not deliberate about ends, but always about means . . . Since, therefore, when we choose, we choose something within our reach which we desire as the result of deliberation, we may describe *prohairesis* as 'the deliberative desire of something within our power'" (*Nicomachean Ethics* III.3 1113a). This belief that one does not deliberate about ends, but that they are given naturally by the ends of the virtues, is a point that Aquinas upholds as well. However, modern democracy and pluralism would seem to demand the capacity to deliberate not only about means, but also about ends. If it is true that our natural inclinations that order the virtues toward their proper ends are underdetermined or underdeveloped, then it would seem that it is possible to deliberate not only about the most fitting means but also about what ends are to be pursued within the political community.

Even though both Aristotle and Aquinas maintain that the goods or ends of human flourishing are fixed, they would likely both concur that this fact does not guarantee that everyone in a given culture will agree on what those ends are. For Aristotle, practical reason can be misled. Hence his polemic against the Sophists. And Aquinas is aware of the effects of sin on the human capacity to perceive and act on the good, which I discussed in Chapter 4. Therefore, Garver's assertion seems correct that "democracy makes possible reasoning about ends,"[51] especially insofar as democracy extends the limits of political participation beyond the purview of only those who govern. In the context of modern pluralism and democracy it is possible to deliberate not only about the means to a fixed or given end, but also about goods and ends themselves. Indeed, even as Christians uphold the common good as a naturally given end in their conception of human nature, it will be essential for them to be able to deliberate together with others about the existence of the common good. Since this end cannot be taken for granted as a starting point for public deliberation, it needs to be not only rationally and passionately defended in public discourse but also witnessed to with integrity in the practices that guide the members of a pilgrim church.

The philosopher Martha Nussbaum provides an important dialogue partner for recognizing both the positive role that emotion can play in public reasoning and just how difficult it is to recognize the common good in modern liberal theory, even when working out of a broadly Aristotelian framework. Her work has contributed much to contemporary discussions on the relevance of Aristotle as a source for contemporary moral deliberation, particularly with regard to the role of the passions and emotions in practical reasoning. In a simple and elegant description she claims that passions are "intelligent responses to the perception of value."[52] There are several important implications of this statement for considering how rhetoric might best function in a democratic context. First, she suggests that emotions are, or at least can be, *intelligent*. The tethering of passions to reason implies that passions can be examined for the manner in which they support or contribute to the process of practical reasoning precisely because they are capable of rational investigation and scrutiny. As discussed in the analysis of passions in relation to justice in Chapter 3, the passions can distract or derail the process of practical deliberation in a negative sense or they can support practical reasoning when they are properly ordered. In a cognitivist

51. Garver, *For the Sake of Argument*, p. 190.
52. Martha Nussbaum, *Upheavals of Thought: The Intelligence of Emotions* (Cambridge: Cambridge University Press, 2001), p. 1.

account of the passions and rhetoric, the appetitive energy of the passions can be harnessed and properly ordered by reason to effectively contribute to a collective process of deliberation about the common good.

Second, Nussbaum's definition implies that emotions are *responses* to what persons *perceive* as having *value*. This second part of Nussbaum's maxim rests on a teleological understanding of human action. That is, humans act in pursuit of the goods that they perceive as having real value and under the impetus that the passions (and, for Aquinas, the affections) provide to motivate their attainment. Garver notes a similar aspect of the passions as he writes that

> the importance of the passions as matter for the ethical virtues comes from what they are — potential desires — and from what they lack, namely determination. Since the passions are a part of the irrational powers of the soul that follows reason, *they are apprehensions of an object.*[53]

In Thomistic terms, to value certain goods or ends as being worthy of drawing our attention or desire (either in the bodily passions or in the spiritual affections of the intellect), human persons must first perceive these goods in the intellect and value such goods or ends in the will. The passions have the capacity to draw the attention of the will toward particular goods, and to present them as objects of deliberation within the intellect. The pursuit of the common good can only function to motivate human behavior if persons perceive this as a real, existent good and believe that the attainment of the common good will contribute to human flourishing or happiness for themselves and for others.

This approach to the role of the passions in rhetoric suggests that the kind of hermeneutical-rhetorical deliberation described above may aid the process of uniting the objective (the common good) and the subjective (the perception of value) components of practical deliberation.[54] Therefore,

---

53. Garver, *Confronting Aristotle's Ethics,* p. 103, italics added. Nussbaum also notes that "the emotions are themselves modes of vision, or recognition. Their responses are part of what knowing, that is truly recognizing or acknowledging, *consists in*" (*Love's Knowledge: Essays on Philosophy and Literature* [New York: Oxford University Press, 1990], p. 79).

54. Note again that this ability to tether one's subjective perception of morality with any external, objective source(s) of morality is precisely what is lacking in many emerging adults and in the broader American culture. Smith writes that it is necessary "to distinguish here between (a) moral claims (that are objectively true) being *embraced* subjectively by individuals through a process in which those individuals come to believe them, versus

Nussbaum adds, "the evaluations associated with emotions are evaluations from *my* perspective, not from some impartial perspective; they contain an ineliminable reference to the self."[55] Nussbaum's insight highlights an essential aspect of what Aquinas refers to as "political prudence," or the kind of reasoning about the common good required of those who participate in the public life of the community. She notes that rhetorical deliberation is exercised from within a particular context that requires careful attention to both a person's perception of the details of the context and the emotional states and particular attachments of the people that form such perception in the first place. Bryan Garsten similarly describes this kind of starting point for public deliberation as "situated judgment" or "deliberative partiality."[56]

This analysis suggests that human persons do not judge from some universal viewpoint, but rather from within the very attachments, concerns, and goals that define who they are as individuals and as a society. As Garver states it, "Rhetorical rationality is both contextually defined and responsive to standards."[57] This insight helps to explain why many have found Rawls's discussion of public reason problematic insofar as it tends to produce what Garsten calls "liberal alienation."[58] Rawlsian public reason seems to assume that there is a universal viewpoint or perspective from which public deliberation can occur. Or at the very least Rawls seems to assume that there is a form of public reason that can be predetermined to be equally accessible to all regardless of their particular thick visions of the good and passionate commitments. But the *Rhetoric* helps us to appreciate in an even more penetrating way than Rawls's analysis in *Political Liberalism* why in public deliberation individuals always work out of a thick, comprehensive philosophy or theology of the good. From the standpoint of public rhetoric, Rawlsian notions of public reason or the veil of ignorance ironically end up limiting the scope of civic trust by confining reason to narrowly agreed on, prede-

---

(b) moral claims (that may not be objectively true) taking on a quasi-true *status* for certain individuals as a result of those individuals believing them to be true . . . few [emerging adults] distinguish between the two meanings" (*Lost in Transition*, p. 23).

55. Nussbaum, *Love's Knowledge*, p. 52.

56. Bryan Garsten, *Saving Persuasion: A Defense of Rhetoric and Judgment* (Cambridge, Mass.: Harvard University Press, 2006), p. 13. In explaining these terms he writes that "we judge best when we are situated within these structures of value, able to draw on their complexity and able to feel, emotionally, the moral and practical relevance of different considerations in as subtle a way as experience has equipped us to do" (p. 192).

57. Garver, "Why Should Anybody Listen?" p. 365.

58. Garsten, *Saving Persuasion*, p. 184.

termined limits. Ironically, according to Garver, "Aristotle would say that reflection, justification, and elaborate articulation, can destroy character and replace it by knowledge."[59] Instead, as persons and groups witness to and defend their vision as a model to be followed by others in the society, an overlapping consensus may emerge on which to ground the shared values and ideals that define the common good of a politically united group of people. These principles and ideals make up the shared notion of the good, the common good, on which legal and political institutions depend, but they can only emerge in a pluralistic context out of the shared commitment to rhetorical discourse based on trust and a minimal level of civic friendship.

As Hunter notes, there is a tradition of liberal political theory, of which Rawls is one representative, "that claims that in a liberal democracy, the state is or should be neutral when it comes to questions of the good. This is wrong mainly because it is impossible. Law infers a moral judgment; policy implies a worldview."[60] Thus, public rhetoric contributes to the cultivation of a coherent, political vision of the good when individuals and groups begin from their specific context and argue passionately and reasonably in defense of their particular vision of the good.[61] As the example of the Catholic Church's dialogue with modernity and liberalism in the nineteenth and twentieth centuries indicates, this rhetorical exchange can lead to a dialectical refinement of insight into practical truths and values.

Engaging in this kind of rhetoric entails an ineliminable element of risk and vulnerability because all parties to the dialogue, if it is truly an exchange of ideas based on trust, are likely to have their vision formed, shaped, and honed by the dialogue itself. Thus, *both the content and the form* of the dialogue matter for how persons are formed in their vision of the common good. Indeed, if Hunter's analysis is correct, then he seems to indicate that Christians have been formed more by the rhetoric of the culture wars than by theological ideals of justice, charity, and civic virtue. If rhetoric can be

---

59. Garver, "Why Should Anybody Listen?" p. 383.

60. Hunter, *To Change the World,* p. 103.

61. I call this a "political" vision of the good, which I model off of Rawls's "political conception of the person" (see *Political Liberalism* [New York: Columbia University Press, 1993], p. xvii) because I want to defend the notion that the state cannot be neutral in regard to the good, but I also want to recognize that the state need not enforce a fully comprehensive doctrine of the good on others. The state must enforce what Stephen Macedo has referred to as a "limited but *pervasive*" vision of the good, one that is sufficient to order a people toward the common good ("Charting Liberal Virtues," in *Virtue,* ed. John W. Chapman and William A. Galston [New York: New York University Press, 1992], pp. 204-32, p. 212).

restored to an Aristotelian notion of public, dialectical pursuit of practical truth, guided by the passionate commitments and most reasonable ideals of a society's members — albeit one that will look and function quite different from ancient Athens or medieval Christendom — then it can also serve as a model for seeking an overlapping consensus on which relatively stable and just political institutions can be built. Indeed, if natural law insists that there are certain aspects of human morality that are embedded within the inclinations and desires of every person, then it should be possible to agree on the basic contours of the needs and rights of all persons, even in the absence of wider cultural agreement on thick notions of the good. The more Christians who practice civic virtue are able to be formed in alternative standards of public rhetoric that conform to standards of public deliberation and seek to build consensus, the more will they be contributing to the restoration of trust and to a form of cultural dialogue and exchange that can more effectively and truthfully pursue the common good and support just institutions for all.

I noted above that Nussbaum is helpful both for our understanding of the role of passions in practical reasoning and for showing the limits of the liberal tradition in cultivating a cognitive grasp of the common good as a real and actionable good. Recall that in Chapter 3 compassion was considered as a virtue that allows a person to experience another's distress as one's own (see *Summa theologiae* II-II 30.2), and that on Aquinas's account this can happen in two ways. The first entails a sympathetic experience of another's suffering due to a union of affection (such as naturally acquired compassion or infused charity), and the second involves the belief that a similar experience may befall oneself. Nussbaum also comments on this second way of cultivating compassion in two of her works, *The Therapy of Desire* (1996) and *Upheavals of Thought* (2001). While I am generally sympathetic with her efforts to develop the virtue of compassion for contemporary moral philosophy, a closer look at her account of compassion indicates why a Thomistic conception of civic virtue, and the account of compassion that it entails, provides resources for thinking about and developing compassion as tethered to the common good that are not as readily available in liberal thought.

One of Nussbaum's goals in *The Therapy of Desire* and *Upheavals of Thought* is to construct a cognitivist account of compassion that combines "logic with compassion,"[62] which draws on a positive account of the role of

---

62. Nussbaum, *The Therapy of Desire: Theory and Practice in Hellenistic Ethics* (Princeton, N.J.: Princeton University Press, 2009), p. 9.

the passions or emotions in practical reasoning,[63] and which is rooted in a broadly Aristotelian, eudaimonistic framework. In developing her account of compassion she notes that it has three cognitive elements:

> the judgment of *size* (a serious bad event has befallen someone); the judgment of *nondesert* (this person did not bring the suffering on himself or herself); and the *eudaimonistic judgment* (this person, or creature, is a significant element in my scheme of goals and projects, an end whose good is to be promoted). The Aristotelian *judgment of similar possibilities* is an epistemological aid to forming the *eudaimonistic judgment* — not necessary, but usually very important.[64]

The first two elements seem relatively straightforward, and I focus on what Nussbaum means by the eudaimonistic judgment and what this entails for her account of compassion. For Nussbaum the rational pursuit of happiness or flourishing *(eudaimonia)* presupposes a distinctive set of human powers and capacities that can be developed through education and practical experience to enable an individual to strive toward happiness.[65] When it comes to developing compassion, Nussbaum draws on the second possible manner of doing so that was noted above — that is, she bases it on the belief that a similar, unjust harm may befall oneself.

Therefore, Nussbaum's eudaimonistic judgment requires that someone must "view the other person as an important part of one's schemes or goals."[66] On her account compassion involves an acceptance of the vulnerability that is involved in recognizing that if unjust suffering can befall someone else in society, then it behooves me qua individual to prevent such suffering from happening (or to redress the situation when it does happen) because a similar fate could befall *me* in the future. This is part of what she means when she claims that, for her, Aristotelian thought always contains an "ineliminable reference to the self."[67] While I agree that from a virtue perspective based

---

63. This account of the role of the passions is even more thoroughly developed in two essays from *Love's Knowledge:* "The Discernment of Perception," pp. 54-105, and "Perception and Revolution," pp. 195-219.

64. Nussbaum, *Upheavals of Thought,* p. 321.

65. She develops these Aristotelian insights into a full-fledged theory of rights in *Women and Human Development: The Capabilities Approach* (Cambridge: Cambridge University Press, 2000).

66. Nussbaum, *Upheavals of Thought,* p. 330.

67. Nussbaum, *Upheavals of Thought,* p. 52.

on the pursuit of happiness or wellbeing there will always be an ineliminable reference to the self, it should be noted that this need not be the *only,* or even the best, manner of cultivating genuine compassion.

Despite the many merits of Nussbaum's account of compassion (and correlatively, rights), there is one thing that her account cannot do. It cannot move beyond the self-referential perspective that defines it and into the kind of union of affection that is the basis for the first way that Aquinas describes as the ground for compassion. Furthermore, Aquinas's first way of construing compassion is ultimately more effective for cultivating greater civic friendship and trust. Moreover, and this is essential to an account of compassion as a subjective part of civic virtue, it cannot do so precisely because there is no recognition of the common good in her account. In Nussbaum's Aristotelianism every ethical judgment remains purely self-referential. For example, Nussbaum writes that

> compassion is our species' way of hooking the good of others to the fundamentally eudaimonistic (though not egoistic) structure of our imaginations and our most intense desires. The good of others means nothing to us in the abstract or antecedently. It is when it is brought into relation with that which we already understand — with our intense love of parents, our passionate need for comfort and security — that such things start to matter deeply.[68]

The reason that it is so helpful to look at Nussbaum's construal of compassion is because she shows exactly how far one can develop an account of compassion from within a liberal paradigm and drawing on an ancient eudaimonistic and teleological construal of humans as subjects (a unique combination to be sure). At the same time, her work shows us what the limits of such an approach are.

Her argument for compassion always starts with the individual and ends with the individual, though it does have the merit of attempting to bring other individuals into one's field of concern. As we saw in the citation above, this self-referential element of her theory does not necessarily make it egoistic. Her approach does not, however, demonstrate any way beyond this self-referential moment, or indicate how goods that transcend the individual might be perceived and function in the motivating structure of virtue. Although Nussbaum's approach is much more philosophically so-

---

68. Nussbaum, *Upheavals of Thought,* p. 388.

phisticated than the perspective held by the majority of emerging adults described by Smith, it seems isomorphic with the same kind of inability to consider morality from a perspective beyond the self. Based on his research and interviews with young adult Americans, Smith indicates that declining civic and political participation among young adults and in American culture is due at least in part because "it is hard for emerging adults *to see an objective reality beyond the individual self.*"[69] A Thomistic construal of compassion as a subjective part of civic virtue tethers each individual person's good to the common good in such a manner that Aquinas's first manner of construing compassion becomes a viable alternative.

In other words, a Thomistic account of civic virtue and compassion provides a realistic cognitive schema for viewing the interdependent nature of human persons, societies, and cultures that is not based solely on *my* subjective needs, desires, and perspectives. The recognition of such a shared, common good is also necessary for moving beyond the reference to the self, without ever leaving the self-referential element entirely behind, that is demanded by a full development of the architectonic virtues of the will — that is, of justice and charity. A critical conception of the common good allows one to engage in the kind of union of affection that enables an agent to feel compassion for another's unjust suffering out of a sense of a shared good precisely because there are real standards of judgment beyond the self that make demands on a person's moral decision-making. This first kind of compassion — the one grounded in a shared conception of the good — is an important result of having interiorized and perfected civic virtue.

Of course, an objective sense of the good is never completely divorced from one's subjective perception of one's own good being intimately tied into the common good. But this is a different way of construing the self in relation to the wellbeing of others and to the common good than we find in Nussbaum and liberal thought. The fact that both justice and charity, as virtues of the will, lead the agent to act on goods higher than the individual's good raises a paradox within Aquinas's own thought. For he maintains throughout his moral anthropology, following Aristotle's opening lines of the *Ethics,*[70] that the motivational structure of all human action is grounded in the innate search for the agent's own happiness. Therefore, the assertion

---

69. Smith et al., *Lost in Transition*, p. 221.

70. "Every skill and every inquiry, and similarly every action and rational choice, is thought to aim at some good; and so the good has been aptly described as that at which everything aims" (*Nicomachean Ethics* I.1 1094a1-3).

that the fullness of virtue simultaneously entails acting in pursuit of one's individual happiness and the pursuit of goods that transcend than the individual's good (that is, the common good for justice, and God as the supreme good in charity) seems to present a conundrum for an account of civic virtue as an expression of general justice.[71] In other words, how can I, as an agent, desire my own good as my ultimate goal and motivating force for action while simultaneously believing that the fullness of virtue is only found in seeking to secure the good of others through the virtues of justice and charity?

This paradox is resolved, however, if it remains objectively true that each agent's individual good is intrinsically tethered to certain goods that transcend an individual's self-interest. It must be the case that human happiness and virtue is distinctively and intrinsically bound up with the pursuit of the common good of one's community, and it is here where a Thomistic account differs from the manner in which Nussbaum construes the self-referential element of all human action. In a Thomistic account of civic virtue, the flourishing or happiness of each individual agent does not need to be "hooked" to the "eudaimonistic . . . structure of our imaginations," as Nussbaum describes it (although this kind of thought experiment may be quite helpful). Rather, there is a natural recognition that the common good is an essential element and precondition of individual human flourishing. Indeed, it is an essential condition for the flourishing of individual human agents to such an extent that human flourishing cannot be conceived of without being tethered to the common good in such an intrinsic and natural manner. Of course, this is no longer a widely recognized facet of human existence in late modern culture, in part due to the predominance of the notions of market freedom that I discussed in the previous chapter. But this is precisely why a rhetoric for speaking about the common good as a real, subsistent good is so necessary. Although not the sole intellectual possession of the Catholic tradition, this is one moral truth that has survived in a distinctive manner in the institutional and intellectual structures of the Roman Catholic Church, and we have a distinctive responsibility to witness to and defend its objective reality and its significance for human wellbeing.

---

71. I am particularly grateful to Jean Porter for pointing out this paradox to me in an essay that she has prepared for a festschrift in honor of Gene Outka, "The Desire for Happiness and the Virtues of the Will: Resolving a Paradox in Aquinas' Thought" (personal copy). This same tension is also noted by M. S. Kempshall in *The Common Good in Late Medieval Political Thought* (Oxford: Clarendon, 1999) when he writes: "It is the corollary between happiness and goodness in the political community which makes Aquinas' interpretation of the relationship between the individual and the common good so problematic" (p. 79).

There is one other dimension of Aristotle's work that requires further development to be applicable in late modern cultures. I believe that it is possible to infer from what Aristotle says about rhetorical persuasion to say more than he does about what kind of audience the members of the body politic must be to participate in the kind of deliberation about the good for which a Thomistic account of civic virtue advocates. This consideration brings us back to addressing the problems of elitism and epistemological hubris noted in the previous discussion of natural law in the work of John Courtney Murray and Steven Long. If the account of civic virtue and rhetoric defended here is to be applicable in modern democratic regimes, then all citizens and members of civil society must have a justiciable right to participate in the process of communal deliberation about the best political ends and means to be pursued. As Perreau-Saussine writes, "Democracy has at its root a striking politicization of human society. Politics is no longer confined to a little group of oligarchs or aristocrats. The people, as such, have come onto the scene, and with them a new demand for collective autonomy as well as a new passion for individual liberty."[72] A democratic theory of Thomistic civic virtue entails an extension of civic and political responsibility to all members of a community. Correlatively, it demands an extension of a distinctive kind of civic friendship that fosters the conditions of trust in which each member is empowered to participate in public deliberation. Ultimately, the extension of trust and civic virtue may become an act of both civic virtue and Christian charity.

Overall, Aristotle does not seem to endorse primarily democratic forms of government, but he does give one indication of the possibility of a healthy form of democratic deliberation. For example, he writes in the *Politics:*

> The principle that the multitude ought to be in power rather than the few best might seem to be solved and to contain some difficulty and perhaps even truth. For the many, of whom each individual is not a good person, when they meet together may be better than the few good, if regarded not individually but collectively, just as a feast to which many contribute is better than a dinner provided out of a single purse. For each individual among the many has a share of excellence and practical wisdom *(phronē-sis),* and when they meet together, just as they become in a manner one person, who has many feet, and hands, and senses, so too with regard to their character and thought. (*Politics* III.XI 1281b1-7)[73]

---

72. Perreau-Saussine, *Catholicism and Democracy,* p. 149.

73. It is interesting to note here the similarity between this kind of corporeal metaphor,

This comment can be combined with the insights into the nature of rhetorical deliberation discussed above to provide further support for the claim that the process of collective practical reasoning in regard to the good and the means toward the good is best fostered in something like modern democratic forms of government, where the maximum amount of freedom compatible with defense of the common good also facilitates the maximum amount of participation among citizens. This suggests that the kind of negative freedom from interference advocated by most liberal perspectives on rights is a necessary but insufficient precondition for broader political participation of the members of a community. The discourse of social media elites that most influence the rhetoric of the culture wars creates the conditions in which moderate voices seeking to work out practical solutions — those who are working out the middle norms of natural law — are mostly ignored or overlooked in public debates. We will need new and wider public and institutional spaces that serve to foster this kind of participatory deliberation.[74] Given the slow and unpredictable process by which cultures change there is no guarantee that this kind of change will happen, but those who practice civic virtue can at least more wisely channel their efforts toward creating the kind of conditions that foster greater civic friendship and trust so that healthy debate has a greater possibility of occurring.

It is within these kinds of public and institutional spaces that a different approach to the working out of the middle axioms of natural law may occur than the ones suggested by Murray's elitism and Long's epistemological superiority in natural law reasoning. Here we can turn again to the sociological notion that Christian Smith has called the "sociological imagination,"[75] and what Charles Taylor describes as the "social imaginary."[76] Both concepts are

---

which we have seen Aquinas also uses in discussing the common good, to the way that Paul writes about the church as the body of Christ made up of many members working together in one body (cf. 1 Cor. 12:12-17; Eph. 4:11-16).

74. One area where this is occurring is in the movement of "deliberative democracy" that brings together groups of citizens to deliberate on practical solutions to difficult or intractable political issues. See, for example, *The Deliberative Democracy Handbook: Strategies for Effective Civic Engagement in the Twenty-First Century,* ed. John Gastil and Peter Levine (San Francisco: Jossey-Bass, 2005).

75. "The sociological imagination seeks to understand the *personal experiences of individual people,* on the one hand, and *larger social and cultural trends, forces, and powers,* on the other, by *explaining each in terms of the other*" (*Lost in Transition,* p. 4).

76. Taylor describes the social imaginary as "the ways people imagine their social existence, how they fit together with others, how things go on between them and their fellows, the expectations which are normally met, and the deeper normative notions and images

descriptive terms that capture the shared conception of the good, values, and ideals that emerge in the complex, dialectical relationship between individuals' thick conceptions of the good and the public culture. In the process of rhetorical deliberation the sociological imagination and the social imaginary may function like what Aristotle calls *enthymemes* — those commonsense ideals that are shared, often implicitly, by the majority of the members of a political community. If these are engaged using the rhetorical tools of reason, emotion, and character, the middle axioms of natural law may emerge from the collective experience and public dialogue that constitutes the complex trialectic between ideals, persons, and the institutions and practices that make up pluralistic, democratic communities.

Finally, there is one further aspect of Aristotle's discussion of *Rhetoric* that I want to consider before closing this section. Aristotle notes that there are three kinds of rhetorical speech: "deliberative, forensic, and epideictic" (*Rhetoric* I.III 1358b3). Deliberative speech for Aristotle has to do with deliberation about the best and most expedient means toward a given end. Forensic speech has to do with particular justice and whether or not an act is judged just or unjust, lawful or unlawful, and it is practiced especially in the judicial system. Forensic speech is the most technical of the three, while deliberation and epideictic speech are atechnical forms of reasoning. Finally, epideictic speech has to do with assigning praise or blame to that which is considered good, excellent, and noble, or evil and shameful. As such, it is intimately connected with the way that persons perceive and make actionable the ideals and values that inform culture. Both deliberative and epideictic rhetoric, however, are particularly salient for the kind of public witnessing that I am suggesting the members of a pilgrim church should practice as an essential modality of civic virtue. I want to suggest in particular that epideictic rhetoric is the best resource for witnessing to, arguing for, and demonstrating (in an enthymatic, rather than a strictly logical, syllogism) the existence of the common good in the context of plurality and modern democratic societies. Both logical (analogical/metaphysical and technical) arguments for the existence of the common good and rhetorical (enthymatic and atechnical) arguments can be combined to facilitate a critical, rational grasp of the common good, supported by well-ordered passions, as the foundation of acts of civic virtue.

It is now possible to bring this supplemental discussion of Aristotelian

---

which underlie these expectations" (*Modern Social Imaginaries* [Durham, N.C.: Duke University Press, 2004], p. 23).

rhetoric more directly back into the development of a Thomistic conception of civic virtue. First, one notes that not all of the scholars I have engaged here are using the language of passions, affections, and emotions in the distinctive ways that Aquinas himself does. In speaking specifically about Aristotle's *Rhetoric* I have tried to use the word "passions" to refer to the bodily sensations of pain or pleasure that are constitutive of deliberative desire. Nussbaum, on the other hand, frequently refers to emotions in general and sometimes to passions in particular without much linguistic distinction, and this also seems to be in line with our common, cultural language, especially to the extent that it is informed by modern psychology.[77] Yet I have already noted that Aquinas distinguishes between passions and affections; and moreover, this distinction is derived from his positing of the faculty of the will (the intellectual appetite) in the human soul, a faculty that was not present in Aristotle's analysis. Bringing the notion of the will back into our discussion of civic virtue requires placing these Aristotelian insights into the system and language of Aquinas. In doing so, I do not believe that we are doing a disservice either to Aristotle or to Aquinas, but rather attempting to continue developing a tradition of thought that can be traced back to both thinkers in a coherent and intelligible manner — a tradition that continues to develop and take on new and distinctive features in the contemporary context of pluralism and democracy.

On the one hand, Christians have recourse to the dialectical, analogical, and philosophically technical argument about the existence of the common good developed in Chapter 2. This includes Aquinas's metaphysical discussion of God as the highest common good of all of creation, and the temporal common good of the human community as analogically related to God as Creator. A Thomistic anthropology adds the fact that both of these modalities of the common good are naturally perceived and desired by all persons (no matter how inchoately). The use of analogical comparison here suggests that there is both congruence and dissimilarity between these two forms of the common good, insofar as the temporal common good can be rationally perceived and function as a good that motivates human action, even without direct reference to God as the source of all common goods. The acquired form of civic virtue is capable of at least a basic recognition of this terrestrial common good. This congruence and dissimilarity is isomorphic to the dis-

---

77. For a more in-depth evaluation of these linguistic and conceptual notions regarding emotion, see Nicholas E. Lombardo, O.P., *The Logic of Desire: Aquinas on Emotion* (Washington, D.C.: Catholic University of America Press, 2011), pp. 224-27.

cussion on the analogical distinction between nature and grace, especially in recognizing that grace does not destroy but rather perfects nature. The infused form of civic virtue will consider the analogical relationship of the temporal common good as tethered to and dependent on God as the source of being and truth. Furthermore, the habits of the infused forms of charity and justice underscore the intrinsic connection between love of God, self, and neighbor (in the order of charity), and the call to meet the requirements of justice (both particular and general) in the temporal realm, even as the acquired form of justice can similarly be a motivating virtue for those who have not received the gift of grace.

Some version of this kind of metaphysical deduction regarding the existence of the temporal common good is something that (ideally) would be shared by all Christians who believe in God as the supreme good of the universe (or indeed anyone who upholds some form of metaphysical theism, no matter how generally construed). For Christians arguing in favor of the common good in a contemporary context of pluralism, this would serve as the logical, dialectical, and technical proof of the existence of the temporal common good of the community. In other words, this argument is the *logos* at the heart of the Christian claim that the common good is a real and existent good. However, in moving from theological or philosophical proofs of the existence of the common good into the public forum of collective deliberation, *ethos* and *pathos* also need to be wisely engaged through less technical means of witnessing.

As noted above, it cannot be taken for granted that all members of a late modern democracy will agree on the existence of the common good, at least not as the starting point for an argument. In stating this, I do not claim that Christians should cease efforts trying to convince others about the truth of the analogical relationship between the existence of God and the temporal common good, but rather that their strictly logical arguments about the existence of the common good (or their attempts simply to assert this fact, especially when couched in the language of the culture wars) have heretofore been unsuccessful in convincing the majority of those who are educated and formed in liberal cultures that such a thing exists. This is precisely the point at which the rhetorical tools of deliberative and epideictic speech, involving both *ethos* and *pathos,* can be Christians' most persuasive means of reasoning together with their fellow citizens into *a critical conception and perception of the common good* as a real, existent good, and thus as the cognitive structure that forms the foundation for acts of civic virtue.

Although analytically separable, epideictic speech regarding the common good, *ethos* (the character of individual Christians and church bodies engaging in public deliberation about the existence of the common good) and *pathos* can function together to underscore the existence of the common good and to articulate the middle norms of natural law in the atechnical forms of rhetorical and practical deliberation. For example, Garver claims that "successful epideictic rhetoric is a development of self-knowledge,"[78] as he writes that

> when each citizen knows something, then epideictic rhetoric, through symbolic affirmations and rituals, including ritual trials, can convert knowledge from something that each person knows [individually] to something that everybody knows [collectively] and which therefore can figure in deliberations. . . . Making common knowledge truly common is the function of epideictic rhetoric, as opposed to the deliberative rhetoric that calculates means to an end and judicial or forensic rhetoric that determines guilt or innocence in the past. It concerns *collective responsibility* as opposed to individual guilt.[79]

Thus, when Christians want to demonstrate the existence of the temporal common good, it is possible to begin with the logical assurance that it is a truly existent good, but then deliberate together with their fellow citizens toward demonstrating it as a truly existent good. In this process, their fellow deliberators may not be immediately convinced by technical arguments such as those adduced in moral theology, but rather they may grow into awareness of the common good as all discover together the middle axioms of natural law that point toward the shared aims of the common good. Doing so requires that Christians who engage in public rhetoric need to risk trusting that others will reason together with them, in part based on others' perception of their characters. But this character itself is already witnessed by the fact of placing trust in the audience and one's fellow community members. This will be a gradual process of self-discovery that members of the pilgrim church undertake with others from a multitude of religious and philosophical backgrounds, and they are not likely to secure 100 percent agreement on its existence. But it is at least possible for a community's self-understanding and knowledge of the common good to grow and expand through the process of dialogue, critical reflection, deliberation, and lived experience together. Aristotle's *Rhetoric* helps to demonstrate in particular how logical

78. Garver, *For the Sake of Argument*, p. 38.
79. Garver, *For the Sake of Argument*, p. 39, italics added.

argument alone will not be persuasive, but that character and humble but passionate commitment can serve to foster not only greater trust and civic friendship but also a more accurate perception of moral truth.

Therefore, a correlative to this need to engage in epideictic speech that praises the nobility of the common good is the need to continue to develop an *ethos* that fosters a sense of the common good, not only within the pilgrim church itself, but also in the manner in which Christians and Christian communities speak and act toward those who do not share the same biblical or theological presuppositions. Religious arguments in democratic contexts tend to be problematic to the extent that there is a tendency to enter the public forum as if already in possession of absolute moral certainty. But there is an important distinction between moral certainty within a coherent historical, institutional, philosophical, and theological tradition such as the Catholic Church and the expectation, or worse, the demand, that this certainty is to be shared by all members of a democratic society.

This call to character and authentic witness may seem tautological, but it is necessary for Christians to speak and act *as if* the common good were truly their goal when they engage in public acts and deliberation if they expect anyone else to trust and believe them on this particular point. Garver indicates that "Aristotle's great idea . . . is that the *ethos* that is, and ought to be, the most powerful and authoritative source of belief must be an *ethos* created by argument (*Rhetoric* I.2.1356a5-13)."[80] Thus, when it comes to showing others the way to a critical conception of the common good following an epideictic form of deliberation, logical argument and character are both essential ingredients in demonstrating what Christians believe to be an essential truth about human existence — that is, the belief that the common good is the highest natural good of human life.

Public rhetoric thus represents a distinctive manner of witnessing to the moral realism that is foundational to natural law reasoning. First, Aristotle believes that rhetorical proofs will ultimately be persuasive only if they reflect a general congruence between the beliefs that individuals and communities hold and the lived experience of those who deliberate (that is, a connection between thought and reality — that is, a critical moral realism). This is nothing less than aiming at moral truth in the kind of practical reasoning that I am recommending that combines *logos, ethos,* and *pathos.* For example, in developing Aristotle's conception of the emotions Nussbaum insists that ethical reflection must meet three criteria to be considered rea-

---

80. Garver, *For the Sake of Argument,* p. 33.

sonable: internal consistency, correspondence, and broad coherence and fit.[81] In her case, this does not require any kind of "metaphysics of internal representations that allegedly mirror the world,"[82] such as Aquinas's conception of *phantasms* (*Summa theologiae* I 76). Without some kind of moral realism, however, attempts to cultivate compassion and to defend the common good are doomed to be short-circuited by the forces of cultural dissolution and nihilism. For the purposes of Christians engaging in public deliberation from within natural law tradition it is important to recognize that the existence of the common good is an implicitly, if also inchoately, desired good of all human persons. As one of the natural inclinations that orders the virtue of general justice toward the common good, we can recognize it as a universally shared human longing — albeit one that has been significantly underdeveloped in the late modern cultural, philosophical, linguistic, and free market paradigm.[83] The starting point for deliberation should thus not be an *assertion* of the existence of the common good (recall that the more authoritarian these assertions become the more they erode trust), but rather a charitable act of *trust* in our fellow humans' innate desire for and capacity to rationally discern the middle axioms of natural law and the rough contours of the ideals and practices that constitute common good. This is precisely where we should expect to begin the effort to move the idea of the common good from something that is universally but inchoately desired by many, if not all, individuals into something commonly recognized. Only then will it become an actual good capable of being articulated, grasped, perceived, and acted on as a guide to practical reasoning in law and politics.

81. Nussbaum, *The Therapy of Desire*, pp. 23-24.

82. Nussbaum, *Upheavals of Thought*, p. 37.

83. Smith provides two observations with regard to this phenomenon among emerging adults that are quite fascinating. In analyzing the moral reasoning of young adults he notes that the majority of them believe that the only reliable sources of moral authority are subjective feelings and personal experience, but that when pushed to explain the sources of their moral beliefs, they "in fact, turn out to be highly oriented to the interests, needs, or desires of *social* relations" (*Lost in Transition*, p. 35). He also adds that most emerging adults report "just knowing" right from wrong at an intuitive level, as if everyone has a natural, innate knowledge of right versus wrong. He concludes his analysis by stating that "in very many ways, emerging adults today express many of the difficulties that beset modern and postmodern moral philosophy — skepticism, relativism, subjectivism, and the interminability of debates due to the inability of any one school or approach to decisively win the argument . . . despite all the individualism and social constructionism that is evident in so much emerging adult moral reasoning — on this point most emerging adults seem to be giving voice to something like the very premodern notion of a *natural law*" (p. 55).

If our emotional states (including passions and affections) function as Nussbaum describes them (as "intelligent responses to perceptions of value") then it is possible, indeed even necessary, to *feel* a certain passionate commitment toward the common good. And the more that character or *ethos* is utilized to cultivate civic trust, the more will such appeals to emotion be capable of being harnessed in support of rational deliberation. For example, anger toward those who harm individuals in society or the common good as a whole can be a valuable tool in cultivating this kind of rhetoric. The role of anger in regard to justice is a phenomenon recognized by both Aquinas and Aristotle (*Summa theologiae* I-II 47; *Rhetoric* I.13 1373b3; II.2 1378a9). Recall that anger is the principal passion located in the irascible part of the soul, and is thus moderated through the cardinal virtue of courage or fortitude. Insofar as anger is brought into the participation of reason through the exercise of fortitude, the passion of anger becomes the subject of a human virtue, thereby following the political rule of reason and the mean (see *Summa theologiae* I-II 56.4). Because anger can also be left outside the domain of reason, it can either contribute to the increase in virtue or detract from it. Anger can be experienced at inappropriate times or in response to inappropriate situations (such as becoming angry when no slight has been done toward one or one's friends). In such cases it is out of line with reason. Or anger can be experienced in too great a degree (for example, too much anger as it is fostered toward one's perceived enemies, as we have witnessed in the rhetoric of the culture wars), or too little of a degree (as in apathy toward injustice). In such cases anger does not follow the mean.

However, when anger is channeled by courage according to reason and the mean, it draws one's attention to a harm done to an individual, a vulnerability group, or the common good, and leads one to seek appropriate restitution. Restoring the balance of equality that is harmed in acts against the common good is an act of general justice, and requires the faculty of judgment in determining what will be an appropriate amount of restitution. Finally, a proper judgment with regard to the particulars of a just amount of restitution requires the intellectual virtue of prudence, and it requires a movement of the will to seek and desire justice. This movement toward justice and the common good can be supported by well-ordered anger leading to the restoration of the balance and equality that justice seeks to uphold.

Therefore, in order for one to be motivated to seek justice and restitution after becoming justifiably angered, one must also have a particular affection for the common good as the foundation for acts of civic virtue. In many cases — though not always — this affection will be sparked into action through the passion of anger that draws one's attention to the injustice in the first place. A passion, in this case anger, can ignite a process that although it involves a movement of the irascible faculty, is moderated by reason and the mean as it is brought under the control of the virtue of fortitude. Fortitude demands not the extermination of anger, but rather its regulation according to the rule of reason and the mean.

Anger, through a movement of the embodied, sensible (irascible) appetite, when it is moderated by reason through fortitude, draws the attention of the intellect and will to a situation of injustice against the common good such that the will can thus experience an affection that moves it to engage in acts of civic virtue. As Nicholas Lombardo writes, "anger, however, stops short of making a decision: it presents itself, but then waits for us to make a judgment about the situation and decide upon a course of action."[84] I noted above that one of the social consequences of the kind of collective resentment fostered by the rhetoric of the culture wars is that we have lost our ability to wisely channel our anger toward justice. Consider the example of the collective public anger after the "financial meltdown" in the United States in 2008. The general sense of anger experienced individually and collectively, if wisely harnessed, could potentially lead Americans as a people into a process of collective deliberation about the best means of creating and sustaining laws and institutions that provide greater financial accountability and protection to the members of the body politic. Such deliberation toward and through the middle axioms of natural law would also lead toward a deeper appreciation for the existence of the common good and for the manner in which the passions can spur Americans as a people toward justice rather than division. This kind of communal deliberation would simultaneously form Americans as a people into the kind of persons who can wisely moderate anger and cultivate the kind of civic virtue necessary to sustain democratic institutions.

The tools of rhetoric can point to a general emotional experience that is common to many persons in our culture (an enthymeme), and provide more healthy ways of channeling that anger into greater justice and support for the common good. As noted above in Hunter's analysis of the culture wars, anger at injustice is a hallmark of contemporary public and political discourse, but we have developed very few cultural resources for channeling this anger into effective means of pursuing greater justice. In and of itself, and when properly brought into accord with reason and the mean, this kind of anger is healthy and can lead to restitution and the restoration of justice.

84. Lombardo, *The Logic of Desire*, p. 239.

Paul's admonition to "be angry but do not sin" (Eph. 4:26) suggests that anger may be put to virtuous use. Aquinas calls this "zealous anger" (*ira per zelum; Summa theologiae* II-II 158.2). It seems, however, that our sense of anger remains incapable of guiding us toward greater justice and equality in contemporary democracies, precisely because we have lost the capacity to channel our anger into reasonable forms of deliberation that will lead us to seek justice in regard to harm done to the common good. Without proper channeling of anger it turns into Nietzschean resentment and is destructive of the common good and the moral character of the body politic.

In response, many forms of liberal discourse, such as Rawls's public reason, have sought to remove anger from the discourse in an appeal to a higher, sovereign, "rational" discourse where questions of justice can be sorted out. According to Garver, "Aristotle would say that [narrowly restricted forms of] reflection, justification, and elaborate articulation, can destroy character and replace it by [technical] knowledge."[85] The move toward this kind of technocratic, bourgeois liberalism is precisely what thinkers like MacIntyre, Cavanaugh, and Baxter critique about the modern liberal state. The point, however, is not to downplay the necessity of knowledge, but rather to note that attempts to achieve consensus that seek to eliminate emotion and character end up unnecessarily restricting the range of knowledge or reason that is necessary to deliberate well together as a community. Meanwhile, those who are excluded from this kind of discourse seem to become only angrier and louder in their expression. As Aquinas notes, reasonable anger that cannot be appropriately expressed and addressed can quickly lead to "mania" or to "vindictiveness" (*Summa theologiae* I-II 46.8). It is no wonder then that our public discourses are frequently reduced to ad hominem attacks against individuals or groups who are perceived as a threat to our own sense of safety and security.

What has been lost is the effective capacity to express anger in reasonable ways that lead to the pursuit of general justice and the common good, and to discovering the middle norms of natural law. Part of the difficulty in practicing this kind of civic virtue is that although we have institutions in which forensic rhetoric can be expressed and practiced (in the judicial system), and in which deliberation about the creation of laws can take place (usually in congresses or parliaments), late modern culture on the whole lacks institutions that support epideictic rhetoric of the sort that would help us to make sense of our collective anger at injustice against the common

85. Garver, "Why Should Anybody Listen?" p. 383.

good.[86] The frustration that results from this only seems to feed into deeper confusion and resentment.

Therefore, what emerges from a Thomistic account of civic virtue is a different set of conclusions about what it means to witness to moral truth in public discourse than are typically offered in the debates between religious believers and liberal theorists. First, civic virtue proposes a positive vision for moving forward that makes the total rejection of the liberal nation-state system unnecessary. Second, it remains rooted in the natural law tradition and the church's basic theological commitments so that Christians can provide the necessary criticisms of the more aggressive forms of secularism and militant liberalism that tend to exclude religious arguments from public deliberation. Third, rather than ruling out the conditions for the possibility of anything beyond basic agreement on the procedural principles of justice as a mere modus vivendi, incorporating a more democratic construal of practical deliberation creates greater opportunity to seek the good together as a society. As Garver states it,

> Pluralism creates an ethical middle ground between negative respect and the positive love of intimates, between rights and politeness, between instrumental rationality between strangers and the sort of friendship or love that disposes of personal identity. . . . We find this middle ground in the intellectual virtues of political friendship and trust.[87]

Elsewhere he adds that practical solutions emerge from within the "deliberative space that lies between rights and etiquette."[88] Although this approach is not a magic bullet that will end the kind of vitriolic public debate that defines much of our current public discourse, it is at least a way to envision a path that would move forward with a form of deliberation together about the common good that seeks to rebuild political friendship and trust. A Thomistic account of civic virtue seeks to bring these virtues back into the common *ethos* of late modern constitutional democracies by providing a charitable witness to this kind of dialogue and deliberation.

---

86. Garver, *For the Sake of Argument*, p. 189.
87. Garver, *For the Sake of Argument*, p. 17.
88. Garver, "How Can a Liberal Listen to a Religious Argument?" p. 167.

Politics for a Pilgrim Church

Finally, beloved, whatever is true, whatever is honorable, whatever is just, whatever is pure, whatever is pleasing, whatever is commendable, if there is any excellence and if there is anything worthy of praise, think about these things.

Philippians 4:8

My goal has been to consider how the insights into the nature of general justice or civic virtue in the work of Thomas Aquinas continue to provide guidance to the members of the pilgrim church for engaging in the liberal, democratic societies of the late modern world. My concerns have not been merely archaeological. Renewed insight into what Aquinas held to be true of the nature of the human person, of political institutions, and of the nature of law (in all of its modalities — eternal, divine, natural, positive) can continue to guide the moral witness of Christians today. There is a sense in which the cultivation of civic virtue as *a firm and stable disposition to direct the acts of the virtues toward the common good of one's society* is a universal component of what it means to strive for the kind of perfection or wellbeing that human persons can achieve in this earthly existence. Civic virtue reflects the aims of the Christian wayfarer insofar as her pursuit of her ultimate good in the kingdom of God entails a commitment to the common good and the good of others, expressed paradigmatically through the two architectonic virtues of justice and charity.

A general notion of civic virtue, however, no matter how well defined on a theoretical level, would remain sterile if not put into practice in particular communities, places, and times. Indeed, the need to move from general categories and norms toward specific precepts and acts in contingent, historical circumstances is congruent with the method of natural law described in Chapter 4. Therefore, I have tried to provide an analysis of the historical relationship between the Catholic Church and modern liberal states, as well as the cultural and political conditions of late modern democratic societies within which the members of the pilgrim church are called to live out their commitment to the common good. An accurate grasp of the current context makes possible the wise and prudent means of implementing civic virtue in late modern democratic societies.

I claimed initially that a full appreciation of a theological construal of civic virtue has remained underdeveloped, in part because of the church's historical struggle to come to terms with liberal political thought and the practices of modern, secular states. One of the central insights that emerges from a consideration of this history is an appreciation for the delicate manner with which the church maintains a critical stance toward more doctrinaire forms of liberalism while also affirming moderate liberalism's commitment to universal, natural human rights, not least of which is the right to religious freedom. Understanding these two sides of the Catholic tradition's magisterial stance toward liberalism and the modern state is essential to understanding and applying the church's political thought today. Emile Perreau-Saussine explains this dialectic of affirmation (of positive laicity) and critique (of negative laicity) in the following manner:

> In bourgeois democracy, the issue today is no longer between liberal and illiberal regimes. It is more a matter of which liberal regime is truly liberal. In the sphere of politics, given the choice between liberalism and totalitarianism, the church is firmly on the side of liberalism. But in the moral dimension, the church seems cold, hostile to pleasure and progress, and out of sympathy with liberal public opinion. The church's hostility, however, is not directed toward human rights or political liberalism. What concerns the church are the moral consequences of liberalism envisaged as individual autonomy.[1]

Christian civic virtue seeks to maintain and support what is true, right, and good about moderate liberalism, while providing both the theoretical, philosophical, and theological paradigm and the civic practices necessary to avoid the cultural drift from moderate to doctrinaire liberalism.

---

1. Emile Perreau-Saussine, *Catholicism and Democracy: An Essay in the History of Political Thought,* trans. Richard Rex (Princeton, N.J.: Princeton University Press, 2012), p. 134.

While a general theory of civic virtue, such as the one provided in Part I, does not immediately yield a set of universal and concrete practices, careful attention to the cultural and political context of late modern liberal societies such as I have developed in Part II can begin to suggest positive directions for the instantiation of civic virtue now and into the future. In the context of contemporary liberal thought, a Thomistic account and practice of civic virtue can help to demonstrate the need for liberal societies to recognize the limited but pervasive goods and virtues that democratic societies seek to cultivate. Cathleen Kaveny suggests that two such substantive virtues that are needed in liberal societies are autonomy and solidarity, and these are entirely congruent with a Thomistic account of civic virtue.[2] Indeed, Catholic social thought and a Thomistic account of civic virtue insist that liberal societies must recognize certain virtues and goods necessary for all members of the body politic to foster the common good of all and to sustain the long-term stability and viability of democracy itself. Although Aquinas's moral theology provides what John Rawls would call a thick, comprehensive, and theological vision of virtue and the good that would not be appropriate to expect of or impose on all members of a pluralistic society, a Thomistic account of civic virtue offers an image of the flourishing of the human person as passionately oriented toward the common good. This is an image that may be inspiring for all members of the body politic. In this sense, it may have broad humanistic appeal even as it remains tethered to distinctively theological principles and commitments.

I claimed in Chapter 1 that an ecclesiology grounded in the image of the pilgrim church and developed at Vatican II is both congruent with Aquinas's image of the human person as *homo viator* and provides a fitting metaphor for guiding the practice of civic virtue. This image keeps a pilgrim people's eyes focused on the goal of the kingdom of heaven, while also keeping them open to the suffering of others and focused on the common good insofar as it can be instantiated in this earthly existence. This ecclesiological vision that emerges from the texts and the event of Vatican II focuses on the entire people of God as those who hear the Word of God, are gathered together to form the church as the worshiping *congregatio fidelium,* and whose essential mission is to witness to and proclaim the gospel. In Chapter 6 I claimed that amid the contemporary conditions of social communication within the

---

2. Cathleen Kaveny articulates her thesis regarding these two virtues on p. 33, but then builds her case throughout *Law's Virtues: Fostering Autonomy and Solidarity in American Society* (Washington, D.C.: Georgetown University Press, 2012).

culture wars, Aristotelian notions of rhetoric provide important clues for an effective manner of Christian witness to the practical and moral truths that civic virtue and Catholic social thought envisions for pursuing the common good. In particular, I claimed that reason *(logos),* character *(ethos),* and passionate commitment *(pathos)* may be put to use in the practice of civic virtue to build trust, cultivate civic friendship, and facilitate a process of collective deliberation in the pursuit of just practical solutions to political dilemmas. Thus, an exploration of a Thomistic account of civic virtue has come full circle in focusing on the centrality of authentic and truthful witness as the core practice of the politics of a pilgrim church. The ecclesiological emphasis on witness and proclamation by the members of a pilgrim church begun in Chapter 1 is intimately connected with a rhetoric in pursuit of the common good that concluded the previous chapter. The analogical relationship between nature and grace articulated in Chapter 4 helps us understand how the different modalities of witness function in different contexts. In other words, witness will be of one kind when the congregation of the faithful is gathered together for worship and when it proclaims the gospel, but it will be of a slightly different — albeit analogically related — kind when undertaken in regard to the pursuit of the common good. In either of these public modalities, witness becomes central to the task of evangelization such as Pope Francis has recently emphasized in his apostolic exhortation *Evangelii gaudium.*[3]

In fact, one of the insights provided by Pope John XXIII's emphasis on a pastoral *aggiornamento* of the means by which the Catholic Church proclaims the doctrines of the faith and that is highlighted in an Aristotelian notion of rhetoric is that *the medium is the message.* Christoph Theobald suggests that one of the most urgent needs in the current stage of the implementation of the vision for the church in the modern world provided by Vatican II is "to develop an 'argument of credibility.'"[4] The predominant models of cultural and political engagement utilized by Christians to "win" the culture wars have not contributed to the development of greater credibility for the church's moral witness. In fact, many of the more public stances of denunciation such as the threat of denial of communion to political leaders who hold stances incongruent with Catholic moral thought,

---

3. See Francis, *Evangelii gaudium* (Vatican City: Libreria Editrice Vaticana, 2013), chapter IV, "The Social Dimension of Evangelization."

4. Christoph Theobald, "The Theological Options of Vatican II: Seeking an 'Internal' Principle of Interpretation," in *Vatican II: A Forgotten Future?* ed. Alberto Melloni and Christoph Theobald, trans. Paul Burns (London: SCM, 2005), pp. 87-108, p. 105.

even when canonically legitimate and undertaken with good intentions, ultimately serve to underwrite the very conditions of moral dissolution and resentment described by Hunter. I think John XXIII intuitively understood this connection between character, *ethos,* and moral truth, when he stated in his opening address to the council that "the spouse of Christ prefers to use the medicine of mercy rather than the weapons of severity; and, she thinks she meets today's needs by explaining the validity of her doctrine more fully rather than by condemning."[5] In addition, both *Unitatis redintegratio* (§11) and *Dignitatis humanae* (§3) highlight the common search for truth that the members of a pilgrim church undertake with all persons of good will.[6] Finally, Pope Francis suggests that "it is time to devise a means for building consensus and agreement while seeking the goal of a just, responsive and inclusive society. The principal author, the historic subject of this process, is the people as a whole and their culture."[7] The Thomistic account of civic virtue developed here is well situated to support just such an endeavor of cultural dialogue and deliberation about the good of liberal societies. Given how entrenched the church has become in the forms of rhetoric endemic to the culture wars, particularly in America, the practice of civic virtue suggests that we might step back and reassess our predominant forms of engaging culture and politics.[8]

I want to conclude, therefore, by noting a few practical examples of the ways in which members of the pilgrim church have practiced the kind of positive witness and constructive rhetoric that I am advocating as an essential component of Christian civic virtue. I noted in Chapter 1 that one of the ways in which civic virtue survived during the period of the Catholic Church's more reactionary stance toward the modern state was in lay apos-

5. John XXIII, "*Gaudet mater ecclesia:* Pope John's Opening Speech to the Council" (October 11, 1962), trans. Joseph Komonchak. http://jakomonchak.files.wordpress.com/2012/10/john-xxiii-opening-speech.pdf. Accessed April 28, 2014.

6. See also Christoph Theobald, "The Principle of Pastorality at Vatican II: Challenges of a Prospective Interpretation of the Council," lecture presented at *The Legacy of Vatican II,* Boston College, September 26, 2013, translated by Andrea Vicini, S.J. http://www.bc.edu/content/dam/files/schools/stm_sites/c21online/pdf/legacy-translation.pdf. Accessed March 20, 214.

7. Francis, *Evangelii gaudium,* §239.

8. James Davison Hunter also suggests in *To Change the World: The Irony, Tragedy, and Possibility of Christianity in the Late Modern World* (New York: Oxford University Press, 2010) that *"it may be that the healthiest course of action for Christians, on this count, is to be silent for a season and learn how to enact their faith in public through acts of shalom rather than to try again to represent it publicly through law, policy, and political mobilization"* (p. 281).

tolates such as Catholic Action.[9] I also noted in Chapter 4 that the sisters of Bluffton studied by Meg Wilkes Karraker provide an excellent example of civic virtue.[10] In particular, they demonstrate the kind of authentic public witness to the gospel that spans both ecclesial and political boundaries to create trust, or what Karraker describes as social and caring capital. This cultural capital and trust establish conditions under which a more effective public rhetoric of the common good may be undertaken by all members of civil society. In the case of the sisters of Bluffton this led to practical solutions that adequately, though by no means perfectly, addressed racism and immigration in their community.

Similar examples of public witnesses by the members of the pilgrim church that build trust and civic friendship that can be leveraged to deliberate toward the common good can be found in the lay apostolates such as the community of Sant'Egidio and the Focolare movement. The community of Sant'Egidio began with a group of high school students who gathered together to support one another in faith in the church of Santa Maria in Trastevere in Rome in 1968. They began simply by reading Scripture and praying together, and then asking what God was calling them to do in response. Their first ministry was feeding and reaching out to the homeless in Rome. Within forty years, simply by cultivating "prayer and friendship" they have built an international network of communities that helps to administer one of the most successful AIDS treatment and malnutrition services in sub-Saharan Africa through DREAM (Drug Resource Enhancement against AIDS and Malnutrition), helped to pass a UN vote in favor of a worldwide moratorium on the death penalty, and has facilitated the peace process in Mozambique, Algeria, Guatemala, Albania, Kosovo, Liberia, and Ivory Coast.[11] Sant'Egidio

9. For more in-depth studies of this movement, see the references from Chapter 1, but also Jeremiah Newman's *What Is Catholic Action?* (Westminster, Md.: Newman, 1958), and Martin Quigley Jr. and Monsignor Edward M. Connors, *Catholic Action in Practice: Family Life, Education, International Life* (New York: Random House, 1963).

10. See Karraker's *Diversity and the Common Good: Civil Society, Religion, and Catholic Sisters in a Small City* (Lanham, Md.: Lexington, 2013).

11. For a general overview of the history of Sant'Egidio and their apostolates, see Kathy Gilsinon, "Sant'Egidio: linking friendship and service in world-changing ways: though previously little known in the United States, a Catholic lay movement started 40 years ago by high school students in Rome is gaining members in U.S. cities," *National Catholic Reporter* (May 16, 2008): 13+, *Expanded Academic ASAP*, Web. Accessed March 26, 2014. For more in-depth research on Sant'Egidio, see the invaluable study by Roberto Morozzo della Rocca, *Making Peace: The Role Played by Sant'Egidio in the International Arena* (London: New City, 2013).

provides an excellent example of the kind of atechnical witness to moral truth described in the previous chapter that can help to create the kind of public spaces in which a communal process of deliberation about the goods to be pursued by the members of the body politic and by the state (and by international actors, such as the UN and NGOs) may move toward technical solutions in law, institutions, and social justice programs that enhance the common good, especially by serving those most in need.

Similarly, the Focolare movement grew out of the founder Chiara Lubich's desire to witness to the gospel of love amid the destruction of World War II. Like Sant'Egidio it has grown into an international movement that is dedicated to witnessing to the unity of all humankind through dialogue and a multitude of lay apostolates. In 2003 Pope John Paul II referred to the members of Focolare as "apostles of dialogue."[12] The movement has similarly grown from offering simple hospitality and direct service to becoming engaged in education, art and media, interreligious dialogue, and support for seeking the common good amid a pluralistic society on both a local and a global scale. While further comment and study on the specific details of the practices of movements like Sant'Egidio and Focolare are warranted, both truly practice civic virtue and witness to a politics for a pilgrim church.

The account of civic virtue developed here remains committed to democracy and moderate liberalism precisely insofar as it is necessary for the members of a pilgrim church to appreciate and to continue to defend the positive contributions to human freedom and the possibilities for communal deliberation that moderate liberal regimes make possible. The members of the pilgrim church have a positive stake in defending these aspects of modern liberal practices, even as they may want to witness to more robust notions of virtue, unity, rhetoric, dialogue, and the good than liberal theorists are comfortable in admitting. In upholding Sant'Egidio and Focolare as exemplary communities of civic virtue, I do not wish to suggest that these are the only ways in which Christians may practice civic virtue. A Thomistic account of civic virtue provides a normative paradigm for orienting all the acts of the virtues — whether the acquired cardinal virtues or the infused forms of the cardinal and theological virtues — toward the common good of the body politic. As such, it is capable of providing a positive vision of

12. John Paul II, "Message to Ms. Chiara Lubich on the Occasion of the 60th Anniversary of the Birth of the 'Work of Mercy'" (Focolare Movement), December 5, 2003. Cited by Thomas Masters and Amy Uelmen, *Focolare: Living a Spirituality of Unity in the United States* (Hyde Park, N.Y.: New City, 2011), p. 33.

striving for the common good for all persons of good will. It may indeed inspire those great-souled persons that late modern culture so desperately needs. But in addition to great-souled men and women, we also need well-supported institutions that foster the civic virtue of the members of the body politic so that we may move away from the predominant forms of rhetoric in the culture wars. It remains the task of the members of the pilgrim church to continue to find creative ways of witnessing to the gospel and to the common good by practicing civic virtue during their journey through this earthly existence. I find it fitting to close with the quote from Pope Francis that I noted in the introduction, as a way to summarize the ideal politics for a pilgrim church and of a Thomistic notion of civic virtue:

> We must never forget that we are pilgrims journeying alongside one another. This means that we must have sincere trust in our fellow pilgrims, putting aside all suspicion or mistrust, and turn our gaze to what we are all seeking: the radiant peace of God's face.[13]

13. Francis, *Evangelii gaudium*, §244.

Works Cited

Acta Sanctae Sedis. 41 vols. Rome: Typis Polyglottae Officiniae S.C. de Propaganda Fide, 1865-1908.

Aquinas, Thomas, O.P. *Commentary on the Nicomachean Ethics, Volumes I-II.* Translated by C. I. Litzinger, O.P. Chicago: Henry Regnery, 1964.

———. "Commentary on the Politics." Translated by Ernest L. Fortinn and Peter D. O'Neill. In *Medieval Political Philosophy.* Edited by Ralph Lerner and Muhsin Mahdi. Translated by Ernest L. Fortin and Peter D. O'Neill. New York: Free Press, 1963.

———. *Summa Theologica.* 5 vols. Translated by the Fathers of the English Dominican Province. Notre Dame, Ind.: Christian Classics, 1948.

Aristotle. *Nicomachean Ethics.* Translated and edited by Roger Crisp. New York: Cambridge University Press, 2000.

———. *The Politics and the Constitution of Athens.* Edited by Stephen Everson. New York: Cambridge University Press, 2007.

———. *Rhetoric.* Edited by Edward Meredith Cope and John Edwin Sandys. New York: Cambridge University Press, 2010.

Augustine. *The City of God against the Pagans.* Edited by R. W. Dyson. New York: Cambridge University Press, 1998.

Balthasar, Hans Urs von. *The Theology of Karl Barth: Exposition and Interpretation.* Translated by Edward T. Oakes. San Francisco: Ignatius, 1992.

Barbieri, William A., Jr. "Beyond the Nations: The Expansion of the Common Good in Catholic Social Thought." *Review of Politics* 63, no. 4 (Fall 2001): 723-54.

Baxter, Michael J. "Murray's Mistake." *America* 209, no. 7. EBSCO*host.* Web. Accessed January 6, 2014.

———. "The Non-Catholic Character of the 'Public Church.'" *Modern Theology* 11, no. 2 (April 1995): 243-58.

Benedict XVI. "Ad romanam curia ab omnia natalicia." *Acta Apostilicae Sedis* 98 (January 6, 2006): 40-53.

———. "A Proper Hermeneutic for the Second Vatican Council." In *Vatican II: Re-*

newal Within Tradition, edited by Matthew L. Lamb and Matthew Levering, pp. ix-xv. New York: Oxford University Press, 2008.

———. *Values in a Time of Upheaval.* Translated by Brian McNeil. San Francisco: Ignatius, 2006.

Berlin, Isaiah. *Two Concepts of Liberty.* Oxford: Clarendon, 1958.

Bonino, Serge-Thomas, O.P., ed. *Surnaturel: A Controversy at the Heart of Twentieth-Century Thomistic Thought.* Translated by Robert Williams. Ave Maria, Fla.: Sapientia, 2009.

Bouyer, Louis. *Church of God: Body of Christ and Temple of the Spirit.* Translated by Charles Underhill Quinn. San Francisco: Ignatius, 2011.

Boyd, Craig A. "Participation Metaphysics, the *Imago Dei* and Natural Law in Aquinas' Ethics." *New Blackfriars* 88 (May 2007): 274-87.

Brach, Tara. *Radical Acceptance: Embracing Your Life with the Heart of a Buddha.* New York: Bantam, 2004.

Bradley, Dennis J. *Aquinas on the Twofold Human Good: Reason and Human Happiness in Aquinas's Moral Science.* Washington, D.C.: Catholic University of America Press, 1997.

Braine, David. "The Debate between Henri de Lubac and His Critics." *Nova et Vetera* 6, no. 3 (2008): 543-90.

Brown, Peter. *The Body and Society: Men, Women and Sexual Renunciation in Early Christianity.* New York: Columbia University Press, 1988.

Burrell, David. *Analogy and Philosophical Language.* New Haven, Conn.: Yale University Press, 1973.

Cahill, Lisa. "Toward Global Ethics." *Theological Studies* 63, no. 2 (2002): 324-44.

Carlen, Claudia, ed. *The Papal Encyclicals: 1740-1878.* Vol. 1. Beloit, Kans.: McGrath, 1981.

Cavanaugh, William T. *Migrations of the Holy: God, State, and the Political Meaning of the Church.* Grand Rapids: Eerdmans, 2011.

Cavanaugh, William T., and Michael Baxter. "Reply to 'A View from Abroad' by Massimo Faggioli." *America Magazine Online Edition* (March 31, 2014). Accessed April 11, 2014.

Cessario, Romanus, O.P. *The Moral Virtues and Theological Ethics.* 2nd ed. Notre Dame, Ind.: University of Notre Dame Press, 2009.

Congar, Yves, O.P. "The Idea of the Church in St. Thomas Aquinas." In *The Mystery of the Church,* pp. 97-117. Translated by A. V. Littledale. Baltimore: Helicon, 1960.

———. "L'idee de l'Eglise chez saint Thomas d'Aquin." *Revue des sciences philosophiques et theologiques* 29 (1940): 31-58.

———. "La theologie au Concile: Le 'theologiser' du Concile." In *Situation et taches presents de la theologie,* pp. 51-56. Paris: Editiones du Cerf, 1967.

Congregation for the Doctrine of the Faith. "Letter to the Bishops of the Catholic Church on Some Aspects of the Church Understood as Communion." May 28, 1992. http://www.vatican.va/roman_curia/congregations/cfaith/documents/rc _con_cfaith_doc_28051992_communionis-notio_en.html. Accessed August 23, 2013.

Couture, Roger A., O.M.I. "The Use of *Epikeia* in Natural Law: Its Early Developments." *Eglise et Theologie* 4 (1973): 71-103.

de Koninck, Charles. "On the Primacy of the Common Good: Against the Personalists" (1946). In *The Writings of Charles de Koninck*. Edited and translated by Ralph
McInerny. Notre Dame, Ind.: Notre Dame University Press, 2008.

della Rocca, Roberto Morozzo. *Making Peace: The Role Played by Sant'Egidio in the
International Arena*. London: New City, 2013.

de Lubac, Henri, S.J. *Augustinianism and Modern Theology*. Translated by Lancelot
Sheppard. New York: Crossroad, 2000.

————. *The Mystery of the Supernatural*. Translated by Rosemary Sheed. New York:
Crossroad, 1998.

————. *Surnaturel: Etudes Historiques*. Paris: Desclée de Brouwer, 1991.

Denzinger, Heinrich, and Peter Hünermann. *Symboles et définitions de la foi catholique*.
Paris: Editions du Cerf, 1997.

de Tocqueville, Alexis. *Democracy in America*. Translated by Arthur Goldhammer.
Washington, D.C.: Library of America, 2004.

Dionne, E. J. *Our Divided Political Heart: The Battle for the American Idea in an Age of
Discontent*. New York: Bloomsbury, 2012.

Douglass, Bruce R., and David Hollenbach. *Catholicism and Liberalism: Contributions
to American Public Philosophy*. New York: Cambridge University Press, 1994.

Doyle, Dennis M. *Communion Ecclesiology: Vision and Versions*. Maryknoll, N.Y.: Orbis,
2000.

Dulles, Avery Cardinal, S.J. "Nature, Mission, Structure of the Church." In *Vatican II:
Renewal within Tradition,* edited by Matthew L. Lamb and Matthew Levering,
pp. 25-36. New York: Oxford University Press, 2008.

Faggioli, Massimo. "The View from Abroad: The Shrinking Common Ground in the
American Church." *America* 210, no. 6 (February 24, 2014): 20-23.

Feingold, Lawrence. *The Natural Desire to See God According to Saint Thomas and His
Interpreters*. 2nd ed. Washington, D.C.: Catholic University of America Press,
2004.

Finnis, John. *Natural Law and Natural Rights*. Oxford: Clarendon, 1980.

————. "Public Good: The Specifically Political Common Good in Aquinas." In *Natu-
ral Law and Moral Inquiry: Ethics, Metaphysics, and Politics in the Work of Germain
Grisez,* edited by Robert P. George, pp. 174-210. Washington, D.C.: Georgetown
University Press, 1998.

Flannery, Austin, O.P. *The Basic Sixteen Documents of Vatican Council II: Constitutions,
Decrees, Declarations*. Northport, N.Y.: Costello, 1996.

Foner, Eric. *Who Owns History? Rethinking the Past in a Changing World*. New York:
Hill and Wang, 2002.

Forget, Jacques. "Jansenius and Jansenism." In *The Catholic Encyclopedia*, vol. 8. New
York: Appleton, 1910. http://www.newadvent.org/cathen/08285a.htm. Accessed
April 21, 2014.

Fourcade, M. "Thomisme et antithomisme a l'heure de Vatican II." *Revue Thomiste* 108
(2006): 301-25.

Francis. *Evangelii gaudium.* Vatican City: Libreria Editrice Vaticana, 2013.

Galston, William. *Liberal Pluralism: The Implications of Value Pluralism for Political Theory and Practice.* Cambridge: Cambridge University Press, 2002.

Garsten, Bryan. *Saving Persuasion: A Defense of Rhetoric and Judgment.* Cambridge, Mass.: Harvard University Press, 2006.

Garver, Eugene. *Aristotle's Rhetoric: An Art of Character.* Chicago: University of Chicago Press, 1994.

———. *Confronting Aristotle's Ethics.* Chicago: University of Chicago Press, 2006.

———. *For the Sake of Argument.* Chicago: University of Chicago Press, 2004.

———. "How Can a Liberal Listen to a Religious Argument? Religious Rhetoric as a Rhetorical Problem." In *How Should We Talk about Religion? Perspectives, Contexts, Particularities,* edited by James Boyd White, pp. 164-93. Notre Dame, Ind.: University of Notre Dame Press, 2006.

———. "Why Should Anybody Listen? The Rhetoric of Religious Argument in Democracy." *Wake Forest Law Review* 36 (2001): 353-99.

Gastil, John, and Peter Levine, eds. *The Deliberative Democracy Handbook: Strategies for Effective Civic Engagement in the Twenty-First Century.* San Francisco: Jossey-Bass, 2005.

George, Robert P. "The Common Good: Instrumental but Not Just Contractual." *Public Discourse Blog.* http://www.thepublicdiscourse.com/2013/05/10166/ (May 17, 2013). Accessed August 30, 2013.

———. *Making Men Moral: Civil Liberties and Public Morality.* Oxford: Clarendon, 1993.

Gill, Robin. *Churchgoing and Christian Ethics.* Cambridge: Cambridge University Press, 1999.

Gilsinon, Kathy. "Sant'Egidio: Linking Friendship and Service in World-changing Ways." *National Catholic Reporter* (May 16, 2008): 13+. *Expanded Academic ASAP.* Web. Accessed March 26, 2014.

Gregory, Eric. *Politics and the Order of Love: An Augustinian Ethic of Democratic Citizenship.* Chicago: University of Chicago Press, 2008.

Grisez, Germain. *The Way of the Lord Jesus.* Vol. 2, *Living a Christian Life.* Quincy, Ill.: Franciscan, 1993.

Hayek, Friedrich. *Law, Legislation and Liberty.* Chicago: University of Chicago Press, 1973.

———. *The Road to Serfdom.* Chicago: University of Chicago Press, 1944.

Healy, Nicholas. "Henri de Lubac on Nature and Grace: A Note on Some Recent Contributions to the Debate." *Communio* 35 (2008): 535-64.

Hegel, G. W. F. *Elements of the Philosophy of Right.* Edited by Allen W. Wood. Translated by H. B. Nisbet. Cambridge: Cambridge University Press, 1991.

Herdt, Jennifer. *Putting on Virtue: The Legacy of the Splendid Vices.* Chicago: University of Chicago Press, 2008.

Hittinger, Russell. *The First Grace: Rediscovering the Natural Law in a Post-Christian World.* Wilmington, Del.: ISI, 2003.

———. "Introduction to Modern Catholicism." In *The Teachings of Modern Roman*

Catholicism on Law, Politics, and Human Nature, edited by John Witte Jr. and Frank S. Alexander, pp. 1-38. New York: Columbia University Press, 2007).

———. "Pope Leo XIII (1810-1903): Commentary." In *The Teachings of Modern Roman Catholicism on Law, Politics, and Human Nature,* edited by John Witte Jr. and Frank S. Alexander. New York: Columbia University Press, 2007.

———. "Two Modernities, Two Thomisms: Reflections on the Centenary of Pius X's Letter against the Modernists." *Nova et Vetera* 5, no. 4 (2007): 843-80.

Hohfeld, Wesley. *Fundamental Legal Concepts as Applied in Judicial Reasoning: And Other Legal Essays.* Edited by Walter Wheeler Cook. New Haven, Conn.: Yale University Press, 1923.

Hollenbach, David, S.J. *Claims in Conflict: Retrieving and Renewing the Catholic Human Rights Tradition.* New York: Paulist, 1979.

———. *The Common Good and Christian Ethics.* Cambridge: Cambridge University Press, 2002.

———. *The Global Face of Public Faith: Politics, Human Rights, and Christian Ethics.* Washington, D.C.: Georgetown University Press, 2003.

Hunermann, Peter. "The Ignored 'Text': On the Hermeneutics of the Second Vatican Council." In *Vatican II: A Forgotten Future?* edited by Alberto Melloni and Christoph Theobald, pp. 118-36. London: SCM, 2005.

Hunter, James Davison. *Culture Wars: The Struggle to Define America.* New York: Basic, 1991.

———. *To Change the World: The Irony, Tragedy, and Possibility of Christianity in the Late Modern World.* New York: Oxford University Press, 2010.

Hütter, Reinhard. "Aquinas on the Natural Desire for the Vision of God: A Relecture of *Summa contra Gentiles* III, c. 25 *apres* Henri de Lubac." *The Thomist* 73 (2009): 573-79.

———. "*Desiderium Naturale Visionis Dei — Est Autem Duplex Hominis Beatitudo Sive Felicitas:* Some Observations about Lawrence Feingold's and John Milbank's Recent Interventions in the Debate over the Natural Desire to See God." *Nova et Vetera* 5 (2007): 81-131.

———. *Dust Bound for Heaven: Explorations in the Theology of Thomas Aquinas.* Grand Rapids: Eerdmans, 2012.

International Theological Commission. "In Search of a Universal Ethic: A New Look at the Natural Law." http://www.vatican.va/roman_curia/congregations/cfaith/cti_documents/rc_con_cfaith_doc_20090520_legge-naturale_en.html. Accessed September 25, 2013.

Jenson, Robert W. "The Triunity of Common Good." In *In Search of the Common Good,* edited by Dennis P. McCann and Patrick D. Miller, pp. 333-47. New York: T&T Clark, 2005.

John XXIII. *Gaudet mater ecclesia* (October 11, 1962). Translated by Joseph A. Komonchak. http://jakomonchak.files.wordpress.com/2012/10/john-xxiii-opening-speech.pdf. Accessed April 28, 2014.

John Paul II. "Message to Ms. Chiara Lubich on the Occasion of the 60th Anniversary of the Birth of the 'Work of Mercy'" (Focolare Movement), December 5, 2003.

Karraker, Meg Wilkes. *Diversity and the Common Good: Civil Society, Religion, and Catholic Sisters in a Small City.* Lanham, Md.: Lexington, 2013.

Kasper, Walter. *Theology and Church.* New York: Crossroad, 1989.

Kateb, George. "Democratic Individuality and the Meaning of Rights." In *Liberalism and the Moral Life,* edited by Nancy L. Rosenblum, pp. 183-206. Cambridge, Mass.: Harvard University Press, 1989.

Kaveny, M. Cathleen. "Catholics as Citizens: Today's Ethical Challenges Call for New Moral Thinking." *America* 203, no. 121 (2010): *Expanded Academic ASAP.* Web. December 17, 2013.

———. *Law's Virtues: Fostering Autonomy and Solidarity in American Society.* Washington, D.C.: Georgetown University Press, 2012.

Keenan, James, S.J. *A History of Catholic Moral Theology in the Twentieth Century: From Confessing Sins to Liberating Consciences.* New York: Continuum, 2010.

Kempshall, M. S. *The Common Good in Late Medieval Political Thought.* Oxford: Clarendon, 1999.

Kent, Bonnie. "Reinventing Augustine's Ethics: The Afterlife of the *City of God.*" In *Augustine's City of God: A Critical Guide,* edited by James Wetzel. New York: Cambridge University Press, 2012.

———. *Virtues of the Will: The Transformation of Ethics in the Late Thirteenth Century.* Washington, D.C.: Catholic University of America Press, 1995.

Kinnaman, David, and Gabe Lyons. *UnChristian: What a New Generation Really Thinks about Christianity . . . and Why it Matters.* Grand Rapids: Baker, 2007.

Knobel, Angela McKay. "Can Aquinas's Infused and Acquired Virtues Coexist in the Christian Life?" *Studies in Christian Ethics* 23, no. 4 (2010): 381-96.

———. "Relating Aquinas's Infused and Acquired Virtues: Some Problematic Texts for a Common Interpretation." *Nova et Vetera* 9, no. 2 (2011): 411-31.

Komonchak, Joseph A. "Thomism and the Second Vatican Council." In *Continuity and Plurality in Catholic Theology: Essays in Honor of Gerald A. McCool, S.J.,* edited by Anthony J. Cernera, pp. 53-73. Fairfield, Conn.: Sacred Heart University Press, 1998.

———. "Vatican II and the Encounter between Catholicism and Liberalism." In *Catholicism and Liberalism: Contributions to American Public Philosophy,* edited by R. Bruce Douglass and David Hollenbach, pp. 76-99. New York: Cambridge University Press, 1994.

———. *Who Are the Church?* Milwaukee, Wis.: Marquette University Press, 2008.

Kreeft, Peter. *How to Win the Culture Wars: A Christian Battle Plan for a Society in Crisis.* Downers Grove, Ill.: InterVarsity, 2002.

Lamb, Matthew L., and Matthew Levering, eds. *Vatican II: Renewal within Tradition.* New York: Oxford University Press, 2008.

Larmore, Charles. "The Limits of Aristotelian Ethics." In *Virtue,* edited by John W. Chapman and William A. Galston. New York: New York University Press, 1992.

Le Goff, Jacques. *L'imaginaire medieval.* Paris: Gallimard, 1985.

Litzinger, C. I., O.P. *Commentary on the Nicomachean Ethics, Volumes I-II.* Chicago: Henry Regnery, 1964.

Lombardo, Nicholas, O.P. *The Logic of Desire: Aquinas on Emotion.* Washington, D.C.: Catholic University of America Press, 2011.

Lonergan, Bernard. *A Second Collection.* Edited by William F. J. Ryan and Bernard J. Terrell. Philadelphia: Westminster, 1974.

Long, Stephen. *Natura Pura: On the Recovery of Nature in the Doctrine of Grace.* New York: Fordham University Press, 2010.

———. "On the Loss, and the Recovery, of Nature as a Theonomic Principle: Reflections on the Nature/Grace Controversy." *Nova et Vetera* 5, no. 1 (2007): 133-84.

———. "On the Possibility of a Purely Natural End for Man." *The Thomist* 64 (2000): 211-37.

Lottin, Dom Odon. *Principes de Morale.* Vol. 2. Louvain: Editions de l'Abbaye du Mont Cesar, 1947.

Lovin, Robin. *Christian Realism and the New Realities.* Cambridge: Cambridge University Press, 2008.

Macedo, Stephen. "Charting Liberal Virtues." In *Virtue,* edited by John W. Chapman and William A. Galston, pp. 204-32. New York: New York University Press, 1992.

MacGilvray, Eric. *The Invention of Market Freedom.* New York: Cambridge University Press, 2011.

MacIntyre, Alasdair. *After Virtue: A Study in Moral Theory.* 2nd ed. Notre Dame, Ind.: University of Notre Dame Press, 1984.

———. *Whose Justice? Which Rationality?* Notre Dame, Ind.: University of Notre Dame Press, 1988.

Malloy, Christopher J. "De Lubac on Natural Desire: Difficulties and Antitheses." *Nova et Vetera* 9, no. 3 (2011): 567-624.

Mannion, Gerard. *Ecclesiology and Postmodernity: Questions for the Church in Our Time.* Collegeville, Minn.: Liturgical, 2007.

Mansini, Guy, O.S.B. "Henri de Lubac, the Natural Desire to See God, and Pure Nature." *Gregorianium* 83, no. 1 (2002): 89-109.

Maritain, Jacques. *Christianity and Democracy and the Rights of Man and Natural Law.* Translated by Doris C. Anson. San Francisco: Ignatius, 2011.

———. *An Essay on Christian Philosophy.* Translated by Edward H. Flannery. New York: Philosophical Library, 1955.

———. *Man and the State.* Chicago: University of Chicago Press, 1951.

Massingale, Bryan. *Racial Justice and the Catholic Church.* Maryknoll, N.Y.: Orbis, 2010.

Masters, Thomas, and Amy Uelmen. *Focolare: Living a Spirituality of Unity in the United States.* Hyde Park, N.Y.: New City, 2011.

Mattison, William. "Can Christians Possess the Acquired Moral Virtues?" *Theological Studies* 72 (2011): 558-85.

McCann, Dennis P. "The Common Good in Catholic Social Teaching: A Case Study in Modernization." In *In Search of the Common Good,* ed. Dennis P. McCann and Patrick D. Miller, pp. 121-46. New York: T&T Clark, 2005.

McCann, Dennis P., and Patrick D. Miller, eds. *In Search of the Common Good.* New York: T&T Clark, 2005.

McCool, Gerald A. *From Unity to Pluralism: The Internal Evolution of Thomism.* New York: Fordham University Press, 1989.

———. *The Neo-Thomists.* Milwaukee, Wis.: Marquette University Press, 2003.

Melloni, Alberto, and Christoph Theobald, eds. *Vatican II: A Forgotten Future?* London: SCM, 2005.

Milbank, Jon. *The Suspended Middle: Henri de Lubac and the Debate Concerning the Supernatural.* Grand Rapids: Eerdmans, 2005.

Miner, Robert. *Thomas Aquinas on the Passions: A Study of Summa Theologiae 1a2ae 22-48.* New York: Cambridge University Press, 2009.

Misner, Paul. *Social Catholicism in Europe: From the Onset of Industrialization to the First World War.* New York: Crossroad, 1991.

Mulcahy, Bernard, O.P. *Aquinas's Notion of Pure Nature and the Christian Integralism of Henri de Lubac: Not Everything Is Grace.* New York: Peter Lang, 2011.

Murphy, Francesca A. "De Lubac, Grace, Politics and Paradox." *Studies in Christian Ethics* 23 (2010): 415-30.

Murray, John Courtney, S.J. "The Issue of Church and State at Vatican Council II." *Theological Studies* 27, no. 4 (1966): 580-606.

———. *We Hold These Truths: Catholic Reflections on the American Experiment.* New York: Sheed & Ward, 1960.

Nederman, Cary J. *Medieval Aristotelianism and Its Limits: Classical Traditions in Moral and Political Philosophy, 12th-15th Centuries.* Brookfield, Vt.: Variorum, 1997.

Nell-Breuning, Oswald. "The Drafting of Quadragesimo Anno." In *Readings in Moral Theology,* no. 5, edited by Charles E. Curran and Richard A. McCormick. Mahwah, N.J.: Paulist, 1986.

Newman, Jeremiah. *What Is Catholic Action?* Westminster, Md.: Newman, 1958.

Novak, Michael. *Free Persons and the Common Good.* New York: Madison, 1989.

Nussbaum, Martha. *Love's Knowledge: Essays on Philosophy and Literature.* New York: Oxford University Press, 1990.

———. *The Therapy of Desire: Theory and Practice in Hellenistic Ethics.* Princeton, N.J.: Princeton University Press, 2009.

———. *Upheavals of Thought: The Intelligence of Emotions.* Cambridge: Cambridge University Press, 2001.

———. *Women and Human Development: The Capabilities Approach.* Cambridge: Cambridge University Press, 2000.

Oakes, Edward T., S.J. "The *Surnaturel* Controversy: A Survey and a Response." *Nova et Vetera* 9, no. 3 (2011): 625-56.

O'Brien, David J., and Thomas A. Shannon. *Catholic Social Thought: The Documentary Heritage.* Maryknoll, N.Y.: Orbis, 2004.

O'Donovan, Oliver. *Common Objects of Love: Moral Reflection and the Shaping of Community.* Grand Rapids: Eerdmans, 2002.

———. *The Ways of Judgment: The Bampton Lectures, 2003.* Grand Rapids: Eerdmans, 2005.

Okin, Susan Moller. *Justice, Gender, and the Family.* New York: Basic, 1989.

O'Meara, Thomas. "Theology of Church." In *The Theology of Thomas Aquinas,* edited by Rik Van Nieuwenhove and Joseph Wawrykow, pp. 303-25. Notre Dame, Ind.: University of Notre Dame Press, 2010.

Pagan-Aguiar, Peter E. "St. Thomas Aquinas and Human Finality: Paradox or *Mysterium Fidei?*" *The Thomist* 64 (2000): 375-99.

Perkams, Matthias. "Aquinas's Interpretation of the Aristotelian Virtue of Justice and His Doctrine of the Natural Law." In *Virtue Ethics in the Middle Ages: Commentaries on Aristotle's Nicomachean Ethics, 1200-1500,* edited by Istvan P. Bejczy, pp. 131-50. Leiden: Brill, 2008.

Perreau-Saussine, Emile. *Catholicism and Democracy: An Essay in the History of Political Thought.* Translated by Richard Rex. Princeton, N.J.: Princeton University Press, 2012.

Pettit, Philip. *Republicanism: A Theory of Freedom and Government.* Oxford: Clarendon, 1997.

———. *A Theory of Freedom: From the Psychology to the Politics of Agency.* Oxford: Oxford University Press, 2001.

Pieper, Josef. *The Four Cardinal Virtues: Prudence, Justice, Fortitude, Temperance.* Notre Dame, Ind.: University of Notre Dame Press, 1966.

———. *Leisure: The Basis of Culture.* Translated by Alexander Dru. San Francisco: Ignatius, 2009.

Pinckaers, Servais, O.P. *The Pinckaers' Reader.* Edited by John Berkman and Craig Steven Titus. Washington, D.C.: Catholic University of America Press, 2005.

———. *The Sources of Christian Ethics.* Translated by Mary Thomas Noble, O.P. Washington, D.C.: Catholic University of America Press, 1995.

Pius VI. "Charitas." In *The Papal Encyclicals: 1740-1878,* vol. 1, edited by Claudia Carlen, I.H.M., pp. 177-86. Beloit, Kans.: McGrath, 1981.

Pius IX. *"Quanta cura."* In *Acta Sanctae Sedis,* pp. 160-67. Rome: Typis Polyglottae Officiniae S.C. de Propaganda Fide, 1867.

Pohle, Joseph. "Pelagius and Pelagianism." In *The Catholic Encyclopedia.* Vol. 11. New York: Appleton, 1911. http://www.newadvent.org/cathen/11604a.htm. Accessed April 21, 2014.

Pope, Stephen. *Human Evolution and Christian Ethics.* Cambridge: Cambridge University Press, 2007.

———. "Natural Law and Christian Ethics." In *The Cambridge Companion to Christian Ethics,* edited by Robin Gill, pp. 67-87. 2nd ed. New York: Cambridge University Press, 2012.

Porter, Jean. "The Common Good in Thomas Aquinas." In *In Search of the Common Good,* edited by Dennis P. McCann and Patrick D. Miller, pp. 94-120. New York: T&T Clark, 2005.

——— "The Desire for Happiness and the Virtues of the Will: Resolving a Paradox in Aquinas' Thought" (personal copy).

——— "In the Wake of a Doctrine: A Reassessment of the Doctrine of the Natural Law as Developed in *We Hold These Truths.*" In *John Courtney Murray and the Growth of Tradition,* edited by Todd Whitmore and Leon J. Hooper. Kansas City, Mo.: Sheed & Ward, 1996.

————. *Ministers of the Law: A Natural Law Theory of Legal Authority.* Grand Rapids: Eerdmans, 2010.

————. "Moral Language and the Language of Grace: The Fundamental Option and the Virtue of Charity." *Philosophy and Theology* 10 (1996): 169-98.

————. *Natural and Divine Law: Reclaiming the Tradition for Christian Ethics.* Grand Rapids: Eerdmans, 1999.

————. *Nature as Reason: A Thomistic Theory of the Natural Law.* Grand Rapids: Eerdmans, 2005.

————. "Openness and Constraint: Moral Reflection as Tradition-Guided Inquiry in Alasdair MacIntyre's Recent Works." *Journal of Religion* 73, no. 4 (1993): 514-36.

————. "The Subversion of Virtue: Acquired and Infused Virtues in the *Summa theologiae.*" *Annual of the Society of Christian Ethics* (1992): 19-41.

Quigley, Martin, Jr., and Monsignor Edward M. Connors. *Catholic Action in Practice: Family Life, Education, International Life.* New York: Random House, 1963.

Rahner, Karl, S.J. "Concerning the Relationship between Nature and Grace." In *Theological Investigations.* Vol. 1, pp. 301-3. Translated by Cornelius Ernst. London: Darton, Longman, & Todd, 1974.

Rawls, John. *The Law of Peoples: With "The Idea of Public Reason Revisited."* Cambridge, Mass.: Harvard University Press, 1999.

————. *Political Liberalism.* New York: Columbia University Press, 1993.

————. *A Theory of Justice.* Cambridge, Mass.: Belknap Press of Harvard University Press, 1971.

Raz, Joseph. *The Morality of Freedom.* Oxford: Clarendon, 1986.

Riley, Joseph Lawrence. *The History, Nature, and Use of EPIKEIA in Moral Theology.* Washington, D.C.: Catholic University of America Press, 1948.

Rourke, Thomas R. "Michael Novak and Yves R. Simon on the Common Good and Capitalism." *Review of Politics* 58, no. 2 (1996): 229-58.

Sabra, George. *Thomas Aquinas's Vision of the Church: Fundamentals of an Ecumenical Ecclesiology.* Mainz: Matthias-Grünewald-Verlag, 1987.

Sandel, Michael. *Liberalism and the Limits of Justice.* Cambridge: Cambridge University Press, 1982.

Schindler, David. *Heart of the World, Center of the Church: Communio Ecclesiology, Liberalism, and Liberation.* Grand Rapids: Eerdmans, 1996.

Schuck, Michael. "Early Modern Roman Catholic Social Thought: 1740-1890." In *Modern Catholic Social Teaching: Commentaries and Interpretation,* edited by Kenneth R. Himes, O.F.M., pp. 99-124. Washington, D.C.: Georgetown University Press, 2005.

Sherwin, Michael, O.P. "Infused Virtue and the Effects of Acquired Vice: A Test Case for the Thomistic Theory of Infused Cardinal Virtues." *The Thomist* 73 (2009): 29-52.

————. "St. Thomas and the Common Good: The Theological Perspective; An Invitation to Dialogue." *Angelicum* 70 (1993): 307-28.

Shklar, Judith. "The Liberalism of Fear." In *Liberalism and the Moral Life,* edited by Nancy L. Rosenblum, pp. 21-38. Cambridge, Mass.: Harvard University Press, 1989.

Simon, Yves R. *Philosophy of Democratic Government*. Chicago: University of Chicago Press, 1951.

Smith, Christian, et al. *Lost in Transition: The Dark Side of Emerging Adulthood*. New York: Oxford University Press, 2011.

Southern, R. W. *Scholastic Humanism and the Unification of Europe*. Vol. 2. Cambridge, Mass.: Blackwell, 2001.

Tanner, Norman P., S.J., ed. *The Decrees of the Ecumenical Councils*. Vol. 2. London: Sheed & Ward, 1990.

Taparelli, Luigi, S.J. *Saggio Teoretico di Dritto Naturale*. Rome: Edizioni "La Civilta Cattolica," 1949.

Taylor, Charles. *Modern Social Imaginaries*. Durham, N.C.: Duke University Press, 2004.

———. *A Secular Age*. Cambridge, Mass.: Belknap Press of Harvard University Press, 2007.

Theobald, Christoph. "The Principle of Pastorality at Vatican II: Challenges of a Prospective Interpretation of the Council." Lecture presented at "The Legacy of Vatican II," Boston College, September 26, 2013. Translated by Andrea Vicini, S.J. http://www.bc.edu/content/dam/files/schools/stm_sites/c21online/pdf/legacy -translation.pdf. Accessed March 20, 2014.

———. "The Theological Options of Vatican II: Seeking an 'Internal' Principle of Interpretation." In *Vatican II: A Forgotten Future?* edited by Alberto Melloni and Christoph Theobald, translated by Paul Burns, pp. 87-108. London: SCM, 2005.

Tierney, Brian. *The Idea of Natural Rights: Studies on Natural Rights, Natural Law, and Church Law, 1115-1625*. Atlanta, Ga.: Scholars, 1997.

Torrell, Jean-Pierre, O.P. "Nature and Grace in Thomas Aquinas." In *Surnaturel: A Controversy at the Heart of Twentieth-Century Thomistic Thought*, edited by Serge-Thomas Bonino, O.P., translated by Robert Williams, pp. 155-88. Ave Maria, Fla.: Sapientia, 2009.

———. *Saint Thomas Aquinas*. Vol. 1, *The Person and His Work*. Rev. ed. Translated by Robert Royal. Washington, D.C.: Catholic University of America Press, 2005.

———. *Saint Thomas Aquinas*. Vol. 2, *Spiritual Master*. Translated by Robert Royal. Washington, D.C.: Catholic University of America Press, 2003.

Van Nieuwenhove, Rik, and Joseph Wawrykow. *The Theology of Thomas Aquinas*. Notre Dame, Ind.: University of Notre Dame Press, 2010.

Vogt, Christopher. "Fostering a Catholic Commitment to the Common Good: An Approach Rooted in Virtue Ethics." *Theological Studies* 68 (2007): 394-417.

Wadell, Paul. *The Primacy of Love*. New York: Paulist, 1992.

Weigel, George. "*Caritas in Veritate* in Gold and Red: The Revenge of Justice and Peace (or So They May Think)." *National Review Online Edition* (July 7, 2009). Accessed January 3, 2014.

———. *Catholicism and the Renewal of American Democracy*. Mahwah, N.J.: Paulist, 1989.

Westberg, Daniel. *Right Practical Reason: Aristotle, Action, and Prudence in Aquinas*. Oxford: Clarendon, 1994.

Works Cited

Wetzel, James, ed. *Augustine's City of God: A Critical Guide.* New York: Cambridge University Press, 2012.

Witte, John, Jr., and Frank S. Alexander, eds. *The Teachings of Modern Roman Catholicism on Law, Politics, and Human Nature.* New York: Columbia University Press, 2007.

Witte, John, Jr., and Joel A. Nichols. *Religion and the American Constitutional Experiment.* 3rd ed. New York: Westview, 2010.

Index of Names and Subjects

Index of Scripture References